APPALACHIAN FREE SPIRIT

A Recovery Journey

DUKE TALBOTT

BALBOA.
PRESS

A DIVISION OF HAY HOUSE

Balboa Press books may be ordered through booksellers or by contacting:

Balboa Press
A Division of Hay House
1663 Liberty Drive
Bloomington, IN 47403
www.balboapress.com
1 (877) 407-4847

Because of the dynamic nature of the Internet, any web addresses or links contained in this book may have changed since publication and may no longer be valid. The views expressed in this work are solely those of the author and do not necessarily reflect the views of the publisher, and the publisher hereby disclaims any responsibility for them.

The author of this book does not dispense medical advice or prescribe the use of any technique as a form of treatment for physical, emotional, or medical problems without the advice of a physician, either directly or indirectly. The intent of the author is only to offer information of a general nature to help you in your quest for emotional and spiritual well-being. In the event you use any of the information in this book for yourself, which is your constitutional right, the author and the publisher assume no responsibility for your actions.

Any people depicted in stock imagery provided by Getty Images are models, and such images are being used for illustrative purposes only. Certain stock imagery © Getty Images.

Print information available on the last page.

ISBN: 978-1-9822-3290-0 (sc)
ISBN: 978-1-9822-3292-4 (hc)
ISBN: 978-1-9822-3291-7 (e)

Library of Congress Control Number: 2019911748

Balboa Press rev. date: 08/20/2019

Dedication

This book is dedicated to all veterans of war, especially those who are dealing with Post-Traumatic Stress Disorder from active participation in combat zones. May they see the hope that is available for addressing the consequences of facing the agony and tragedy of that involvement through the spiritual growth and emotional recovery that is available to each and every one of them as they find the God of their understanding and know that they can be whole persons full of serenity and happiness in each moment of life. May God bless them all.

Preface

"The unexamined life is not worth living." - Socrates

This book is the result of taking an in-depth look at the soul of an individual dealing with alcohol and drug abuse stemming from unaddressed Post-Traumatic Stress Disorder from combat. If it has some relevance to any other person in identifying that he or she has a problem with addiction that has become unmanageable and it is time to do something about it then it will be well worth the effort. Addiction to chemicals does not have to be a way of life. It can be addressed and the great wonderful person that was created when a baby was born can become that again. A true life of happiness and fruitfulness can emerge in the recovered person. This is the story of one lost soul who with the help of God and literally hundreds of others found a new way of living and relating to that God. It is not an all-encompassing path for everybody but it is how it has worked for one person. If it helps another it will have accomplished its purpose.

In the process of recovery many other personal challenges would be identified. It is doubtful that any of them would have been found in the absence of addressing chemical dependency. These included especially a long time and unrecognized trait of codependency. With recovery it was possible to confront this, which is an addiction of its own kind, as well as many others. The process of recovery continues throughout a lifetime. And the more we identify and address the happier we will become as we travel our journey.

As a true son of Appalachia. I was born, raised, educated, spent a career (or most of it), and retired in Appalachia. It is home. Although there are a lot of things in Appalachia that I would do a different way, the place is full of warm wonderful people although some of them don't always show it (which is basically true of lots of places around the globe). Although calling Appalachia home I belong wherever I am in the world.

It has been said over the years that the two best places to hide alcoholism and addiction are the Ivory Tower and the military. I believe it, especially with the Ivory Tower part. It is also said that a person who is all wrapped up in himself has a very small package indeed. It has been a difficult task looking and writing about an addictive world because most of life has been spent looking at others. With recovery it has become rather a life of identifying with others and respecting their differences as gifts from God and finding therein the unity of all humanity.

Because most Twelve Step recovery programs are anonymous the names of individuals (who were not publicly known) have been intentionally omitted. Some people may recognize themselves, and I hope I have portrayed them in a fair and conscientious manner. If this has not been the case I offer a sincere apology. There are two exceptions to this anonymity. They are Dahir the Somali houseboy and Thu the Vietnamese hootch girl. If by some incredible and almost impossible chance they should ever have an opportunity to read this I appreciate very much the contribution you both have made to this journey.

CHAPTER 1

Trying to Grow Up

It **is** Sunday morning February 1, 2015, Calle Loiza, San Juan, Puerto Rico. A young man is walking down the otherwise empty narrow sidewalk of the street, a lost look in his eyes. He is carrying an open beer in one hand and a couple of six-packs in a plastic bag in his other hand. A feeling of pity and compassion welled up in me as I saw him. In a fleeting moment, the flashback of yesteryear passed through my soul. Maybe, just maybe, someday, he could take solace within the spiritual realm that lies dormant within him. As I passed beside him and said hello he replied with only a grunt. That young man was me forty years ago and it was an irony that on the morning of arriving in Puerto Rico to get out of the winter cold and snow of West Virginia's Highlands that he was the first person I saw to speak to. I had flown into San Juan for the first time late on the previous day. It was a Saturday night and I had gone directly to bed.

Looking forward to a new experience on "Isla del Encanto" I had gotten up early to take a stroll through this neighborhood located away from the hustle and bustle of the tourist meccas of the city. On a beautiful and sunny Sunday morning the streets were virtually disserted with the young man the only person in sight. Somehow this was maybe a reassurance that I was doing the right thing because I had planned on spending the time in Puerto Rico writing – writing about a life of violence, war, PTSD, addiction, and a host of other challenges that go with it until in final surrender I had accepted the concept of powerlessness over life's events and in desperation turned to a spiritual awakening that would lead to a life of peace and tranquility.

It was a long voyage from the Appalachian mountains of West Virginia to the friendliness and warmth of Puerto Rico in winter – a journey that went through many parts of Europe, Africa, Asia, and Latin America, and through years of peace and violence, love, laughter, intoxication, and intrigue, to acceptance, tranquility, and serenity and an awareness of the spiritual as both human and divine. It was a journey highly influenced by chemical substances to escape from the past and to attempt to preside successfully over the present. It was a life of running away until in total surrender the search for a spiritual path through the various Twelve-Step[1] recovery programs[2] and the recognition that the universality of spiritual traditions within human cultural and religious experiences would lead to the serenity, peace, and acceptance I had always longed for. Much of that would also be influenced by the environment in which I grew up and the cultural and social milieu of small town Appalachia.

Most of our family's ancestors had been in West Virginia for more than two centuries. The progenitors of our nuclear family had come to settle in the rugged hills of Appalachian Virginia in the eighteenth century. Our paternal ancestors apparently originated in Shrewsbury, England. Sometime before 1780 they had immigrated to Alexandria, Virginia, probably as indentured servants. In that year two brothers and a sister, Richard, Cottrell, and Charity Talbott secured a Revolutionary War land grant in the western part of the state, and with that they relocated to the area that is today Philippi, West Virginia. Our dad was a great, great grandson of Richard Talbott.

Our great grandfather whose name was Irvin Benton Talbott was a Confederate soldier. Family legend has it that he was a young man when the skirmish known as the "Battle of Philippi" occurred. This incident was precipitated early on in the conflict when pro-Union troops under the command of the governor of Ohio crossed the Ohio River into seceding Virginia to secure the Baltimore and Ohio Railroad which was that state's principal transportation corridor to the port cities of the eastern seaboard. To protect the railroad Virginia forces had stationed themselves first in Grafton where the branches of the lines connecting Wheeling and Parkersburg on the Ohio River joined to go to Baltimore. Upon the approach of the Ohio troops the Virginia forces retreated south along the Beverly-Fairmont Turnpike to Philippi a location which was considered more hospitable to their cause. They were followed closely by the Ohio forces who soon routed the rebels from their new encampment. The site of the battle that accomplished this victory was adjacent to our great grandfather's family farm and it was from that location that he watched it play out.

When it was over in curiosity he visited the battle site with Union troops still encamped on it. Allegedly a Union solder, ostensibly from New York, told our great grandfather to blacken his boots and when he refused to do so the Union soldier stabbed him in the leg with his bayonet. When great grandfather recovered from the injury he was convinced by this insult that the Union troops were the enemy and he went off to join Virginia's Army of the Shenandoah in which he would serve for the duration of the war. However, before leaving the battle scene he picked up an expended cannonball as a souvenir. It is a token of the war that remains in the family today.

Our paternal grandfather, born after the Civil War was over, eventually migrated to the new city of Elkins which had been established as a railroad center in the 1880s as the Industrial Revolution exploded into West Virginia and the venture capitalists driving it needed a transportation hub to extract the area's rich coal and timber reserves for shipment to the Northeast. There in 1906 he established a general store which specialized in glass. It is a business which still exists in the family today. Both he and grandmother were active members of the community being heavily involved in the American Baptist Church and with grandad serving a couple of terms on the Elkins city council. In the 1920s he was also briefly an active member of the Ku Klux Klan but soon withdrew from the organization condemning it as morally wrong for the attitudes and actions it fostered.

Our maternal grandfather's family were originally Dutch settlers who had immigrated to the Hudson River Valley of New Netherlands near what is today Kingston, New York, sometime in the 1660s or 1670s. Gradually, population pressure forced them first to New Jersey and subsequently to the plateaus of western Virginia in an area called Queens which is today in Upshur County. As West Virginia, which had split from Virginia in the turmoil of the Civil War, began to become industrialized in the latter half of the nineteenth century, his parents when he was still a lad, left Queens and settled in nearby Belington, West Virginia. As the railroad developed in the area and he grew into a young man he was talented enough to eventually become a locomotive engineer for the Western Maryland Railway a position from which he retired in 1961. Our grandmother's family had immigrated to western Virginia from Darmstadt, Germany in the middle of the nineteenth century. As our grandfather's career grew he and grandmother eventually later relocated to the railroad's principal facility in Elkins with their three daughters the eldest of whom was our mother. It was there that our parents met.

Although all our great grandparents were West Virginia farmers, by the time our grandparents were adults they had all made the transition to the emergent industrial economy and their children had ideas of moving even further into the bustling and increasingly urbanized environment of America (and some eventually into various other parts of the world). Our parents, as was true with so many of that generation, were hit by the double traumas of the Great Depression and World War II. Our grandfather's business was kept open for a few years as the economy plummeted, but, similar to so many others, bankruptcy would become the only way out. Although through this process he was absolved of the debts he had accrued, he kept a list of all persons to whom he had bankrupted their accounts payable. Throughout the following years he would work to pay them off in dribs and drabs until finally by the early 1950s everything that had been bankrupted had been repaid with interest. The respect for his honesty and integrity grew proportionally.

Our parents both attempted to go to college in this economic morass. Dad was able to get his tuition paid at the local college by working as a painter on campus. And by being able to live at home, eventually he would graduate in 1934 with his bachelor's degree and a major in General Science and a minor in Math. Although mom attended several colleges throughout the 1930s she had to work to stay in school. She was never able to piece together enough credits to graduate despite several attempts because the funding was never adequate. In her concern for family she also tried to help her younger sister who eventually would graduate with a bachelor's degree and ultimately a master's degree.

My earliest memories are from Dayton, Ohio. Both parents were originally from Elkins, and that is where I was born. From infancy to Five years old we lived in different places in Ohio and Illinois because Dad was working for firms manufacturing various supplies for the Manhattan Project.[3] As such he was draft exempt. He did not know why he was draft exempt except that he understood he was working on something very important to the war effort. On his job he had unlimited gasoline rationing and was gone a lot from home. It was because of his travel and frequent absences from home that when Mom was pregnant with me she went back to Elkins when she was about to deliver to stay with her parents so they could watch my older brother who had been born the previous year. As soon as she delivered and was ready to travel she returned to Danville, Illinois, where they were living at the time. According to Mom we moved every six months or so until finally ending up in Dayton in 1945.

It was in Dayton, when I was five years old, that I was forced to go to kindergarten. I am not sure why but for some reason I hated it. I would not go if I could possibly get out of it. We were picked up for kindergarten in an old station wagon – the kind that still had wooden sides on it. It would be packed full of kids and, of course, at that time no one had seatbelts which were something that were only used on airplanes. The kids would do as kids do in such an environment laughing and being silly and attempting to have a good time in their new educational adventure. There were both boys and girls who went to their early education in this station wagon.

One day I was determined not to go to kindergarten and so I made a plan. There was a small hill (at the time I thought it was a big hill but having since seen it in photos it was, in fact, a small hill). The plan was that I would ride my tricycle up the hill and then pedaling it as fast as I could I would go screeching down the side of the hill and crash it into the station wagon thus taking us all out. I really had not weighed the consequences of such an action but in light of my distaste for kindergarten it seem an appropriate thing to accomplish.

So I got up on the hill and I waited till I saw the station wagon coming and I started pedaling as hard and as fast as I could. The only problem was the tricycle could not go nearly as fast as I thought it would and I had to go past Mom who was watching as we waited for the station wagon. Before I got to it she reached out with one hand – I did not get near the speed I thought I could – and pulled the budding terrorist off the tricycle and into the station wagon. I can remember getting a big resentment sitting in the back of the station wagon and all the other kids were laughing and having fun. I don't think Mom ever knew what evil intentions I had plotted because as she put me into the back of that vehicle she chatted and laughed with the driver who seemed to be also very cheery about going to kindergarten.

Another memory is getting lost in the cornfield. Close to our house was a farm which for some reason we had visited as a family (perhaps to buy produce or homemade dairy products). Adjacent to the farm sales area was a large corn field. For me there were too many people gathered together and besides my wanderlust wanted to find out what was in the cornfield and on its far side. So without telling anyone I wandered into it and promptly got lost because everywhere I turned there was corn and it was all over my head and it all looked the same. Soon I became worried that I did not know how to get out of it. But I firmly believed it was my responsibility to get out of it on my own initiative and so a lot of futile struggle and self-reliance went into the effort, but it did not work. I could not find a way out but I knew I had to do it and so I continued to wonder around in it. There was no way I was going to call for help. After several unproductive attempts at trying to emerge from the corn field going in different directions to get out, I heard Dad calling my name and I answered and he rescued me.

Thoughts even at that early age were on what I had to do to be self-sufficient. Failure to do so was very frustrating because it was necessary to rely on somebody else to get out of a jam.

In December 1948 for unknown reasons our parents decided to move back to Elkins. Dad entered our grandfather's business along with his two brothers. They would spend the rest of their lives there. I never went back to kindergarten.

Growing up in a small Appalachian town in the aftermath of World War II provided a safety net for kids especially those who had good parents with jobs which could fulfill the basic needs children should experience. It was a time of great change nationally and internationally, but the prosperity of the war's aftermath which characterized so much of the United States could not be found in most of West Virginia. As children in a rapidly deteriorating early rustbelt we did not have much materially but, unlike the prosperity that characterized most of the rest of America in the 1950s, very few children at that time and place in our part of the country had very much materially. So we were not particularly different from other kids who were growing up in our town. There was, however, an underlying current that things were not sound economically and that trend was evidenced by the out-migration of so many of our friends during the period as their parents relocated to Ohio or Baltimore with a few even going to California all in search of gainful employment. It was a fairly frequent occurrence for us to have so say goodbye to these friends whose families had joined the Great Out-Migration. Some people said that was what we as children would have to do when we grew up if we expected to get a better life. Many other adults had already become a part of the out-migration caravan and a lot of young men especially, along with a few women, joined the military so that they could earn a living and get training for employment that might be in demand when they had finished their enlistment. Joining the military was a very honorable and respectable thing to do even if a lot of it was motivated by economic and upward mobility concerns. Many would probably never move back to the mountains after their training and tour of duty choosing to stay instead often in places where they had been stationed or relocating to cities with greater opportunities than could be found at home.

At our house every day there were always three meals on the table at breakfast, noon, and at 6:00 p.m. Be there or miss out. We were expected to arrive at meals on time especially lunch and supper because those were family togetherness experiences. That expectation usually included lunch during the school year as well. We walked the mile from the school back home to eat and then walked the mile back to the school for the afternoon session. This rule was only in place when the weather was at least tolerably nice. When it was not occasionally we would take cold lunch or participate in the hot lunch program. Of course, we walked to school in the morning and back home in the late afternoon regardless of the weather because we were considered too close to the school to ride the school bus. Exceptions were made to these meal rules only for school or church activities. In the same manner, we were always expected to be at school on week days and in church on Sunday morning. All family members were to treat each other with respect. Never during childhood did I ever hear our parents in an argument or yelling at each other. And I never once heard Dad use a swear word. And never during childhood was there ever any evidence of alcohol and drug use. (Although our father did smoke cigarettes which he quit shortly after I had started the odorous weed while in high school.)

Like so many others of "the greatest generation" who lived through the Great Depression of the 1930s and World War II our parents expected us to be stoic and responsive to any situation that required work or responsibility. Emotions about life's events especially feelings were not usually permitted. I do not ever remember getting a hug from Dad when I was a kid growing up although they were occasionally forthcoming from Mom.

In fact, Dad paid very little attention to us. I expect out of necessity as much as anything else. Economic circumstances were so particularly bad in Elkins in the 1950s that he was almost compelled to maintain a significant work commitment if he was going to stay solvent and meet his family responsibilities. With five children and operating a business established by his father and in partnership with his brother who also had several kids, he spent most of his time at work usually from 8:00 a.m. to 6:00 p.m. six days a week. In addition, in the summer, there was the garden to tend to which as we got older devolved more and more to the older kids. I swore at one point that when I grew up I would never hoe another row of green beans – a promise which I have kept to myself. In taking that oath to never hoe green beans again I lopped off a plant at its roots so it could never grow and would wither and die. That was, I guess, an early rudimentary reliance on violence to solve the challenges of life.

That garden, however, produced a lot of fresh food for us during the summer as well as providing a source for lots of home-grown canned food for the winter months. These included particularly sweet corn, green beans, bell peppers, leaf lettuce, broccoli, several kinds of squash, cucumbers, green onions, beets, parsley, dill and other herbs. Mom canned especially the green beans, sweet corn and pickles made from the cucumbers as well as apple sauce and grape juice which she made from fruits that came from our grandparents' garden. She also made and canned elderberry jelly and blackberry jam from the wild berries that we kids would pick from nearby bushes. That garden was also something we could eat from when we were playing outside. Go pick off a cucumber or a fresh green pepper and eat it for a snack.

We also had lots of chores such as helping in the kitchen especially washing and drying the dishes, mowing the grass, cleaning out the basement when it flooded which seemed to be a regular occurrence and happened frequently because of the poor drainage, and washing the car. Occasionally we might be paid a nickel or a dime for some of these jobs. Thus a work ethic was instilled in us which would continue with all of us throughout life.

On Sundays we were expected to go to church both Sunday School and morning worship. Sometimes we also went to Sunday evening services and occasionally Wednesday prayer services. By and large, although a little bit of hellfire and brimstone was always present, the predominant message of those services was that of a loving, caring, and forgiving God who could be called upon in times of need. This conceptualization of a God who was concerned for our well-being would in recovery make acceptance of the idea that God could and would be there for us if we let him an easy concept to ultimately incorporate into a clean and sober life.

One troubling central religious theme though throughout those adolescent years was the concept that one needed to be saved by Jesus, but that salvation, it appeared, was not made available to very many people. Even though there were millions of people who did have an opportunity to be "saved," many millions more did not. Somehow this construct seemed imminently unfair. Why would some people have the opportunity for salvation and others not have the opportunity? As a child I never was able to reconcile this concept into a religiously acceptable doctrine.

Another concept that I also had a great deal of trouble with was the idea of Original Sin. I hadn't done anything really bad and I tried to be good so how and why was I to be singled out along with everybody else as having some kind of original sin that I had not had anything to do with, and that I was just naturally bad for what someone else had done thousands of years ago. Sure there were lots of bad people but it was not reasonable that any of them had inherited it as original sin. They became bad because of the actions they took. If God was a loving, caring, and forgiving God how could he lay this on the people he had created. It all seemed so infinitely unfair and something he just would not do. Increasingly I came to doubt that God would limit salvation to so few people and that Original Sin was an idea that had to be jettisoned along the road of life.

Following the same line of reasoning I also could not see how going through some ritual or formality could save an individual. It simply did not add up that if some motion were carried out it would lead to eternal salvation. There was no reason or rationale to it at least so far as I could see. Although baptized at the age of twelve and taking communion thereafter it made no sense that this was the way devout people could make it into heaven. Although I understood that these actions were symbolic, the real need for them was pretty much irrelevant. It was what was in the heart and the actions that came as a result of it that was important. Retrospectively, I think all these doubts helped to pave the way to more readily accept the Twelve Step concept of the "God of our understanding" that would become so important to recovery in later years.

Although this God would be with me throughout the turmoil of adult life it would be primarily in the head and not in the heart. Consequently, the road through a life of reliance on drugs and alcohol was frequently characterized by unplanned but self-induced challenges followed by "fox hole prayers". As an adult during active addiction, God was not a personal God who was a living and vibrant part of life but a separate entity operating independently with little relevance to me or my lifestyle. By adulthood this attitude had become one that pretty much said "God, you go do your thing and I'll go do my thing." One can readily see what the results of that approach would be with such a perspective.

Another moral quandary faced as an adolescent was the dichotomy that although I felt I really wanted to belong as a part of the society at large that somehow or another I did not fit in to it. Juxtaposed against this was the feeling that I wanted to be and act "outside the box." Somehow I was never ever able to reconcile the antithetical concepts of "should I fit in?" or "should I have an individualized path?" In later years addiction would make that choice for me. Today I know that neither have to prevail. We can be fully whole yet both inside the box and outside the box. That is not a choice we have to make in life today. The "box" is a creation of the ego and not a determinant of the relationship with the God of our understanding. Our role is to be in sync with God's will, and life will emerge as a holy creation with the peace and serenity that God has designed for us. It is only to that God that thoughts and actions have to be directed without any external justification coming from others whoever or wherever they might be in the world. It is fulfilled by the singleness of purpose defined in the surrender to the God of our understanding and it is consummated by letting go of ego, becoming one with God's world, and contributing what we can to the rest of God's children no matter who or where they are.

By and large I was a very average student never really excelling at academic work, but never really bombing out – do what was necessary to get by. I got along pretty well with other people and had very few disciplinary problems. At school I generally interacted just fine with the other students. To have done otherwise would have been totally unacceptable behavior in the context of the family values that were being imparted while growing up. It was necessary and expected for us to be a cooperating and congenial part of both the family and the community. To be the object of a constabulary search would have been unfathomable. However, there was one exception to this construct. During the summer between the sixth and seventh grade years a new junior high school was under construction (more about that later). Several of us boys were checking it out especially the new freshly poured concrete sidewalks in front of the building. At the time, since we would be the first class to enter it and go through all three years, we reasoned it would be a good idea to leave something identifying us for posterity. We soon found a stick which would appropriately write in the newly poured concrete and so several of us inscribed our names for future generations of students to know that we had been there.

The powers that be in the community took a less than approving view of our attempts at immortality through wet cement. The constabulary did indeed come looking for us. All those who had signed their names were hauled into municipal court. I really do not know what the official charge was but we were all put on probation for a year. It was scary because there was some talk too among adults that we might be going to 'Pruny Town'"[4] – Reform School! It did not happen, but it certainly did put the fear in all of us of a lifelong stigma and of being exiled from our home town. I went away from this experience thoroughly convinced that I should never again leave any incriminating evidence behind. Our parents never mentioned this incident once it was over.

My first school was white only through the sixth grade. I guess I knew I was white because our parents had told us we were as had many of our friends and acquaintances. Once finished with elementary school after sixth grade, students were transferred to junior high school. In May of 1954 when I was about ready to complete sixth grade I was trying diligently to read the local newspaper. I had begun to take an interest in what was going on in the world and the newspaper was about the only way to do that since we did not have a television which was only slowly beginning to become a fixture in a lot of American homes during that period. The sole other source of news was the movie news reels when I occasionally got to go to a movie, and they pictured and described the national and international events that had occurred during the previous week.

A headline which stretched across the entire top of the newspaper – usually headlines were only two or three columns – was intriguing because I could did not understand it. The headline blared "Segregation Ruled Unconstitutional." I did not know what any of that meant. I knew the word ruler, but this word was "ruled." Asking Mom to explain what the headline was all about, she replied simply "White and colored kids are going to go to school together." She did not elaborate. We accepted the concept that there were two different races simply because that was the way it was. But our parents always maintained that all people were equal in the eyes of God – they made themselves different by how they lived their lives and whether or not they were good or bad in their daily actions.

As a result, segregation was something we acknowledged as reality and did not question as kids. There were white schools and colored schools and white churches and colored churches. At the time we really did not think much about it. We had a black lady who helped Mom clean house and who would occasionally baby-sit us; her husband worked for Dad in his business. At this age there were really no feelings at all about race. It was just basically that people came in different colors. This concept was a little different, however, for my attitude toward Asians. I am not quite sure where this came from, but I suspect that it originated with the international events of childhood. There was so much talk after the Communist victory in China about the challenges and catastrophes that were perceived in the public imagination of what seemed to be happening in Asia. And some of these radical changes I had visibly seen and heard about on the movie newsreels. Of course, it's hard to tell how much of this might have been stimulated by the anti-Communist hysteria of the McCarthy era which was currently underway. So as an adolescent I actually developed some kind of underlying fear of people who looked Asian. And in some part, thanks to the anti-Communist propaganda that was so integral to the early 1950s, the Chinese Revolutionaries seemed so incredibly alien to my latent libertarian values that were slowly beginning to emerge in this period of adolescence. Probably contributing to this unsubstantiated fear of Asians as well were the vicissitudes of the Korean War which raged during a part of early childhood. This self-induced phobia continued at least through junior high school.

Perhaps those fears were augmented by what was expected in elementary school. For some reason drills in school, which had been initiated somewhere along the line during this period possibly related to World War II, the Korean War, or the Cold War were carried out from time to time. These drills were of two kinds and designed to prepare us to readily take cover in the building or to exit quickly from it in the event of an imminent attack. The first type consisted of a bell going off and each student was expected to immediately drop everything and get underneath his or her desk. We would stay under them until the all clear was given. These were explained as necessary in the event of an atomic attack. We also had a second routine holdover from the international challenges the country faced during this time, and that was that when the day ended a different bell went off and to the loud blaring of a John Phillips Souza anthem we all marched out of class with the first grade students going first followed by the other grades in order with all the students marching in a line while the Souza anthem blared. It was an orderly march, one student following after the next until all students had been cleared from the building. No one was allowed to talk until they were outside. The streamlined nature of this exit made it possible to get the students outside in an orderly fashion in the event of a need to evacuate the building quickly if an attack was imminent.

In spite of that strange fearfulness early on of people who looked Asian, by and large during adolescent and undergraduate years I really could not understand what the big deal was about somebody's race or ethnicity. It simply did not seem to be of any importance. Although it was rare to see couples of different races comingling on a social basis as far as I was concerned it did not really matter. On the other hand, there was a little bit of trepidation about association with Roman Catholics because in the very Protestant area in which we lived it was a truer form of Christianity to be Methodist, Baptist, or Presbyterian. Muslims were non-existent and Jews were non-converts seen only from a distance.

Segregated Randolph County in which I lived, like so many other West Virginia county school systems, for the most part welcomed the opportunity to dismantle racially separated schools which were such a drag on the educational resources of the community but were mandated by the state constitution. By the start of school the following September after the May 17, 1954 Brown v. Board of Education decision, the overwhelming majority of West Virginia school systems had integrated most without major incident and this was true as well for our county's school system. The old segregated school system had been put to bed, at least for us.

Rather than race, religion, or ethnicity in 1954, however, I was far more concerned about going to the big brand new consolidated junior high school that had just been built and was opening for the first time in the Fall of that year. It was an unusual sight having so many kids in the hallway and in class.

Although it was a little bit strange seeing the small number of black kids in such a large school it was only a tiny part of being involved in this whole new educational experience. Students went to different classes throughout the day rather than staying in one single classroom. This in itself was very exciting in that we could be left on our own to get from one classroom to another without being led by some adult. We were beginning to enter the world of some expected responsibility for our actions and our movements from place to place. It introduced a new dimension of freedom.

Our parents always put emphasis on education growing up. Not that they expected us to be geniuses, but we were required to do satisfactory work in school. And it was always assumed that we were going to go to college. We had a tiny dining area in our house and it had two corner walls and on one wall they put up a map of the United States (there were only 48 states then) and on the other wall was a map of the world which showed the world wrap around nature of the British Empire in red and that of the French Empire in blue. And then there was the vastness of the expansive and sinister Soviet Union. We could and occasionally did talk about national or world events and made reference to the maps – as I got older this in part contributed significantly to a growing global awareness. It certainly helped with acquiring a significant knowledge of geography.

Although childhood was relatively congenial and devoid of excesses there was one trait which I can remember during virtually all of the years from very early childhood until I came into the rooms of recovery – I always felt that I really did not fit in whether that be at home, with family, in school or church, or at work. Somehow I was not quite good enough, but I could never understand why I had that feeling.

The youthful ideal figure growing up and the individual to whose life I aspired was Huckleberry Finn. He had the best life of anybody in the world. I read his story over and over again. Especially appealing was the freedom, the adventure, and the travel that he got to be involved in. He was a natural guy in a natural world. And that nature provided him with freedom and ensconced him in a role that was pure adventure and fun. He operated without restriction. That was truly a life to live. Often I would go into the woods near our house and, shirtless and with only short pants and tennis shoes on, pretend to be Huckleberry Finn. It was through this close association with nature in summer that a real appreciation for life originated. There was a super polluted creek in the woods near our house and the neighborhood boys were not supposed to go swimming in it. It was a known source of typhoid fever and a variety of other diseases and had been off limits to us kids for as long as I could remember. However, it was too tempting especially on a hot day not to take advantage of it. We had a grapevine strung above the water that we could swing out over the creek and plunge into the natural pool at this location. Occasionally we picked up leeches on our skin or between our toes which had to be burnt off with a match or a cigarette. But to us it was all still fun. Removing leeches was simply a part of the occasion. To avoid detection by our parents of being in the creek we normally skinny dipped so there would be no evidence of the filthy water on our clothes. Skinny dipping was accepted practice for us because when we went to the YMCA pool to swim we had to go butt naked since that was the rule. No swimming trunks for boys. Of course, there were no girls allowed when the boys were swimming and the life guard did wear trunks. Girls had a different rule. They were expected to wear bathing suits during their swim time.

Much more pristine than the creek that ran close to our neighborhood were the rivers of the Monongahela National Forest that was in the highlands east of Elkins. In particular, was the Cheat River with its clean and rapidly flowing water that provided numerous swimming and tubing possibilities. The Cheat had received a lot of attention from the Civilian Conservation Corps in the 1930s and so it had several small parks along its route. One especially was a favorite for people who wanted to get out in nature. That was Stuart's Park and it had a large natural swimming hole and picnic tables and camping sites. The swimming hole had some large boulders adjacent to it which were perfect for diving off. It also had a grapevine swing nearby upstream which could be used for swinging out over the river and dropping into the rapidly flowing water below. We spent a great deal of time at Stuart's Park. It was here that Dad taught us how to swim. He really believed every kid had to be able to swim. It was also here that we ate out on the picnic tables on numerous occasions. Occasionally we camped as a family at the park's campgrounds. Sometimes Mom would take us out in the car for the afternoon where we could swim and hike and play in the woods and then we would cook dinner. Dad would join us after work coming to the park in the company truck when he got off. The national forest was a great place to relate to nature and I loved the freedom and adventure that we could find in it as kids. It was the most natural thing in the world to be a part of the forest and of the river. It had its own kind of freedom.

Possibly the greatest change in youth came when I was fifteen and got a new real job. When I was younger I had had a paper route. It had fifty customers on it and it was located in a two-square block area of downtown Elkins. I could deliver it in about 45 minutes. It was a perfect after school job. It paid a cent and a half for each paper delivered. And I relished the financial and job independence it gave me albeit on a very small scale. Even at this early age making money was more important than doing other things. The paper route provided a little bit of spending cash and it opened up a whole new world because we picked up our papers actually in the press room and got to see how the linotype operated, the "hell box" and how it melted used lead slugs, and the way the giant press rolled out the papers. The noisy rat-a-tat of the teletype machine added to the cacophony. It was all very exciting for a teenager to be a part of this incredibly busy, noisy, hot, and interactive experience. And it was certainly something OSHA would have had an absolute hissy fit over today. But all the processes for printing newspapers today have changed and they are mostly quiet and air conditioned and paper delivery is no longer carried out by young teenage boys who go door to door in their tight packed neighborhoods.

Much as I tried, however, I was not very prudent with money. Even though I really relished earning it, it sure did not take long to spend it. Initially it was candy bars which cost five cents apiece but I soon graduated to more challenging things. Our parents had warned us about pin ball machines. They were not to be played because that was something which could lead to a lot of other unsavory results for teenage boys and it was not a very uplifting experience for a young person to do and it had a lot of potential downfalls. But I no sooner played the first one than I was hooked and wanted to play more and more. They were exciting and a release from other worries. I could stay focused on something fun. So, even though we were not supposed to play them, whenever possible I slipped into a roadside filling station and grill that had one and played the newspaper money away. I never really got caught but it took a lot of explaining about where the money from the newspaper route was going and it produced a number of lectures about being more careful with money.

During the summer when I was fifteen I would get a totally new work experience that would be very different from the paper route. And that new experience was securing, with the help of Dad, a real life, paying job which in light of the economic reality of 1950s Appalachia was a tremendous opportunity and joy for a teenage boy. Money was simply something that most teenagers did not have nor did they have much in the way of opportunity to acquire it. It was quite in contrast to today's teenagers where there are almost always job openings at fast food and related type establishments where virtually everyone could be employed and get in as many hours as they wished.

Actually although lots of students around Elkins had paid temporary work of various kinds during the summer or occasionally part-time gigs during the school year, perhaps only three in high school had real year round or mostly year round jobs. That new job was working in one of the first drive-in restaurants that began emerging during the decade. The starting pay was fifty cents an hour plus food and it was within walking distance from home which was very important because we only had one car and Dad normally took it to work every day. Since I was under sixteen years of age when I started, I had to get a special work permit on initial employment. That job was the greatest opportunity in the world, and I would work my tail off to keep it. And I did.

Although initially beginning on day shift I was soon transferred to evening shift. Evening shift seemed to go faster and I could usually get in more hours and it would not interfere with school once the Fall semester began. I had only been there a few weeks when we were cleaning up after closing and someone produced a bottle of whiskey. This was a totally new experience because I had never before been around alcoholic beverages. Our parents never had alcoholic beverages in the house and very few friends or others had them around. And, with only occasional references by Mom to the damage old "John Barleycorn" had done to so-and-so, the topic was rarely even mentioned.

The people who had brought out the bottle of whiskey offered everyone some. I was not quite sure what to do having never tasted it. But wanting to fit in I said sure I'd have some in as well as I can remember a self-assured sort of way which tried to indicate that they were offering it to an experienced drinker. Little did I know what to expect but I took a big gulp out of the bottle and forced it down. It was the vilest substance I had ever tasted, but when it hit bottom I knew I had arrived. The change it brought was what I considered magnificent. My whole being glowed in the aftermath of that first drink. My environment became one of acceptance and security. I was a part of everything to which I had never before belonged. I was in a new world. Little did I know that I would spend much of life chasing the "buzz" caught on that first evening of drinking.

In what was to become a typical pattern in later years I had another and another and was inebriated that first evening. It would be the same ever after. If I had the first one I did not want to stop. I could not stop. Before long I learned to camouflage the taste with some sort of soft drink or other liquid. In a similar part of the pattern which emerged that evening and was to become such a major aspect of a later drinking and drugging career I got home and although buzzed made it safely and quietly into the house. Everybody was in bed asleep so I did not get caught. There were no repercussions or adverse consequences from that first drinking bout. With the exception of a lot of hangovers, direct repercussions were for the most part largely absent throughout my drinking and drugging career. This contributed significantly as one of the many factors that helped to explain the long-term denial that there was a problem with addiction. As time moved on and other substances became a part of this addictive behavior the same characteristic of few or no repercussions would prevail with whatever I was using to try to recapture that first buzz.

It was not much later that I tasted beer. Initially beer was also a particularly nasty substance. Someone had advised it was an acquired taste so I kept at it until acquiring the taste which did not take very long. And since the drinking age for beer in West Virginia at the time was only eighteen we always had someone to purchase it, and I always had money from the job to pay for it. Beer too would become a significant part of a drinking and drugging career (and also a major part of the later denial that there was a problem). How can you have a problem just drinking beer?

That initial job would also introduce me to the first of two remarkable women who – although they were very, very different from each other in their own special ways – would each have a most profound effect on my early work history and respect for women. Both of them, despite their extreme differences, exhibited a great deal of professional competence, and they both took an interest in their budding young employee. Each of them was willing to spend time on training not only about the job skills involved and how to perform them but also about being able to work for and in a competitive business.

The first woman was the shift supervisor on that initial job. Although our parents had trained us all to be hard workers as family members now was the time to work for somebody else in a wage job. She took a great deal of time not only in teaching the responsibilities of the job but also the responsibilities of being a good employee. She also encouraged me to look more positively on myself as a human being and as an individual who could accomplish many things if the proper effort were put into it.

The second was the editor of the local newspaper. Again with the help of parents I secured a job in my early college years as a cub reporter. Knowing nothing about the newspaper business she apparently thought I had potential so she spent a lot of time with training me especially in how to research a story, confirm an interpretation, and prepare it for publication all under the close timeline scrutiny required by the daily newspaper business. As a result of her instruction and patience writing would become a life-long interest and frequently the means to earn a living. As such, it would include academic papers as well as newspaper columns, position papers, grant applications, op-eds (which I continue to write occasionally), an academic book, and a myriad of other genres.

Both these women left lasting impressions and provided, along with our parents' teachings, a great respect for women in the workforce. They also contributed to the confidence that I could accomplish something as an employee. Their influence would help greatly later on to remain an effective employee despite what would eventually become a significant problem with alcohol and other drugs. It would also make me an early supporter of the Equal Rights Amendment and of the concept of equal pay and opportunity for advancement for equal work for all people regardless of gender.

While in high school I pursued many of the activities that boys undertook as part of their transition to adulthood. As with others when possible I frequented the pool halls and tried to be good at sports. As mentioned, we could get somebody to buy beer for us and, if we were careful and did not make a commotion or bring attention to ourselves, we could usually drink it while shooting pool. The bar tenders simply looked the other way and the rack boys considered it as normal. One thing I did not do in high school though was play team sports, and that was because of an after school work schedule which prohibited participation. And also I rationalized it by saying that I was not as good as my brothers who truly were much better athletes. I was the one cut out to work. Anyway that free spirit attitude toward life in general did not auger well for being involved in the close cooperation required for successful team sports participation. By making money I could be that free spirit, and I did not have to interface with coaches and other team players while everybody was looking.

After graduation from high school as expected I went off to college. The first choice for schools had been to go to the University of Miami. I guess it was appealing because it appeared to be in a different world from the one I was in. But, of course, with the limited financial resources with which we had to work it soon became apparent that that was an impossibility. Although my parents would pay for most of my undergraduate education they had very limited financial resources to rely on – especially since my older brother was also in college at the same time. So it was with a great deal of excitement that I set off to go to West Virginia University. It would be an on-again, off-again relationship that would include four degrees as well as four years of teaching there.

Tuition for the first freshman semester was $51. After three changes in major – first speech as a preparation for law school, then philosophy to satisfy the need for some sort of spiritual framework in life, then finance to get rich on Wall Street, and finally settling on economics with a minor in history to satisfy both the obsession with money and an underlying concern for the affairs of humankind (or perhaps to find a real role in the world). Undergraduate school would see a lot of partying including a fraternity to facilitate it and many hangovers especially on Monday mornings.

While an undergraduate a new dimension was added to this relatively provincial world. My older brother who had decided not to continue in college went to Washington DC to work. There he soon met the girl who would shortly become his wife. She was from a Russian immigrant family in Appalachian Pennsylvania located very close to the state's West Virginia border and to Morgantown and the university where I was going to school. The wedding itself was to be held at the Russian Orthodox Cathedral in Washington. The service was to be in Russian and I was to be the best man. The experience of the pageantry and iconography of the service was fascinating even though I could understand little or nothing of what was being said and performed. And, although both before and after the service we all got drunk, the service itself was an experience as was the reception following it at the home of Mom's sister in Alexandria, Virginia, where we had an opportunity to meet many members of a new sister-in-law's family. Over the years we would all be socially involved and it would be possible to have a close interrelationship with her extended Appalachian immigrant family in southwestern Pennsylvania and to experience the many life transition services of the tiny Russian Orthodox Church there. I always felt welcome. Part of that acceptance was because nobody really cared how much alcohol you drank. It was normal and expected for all social events and for the celebration of life's transitions.

So although undergraduate years were very much a learning experience as they are for so many young people, my world view was slowly starting to change. Unknown at the time this was only the kickoff point in what was about to happen in life. The interest in new things, the cracks in that square but serious box of life, the drinking I thought was a major source of everybody's happiness and a solver of all problems, had already been set in place by the time of graduation in 1964 with a Bachelor's degree in economics and a minor in history. Now it was the opportunity to take on life!

In the five years between 1964 when I graduated from baccalaureate school and entered the Peace Corps in Somalia and 1969 when I finished the tour of duty in Vietnam and returned home, the United States had changed radically just as I had changed radically. The somnolence of the early 1960s had morphed into the turbulence of the late 1960s and early 1970s. Society's radical change had been reflected in my own radical change. Moving from an undergraduate student who greatly admired Barry Goldwater's **Conscience** *of a Conservative,* to a Peace Corps Volunteer in Somalia, to a decorated Vietnam veteran who came to strongly oppose the Vietnam War and our involvement in it was a process of several years duration and included many violent and life threatening experiences. During those years I would build a wall around myself that subconsciously I thought could only be addressed by drinking to excess augmented by various other mind-altering chemicals. That wall would keep all feelings and emotions bottled up inside. That wall would also become so impregnable that I would be outwardly tough enough to be actively recruited as a mercenary soldier at the end of the tour of duty in Vietnam. The cold-heartedness and inner insularity that I had acquired would be an attractive talent for those who were trying to enlist former combat veterans to become paid professional killers. It would also prevent the development of a spiritual relationship with the God of my understanding that is absolutely essential if we are truly going to find happiness and peace in life.

CHAPTER 2

Introduction to a Wider World

In undergraduate school my view had been similar to that of many other young men of the time: have fun – that is, date and party and drink – and get a "Gentleman's C" in your coursework. I joined a fraternity which became an enabling agent for having fun (at least what I thought of as fun) and got by with satisfactory coursework. For the most part I had a pretty conservative social, economic and political attitude toward life's events. Thinking at that time was very much inside the box as far as cultural values and issues and economic philosophy were concerned. There was at this point also a leaning toward a youthful libertarian interpretation of the polity of the day which very much reflected an interest in being independent of parental and societal restraints.

However, in the senior year in undergraduate school a friend had suggested that I sign up for a course from a professor who was for the time considered very much a part of the radical left. The friend, who was also a roommate, thought it might be a good experience to get a different viewpoint. He had had the professor and he said it had substantially changed his outlook and world view. So I dusted off that well-worn copy of Barry Goldwater's **Conscience of a Conservative** and registered for the class. Phew! Little did I know that this instructor would blow my mind in a single class in that last semester of undergraduate school. For the first time in life I began to think critically in terms way outside the box and well beyond anything that had ever been gleaned from **Reader's Digest** which was standard fare during the high school years. He would be without a doubt one of the most convincing and persuasive professors I ever encountered in undergraduate or graduate school. And it is to him that I owe an interest in examining the exciting and positive things that we can do as a people if we take a radical approach to rethinking our relationship to society and the world. As it turned out, this would be only an introduction to extraordinary changes in attitude.

Nonetheless it would take the next five years to fully break the shackles of the conformity thinking of contemporary America and to make a radical transformation to a new philosophy of life, but it was also the beginning of a process of real change that has lasted to this day and continues to grow unabated. I think I can genuinely say that he was the one professor who would begin the shattering of conventional beliefs. After finishing his class and with a radical new way of interpreting the polity and society of the day, different constructs of life and living would emerge during the Somalia and Vietnam experiences. Eventually they would culminate in utilizing the GI bill for post-graduate school working on a Ph.D. in history with a specialization in Africa.

In the sophomore year of undergraduate school a significant presidential initiative occurred that would also have a lasting impact on life over the next several years. That event was President John Kennedy's announcement in 1961 of the formation of a Peace Corps of volunteers to serve in developing countries around the globe. Reading about its announcement thrilled me. Here, at last, was a chance to really get to see the world, to make a total break from a smothering environment, to leave that empty hole that was within me, and to find the true happiness that existed somewhere out there in the world. At the same time this would be pure excitement and it all seemed like a very honorable and laudable thing to do. I could be Huckleberry Finn in an international arena.

Thus it became the goal as the senior year approached to join the Peace Corps upon graduation. As soon as it was possible to apply before graduation I did so. I was super excited after getting the initial acceptance letter. Then I was sent to none other than the Armed Forces Induction Center in Fairmont, West Virginia, where other young men were being evaluated for military service and getting the physical examination which in many cases would soon lead many of them to the rapidly evolving crisis in Vietnam. Apparently, because I was so excited about what I was about to get involved in my blood pressure was over the limit and I was initially rejected. What a crushing blow! How could this happen!

But as fate would have it (I would later come to believe that nothing happens in God's world by accident) a Peace Corps recruiting team was sent to campus. Talking to them and explaining what had happened when I had applied they suggested reapplying and keep reapplying until I got accepted. That is exactly what I did, and eventually the Peace Corps administration in Washington capitulated and I was given another physical exam which was passed with flying colors. Not long after that I was invited to go to training for service in the Somali Republic. On the application form there had been a place to indicate the regional area of the world in which the applicant would like to be a Volunteer. For some reason, maybe for the same reason that led to such respect for Huckleberry Finn, Africa seemed to reflect the greatest potential for excitement and encountering the unusual. So I requested that continent for the preferred location of service.

Life growing up had been one that was virtually free from violence. There were, of course, the occasional scuffles that boys (and sometimes girls) got into. There were also the accidents from cars or sleds or sometimes malfunctioning equipment, but for the most part intentional violence, that is, violence brought on by the determination of one party to instill permanent damage on another was almost non-existent. Guns were an integral part of West Virginia society but people were taught that unless you were on active duty in the military they were to be used only for hunting or for target practice on the rats that could be found in the trash heaps that were a part of the environment.

Most kids started learning about guns early on practicing with a BB gun. It was to be treated with respect and never, ever pointed at another person and always kept away from your face and from little kids. For the most part we followed these rules closely with one exception that I can remember. That exception came about when the boys from Chrystal Springs, which was the next neighborhood over from us, had built a fort made of small logs which they had gathered from fallen trees in the nearby woods. It was located just barely on their side of the international frontier that we had established between them and the boys from Scott Addition where I lived. The boys from Scott Addition decided to evict them from it. So we attacked it with BB guns. Eventually we decided to abandon the attack because one of our guys had a fingernail blown off with a BB shot that came from inside the fort toward us. Shortly after this attack the Crystal Springs boys permanently abandoned their defensive unit and dismantled it. Peace returned to our neighborhoods. Our guys were surprised at this and not quite sure how it had come about, but there was probably some unannounced adult intrusion into this activity to make it happen. Fortunately, at least as far as we were concerned, no adults on our side found out about this insane confrontation, because there would have been extensive and probably severe repercussions for such an abdication of reason and responsibility.

Because home life was characterized by peaceful and tranquil respect and cooperation by all members of our family, by and large growing up as a youth was devoid of any excessive or extensive violence. Our parents disapproved strongly of boys fighting each other and they were emphatic about it, so it was rare that any of us got into a fist fight with another kid. But with entry into the Peace Corps that unfamiliarity with fighting and violence would begin to change. Over a wide spectrum of several of the world's then current hot spots during the next five years daily existence would become increasingly enveloped in violence as a means for settling disputes. It would have a very significant and emotionally traumatic impact on later adult life. Once leaving the relative tranquility and peace of our section of West Virginia I would be surrounded by and in direct contact with violence for much of the next several years.

Thus is was that shortly after baccalaureate commencement, with a great deal of excitement and sense of adventure, I left hometown Elkins and headed to Eastern Michigan University in Ypsilanti for Peace Corps training. There, really for the first time in life, I met people from all over the United States. We had a genuine respect for each other in that group and it felt like I really belonged. It was a fun experience even though we spent intensely long days in class. It seems virtually all the people in the training program had that sense of euphoria that comes from being involved in a potentially positive accomplishment and doing something good together. By and large we all accepted each other for who we were despite our very varied backgrounds.

The training activities at Eastern Michigan University were pleasantly challenging and included intensive Somali language study, broadly a review of the geography and history of the African continent and much more focused instruction in the geography, history, and especially social organization of the Somali people. We also studied the basics of Islam and many of the other cultural factors more particularly related to our region of service. Each day was ended with a physical activity to try to get us in shape for our forthcoming experience. A special effort was made to emphasize to us the physical challenges we were about to be facing. This received particularly intense review over and over again since the first group of volunteers who had preceded us to Somalia had had an enormously high dropout rate with most of it purportedly stemming from the extreme physical hardships of the posts in our new country of assignment. As it would turn out, all the volunteers in our group would complete their terms of services. It may have been that the intense grilling in the physical and emotional depravation that we were about to face had better prepared us to accept the severe lifestyle challenges we had to deal with in Somalia. In addition, a great deal of training was devoted to understanding culture shock when transitioning between two radically different societies and the measures that could be taken to combat it.

At the end of the summer, fully aware of the hardships and lack of material comfort we were about to face, we had a few days of home leave after which we reassembled in New York City for departure as a group for the Horn of Africa. From the Big Apple we left for another brief training and adjustment period at the University of Nairobi in Kenya. In route, our group had a day-long layover in Rome which would be the first time for setting foot in a foreign country. It had a special excitement all its own. From small town Appalachia to the Eternal City! What a thrilling experience!

With the full day layover in Rome we were able to tour many of the historical locations of the city. After visiting the usual tourist attractions, some of us stopped at a bar for a beer. As we were talking among ourselves, a man came over to us and said he had heard us speaking in English and that we were heading to Africa. We said yes and told him were going to Somalia. Surprisingly, he said "Don't go." When we asked him why he replied that he was Portuguese and he had lived in Africa for many years. He added that there was something about the African continent that entranced long time visitors and that it would continually keep calling us back. We brushed it off at the time but his words would resonate for several decades. The call to return to Africa would become a part of post-Peace Corps life for a long time. The continent's pull would also eventually end up leading to pursuit of a doctoral specialization in Kenyan history in the following decade. Others have shared the same concept of the unusual but constant pull to return to Africa – maybe it is that way because Africa is where humankind originated and we were being called back home.

From Rome we flew to Nairobi for our first sojourn in an African country. This was, of course, a new experience for all of us. We bunked in the residence halls and ate in the University of Nairobi cafeteria where there was some opportunity to meet and talk with Kenyan students. We were still in an academic environment when we were at the University of Nairobi and had only a little opportunity for interaction with the other people of the city. After the few days training in Nairobi and adjustment to our new African environment our group was split up with some of us going to northern Somalia, the former British Somaliland, and others to southern Somalia, the former Somalia Italiana. I was with the group going to the north so we boarded an Air India flight and headed for Aden, which at the time was a British colony, but is today a part of the present day Republic of Yemen. An overnight stay there gave us a first glimpse of the Muslim World and how very, very different it was from the predominantly Christian African society of Kenya. This was followed by a short hop over to Hargeisa in northern Somalia where we had another brief stay and orientation to Somali society. Here we met our first real Somalis outside the United States where the only Somalis we had ever encountered had been our Somali language instructors who themselves had been university students. As such, they all spoke relatively fluent English. They had been recruited from many different American institutions and assembled together at our training site. And as university students, of course, they did not represent the average Somali. Now we were going to get a chance to see the real common folks.

After a brief on-the-spot orientation in Hargeisa, the principal city of northern Somalia, for another volunteer and me it was on to Berbera, the country's chief northern port on the Gulf of Aden, to teach English and history at Berbera Intermediate School for boys. To get there we took a trade truck which was the only form of public transport available. It was basically a two-and-a-half ton truck which carried first-class passengers up front in the cab and freight, livestock, and second-class passengers in the back.

The experience would be a year of transformation for both of us. For the first time in life it would necessary to deal with the real "culture shock" of being in an entirely different environment from that in which we had grown up. It would also be a remarkably good preparation which, unbeknownst at the time, would serve well in later adjustment to a military assignment in Vietnam.

The little house which had been assigned for the Peace Corps teachers was a concrete structure with a living room, a bedroom, a room for eating, and a shower room. It had exterior walls all around it with the heavy ends of broken glass bottles mounted in cement on the top of the walls. In front, the wall was lower and we could see over it. There was an iron gate with a lock. It also had a small room in the corner of the yard for a watchman's quarters. In the back of the house was an open space surrounded by a wall that was much higher than in the front which we could not see over. It too had broken glass bottles implanted in cement at the top. On one side it had a heavy wooden door that remained locked all the time. In another corner of this open space was a long-drop latrine. It was a squat kind of latrine which neither of us had ever used so we built a seat very much resembling a small saw horse to sit on. Maybe you have to grow up with the squat kind of facility to ever really feel comfortable using one. Food was cooked on a repurposed large rectangular oil can which had on the top a place for charcoal over which the pots of food were placed to be cooked. Usually we had a "houseboy" who cooked and also washed clothes from time to time. Because Berbera was a small port city we had around the clock electricity (when the service was operational) which made it possible for us to have a small refrigerator something other volunteers could not have. We also had running hot water. Berbera was supplied with water from natural springs on the escarpment going up to the highlands and the water was piped across the hot coastal desert, so by the time it got into the town it was perfectly warm for a shower. We had no mechanical water heater. Again no other volunteers had such a luxury not even in Hargeisa which was the principal city in the north and the location of the Peace Corps Hostel.

The school we taught at was an open air intermediate school for boys. It was long and lean with windows on each side of the classrooms which could be opened for cross-ventilation. There were also doors on each side of the classrooms which opened to covered verandas that served as hallways connecting the rooms together. As with many structures in Berbera it had a long-drop detached outhouse that served as a latrine. There were four classrooms altogether and another smaller room built the same way as the classrooms with a door on each side as well as windows for circulation. This smaller room was used as an office for the principal and teachers. The doors and windows were always open unless there was a sand storm as happened occasionally in which case they were closed. The school also had electricity for lights which made occasional night classes for adults possible.

The school's teachers gathered in the office to drink tea and talk when they were not in class. This was a good way for us to get to know each other. The other teachers by and large had been to teacher training institutes in Somalia. The language of instruction for the classes was English except for religion and Arabic classes which were taught in Arabic. As a result most of the teachers could speak at least some English except the Egyptian teacher (he was on an Egyptian program somewhat similar to the Peace Corps) who taught the Arabic and religion (Islam or Koranic) classes and spoke no English. All the teachers and the principal were very friendly and helpful. The principal had spent some time as an international student studying at a university in the United States.

By and large teaching at the school was a fun experience. The students were usually polite and well behaved and as such they were a joy to teach. I taught Sixth and Seventh Form students who were generally in the age group from about twelve to fifteen or a little older depending on what age they had started to school. For the most part the students were pretty sharp and had an interest in what they were studying. They had started both English and Arabic language instruction in elementary school and by the time they got to intermediate school they were becoming increasingly adept with them. There did seem to be a significant difference in their command of English between Form Six and Form Seven. This might have been due to the age difference and maturity level as much as ability. But it seemed like they were a lot more at ease speaking English by the time they had gotten to Form Seven. We had some enjoyable sessions not only learning English but also being able to take some examples of things from the United States and other parts of the world to illustrate the points of discussion. We had virtually no instructional materials except for the blackboard with chalk and a small reading book which each student had for use in class. The students brought their own tablets to write on. Most of the students' families were business people associated with the port and its offshoot industries, or their families were employed by the small government sector in Berbera.

There were some interesting experiences that occurred throughout the year. One in particular that comes to mind was trying to teach the English word "soul." The word was in one of the stories in the little reading book the students had. After several vain attempts to try to explain it with all the concepts I could conjure up I could see that none of the students was comprehending what I was trying to explain. So in a sort of desperation after several failed attempts I went and got the principal and asked him if he would come to the classroom and write the Arabic word for "soul" on the blackboard. He looked at me kind of funny like what are you doing teaching this word when you're supposed to be teaching English. I told him the word was in our workbook which it was. At any rate he came into the classroom and wrote the word in Arabic on the blackboard. The students, of course, immediately grasped the concept since they had been studying both Arabic and religion for several years by this time in their academic life. If you reflect on it for a minute the difficulty in conveying this word to another culture and language is readily apparent. Later that day on break in the teacher's and principal's room that topic became the subject of discussion and we all agreed that it was a difficult concept to teach, and the Egyptian Arabic and religion instructor even got in on the conversation with one of the other instructors acting as an interpreter because he spoke no Somali or English.

Our time in Berbera would also be an opportunity for a great deal of reflection and meditation and for the first time in adult life for beginning to critically think and act "outside the box." A November letter to family contained the following commentary:

> I can't decide if I'm just beating in time until my service is over or whether I'm really enjoying it. Try to imagine yourself in a town that looks exactly like a picture in the Bible, with everyone speaking a foreign language you don't understand, with foods that are completely different from the ones you're used to, not knowing if you're acting properly within the culture around you, the unbelievable ignorance of the people around you, and the lack of Western education and culture. At times it makes you wonder when you know that what you're doing isn't going to be a drop in the bucket in improving the situation of these peoples. About the only thing that compensates for it is the patience and friendliness of most of the people we've come in contact with. This town could easily be ancient Nazareth or Tyre (but not Babylon). There are benefits personally though. It's a wealth in experience, I'm getting a good tan, I can kill flies with a wack [sic] of the hand, and I'm learning what it's like to be on your own in a foreign country with all the different cultures, currencies, languages, prejudices, and ideas. I guess I've found out that the one thing that's common to all the

people of the earth is that each and every one of them has personal feelings and emotions. That each one is a human being --well enough of soul-searching for now. I guess all I can say is it's great to be alive.[1]

With the thorough training we had had at Eastern Michigan University and at the University of Nairobi it was a relatively easy transition into teaching intermediate school English and history to Somali boys. The strict discipline and sometimes cruel punishment for those boys who got out of line was a little unexpected but by and large it was a pleasant experience albeit a bit on the dull side for someone accustomed to working a full day and staying busy most of the time. This was especially true since we only taught half a day in the morning because Somalis thought that Berbera with its location on the coast making it a lot hotter than the rest of the region was too unhealthy to work in during the afternoon. Most of northern Somalia is a high plateau which tended to be much cooler in the afternoons than the coastal areas. Because of the relative paucity of other things to do in the heat and since nowhere in the city was there air conditioning, we spent a great deal of time at what has to be one of the most beautiful beaches in the world located near Berbera on the Gulf of Aden. After a few months in-country the following letter went back to West Virginia.

Decided it was time for a semi-annual report of the pros and cons of being in the Peace Corps as far as I'm concerned. The positive list is: know what a blessing God has given Americans, have visited six countries on three continents, ... excellent suntan, read two or three books a week, change and convert currencies, in the process of learning how to live in a different country, know how to use and handle passports and visas. Have flown in virtually every kind of airplane, have visited various ships from rowboats to cargo steamers, have seen deserts, the value of water, camel caravans, oases, have learned how to handle numerous different situations on my own, know what it is to live without television, paved streets, hot water, pure water, beef, ham, chicken, bacon, sausage, flush commodes, etc., have learned how to live with sand, poverty, ignorance, language barriers, beggars, etc., I suppose I could list several more advantages. I could list the negative aspects, but that only leads to a negative attitude so I'll stop.[2]

Although upbeat in a tone which reflected the by-and-large very positive demeanor of the Peace Corps experience, the last sentence which contains a rejection of dealing with any sort of negativity is a foreshadowing of what would emerge as a way of life from the Somali Peace Corps experience followed by later military involvement in Vietnam. Build a wall around what is bothering you and refuse to deal with it. Don't talk about it because it will lead to negative attitudes. That process of failing to deal with unsettling issues would become a way of life in the chaotic aftermath following discharge from the military a few years later. It was a way of life that would be resolved by drowning feelings about uncontrollable life events in a sea of alcohol and other chemicals rather than addressing personal issues head-on and resolving them as they were encountered.

Another pattern that would emerge in this initial Peace Corps year at Berbera Intermediate School was the first introduction to non-alcoholic drug use. Some of the other teachers in the school tended to be young and since we were also young they invited us to chew *qat*[3] (also known as kat) with them one afternoon. Although the folks at our training program had talked about it I had no idea what actually happened when it was chewed. But true to a pattern of addictive behavior I readily agreed to join them. It would represent the first actual use of non-alcoholic drugs. Quite frankly there was not a substantial buzz to it but the experience was somewhat enjoyable although the Somali teachers seemed to get much more buzzed than I did. Maybe I wasn't doing it right. But at any rate we had a good time and were invited to join them again on several occasions during the school year. Thus that first additional chemical was added to alcohol in what would become a repertoire of various addictive substances.

We had a small Vespa motor scooter in Berbera. It was great for getting around town and it used very little petrol. We also rode it to the school where we taught. It was especially useful particularly with the heat in Berbera which made walking in the afternoon almost unbearable. The motor scooter also made going to the beach a lot easier. The beach was about three miles away but easily accessible with the motor scooter. One day I got the idea that I could catch a gazelle by following it on the motor scooter in the bush to catch it. We normally had very little fresh meat and gazelles were good eating. I could trail it on the motor scooter in the bush, and after chasing it for a while and wearing it out, jump off the motor scooter, tackle it by its hind legs and then bring it down. Once tackled and having it down we could skin it and gut it and have it for dinner.

So I proceeded to do this late one afternoon. I went out not too far into the bush until I spotted a gazelle. I followed it for a while to make sure it got good and tired from being chased. Getting close enough to it I jumped off the motor scooter at whatever speed the gazelle was going. I was able to grab its hind quarters but it quickly slipped through my arms and got away. It seemed like its hide was super smooth and slippery and I could not keep hold of it. Banged and bruised I got up and tried to start the motor scooter, but apparently as it crashed when jumping off, it had been damaged and there was no way to get it going again.

By this time it was almost dark and without a moon it was going to get pitch black in the night. I knew I was going to have to act quickly if I did not want to spend the night alone sleeping in the bush. Soon passing in the distance there was a caravan of tethered camels being led by a couple of Somali herdsmen in the front. So I sprinted over to the last of the camels and grabbed its tail. I don't think the Somali men in the front of the caravan even knew I was there. Or, if they did, they did not pay any attention to me.

Soon it was pitch black out but I knew I was headed back to Berbera because that was where the livestock markets were located. It was there that the dhows were anchored. They would take the camels, sheep, and goats, which were the chief exports passing through the Port of Berbera, for transport to Saudi Arabia, their ultimate destination. So logically that is the only place a string of tethered camels would be headed. As a result, I felt confident that as the caravan of camels got closer to Berbera I would recognize the surroundings and could head on home once on familiar turf.

It was not to be the most pleasant journey, however. Camels defecate by expelling excrement that looks like a half a tootsie roll usually several at a time and occasionally more than one time in a row. All of a sudden half tootsie roll type items accompanied by a totally obnoxious smell started blasting away coming from the camel whose tail I was holding. I couldn't let go of the camel's tail because I would soon be lost in the pitch black of the night. So there was nothing left to do but face life on life's terms. It was reflective of the growing stoicism and the ignoring of unpleasantries which was rapidly becoming a way of life in this new African environment.

Eventually, we made it to a spot that I recognized and left the caravan and the camel's tail and hurried back to the Peace Corps cottage. Fortunately, the next day I was able to find an Italian businessman who was a friend and ask him for help. In the daylight I could remember which direction I had gone and we went in his truck out into the bush, found the motor scooter, brought it back to Berbera, and got it repaired. It left a lasting memory. What a lesson in accepting life on life's terms!

A somewhat similar experience would occur later after relocating to southern Somalia to work on a school building project on the Juba River. It was an area with a great deal more water than there was in Northern Somalia and as a result had different types of flora and fauna. One day one of the other Volunteers near the school project we were working on discovered a small little monkey on the ground and walked with it holding its hand to where we were standing and talking. We fed it several bananas and played with it although, even though it seemed to be relishing in the activity, it never moved off the ground. After a while I thought it would be cool to put it on my shoulder and walk around the *megala* (open market) with it.

As soon as picking it up and putting it on my shoulder, however, it started screeching and making all kinds of noise. It became super agitated and soon jumped on top of my head and clung on with all 20 digits clamped tightly to my hair. It would not let go and just kept screeching. The more I tried to pull it off the more it screeched and desperately tightened its grip. Soon it began defecating and the more I pulled the more it defecated. I had no idea what to do although I was sure the monkey must have been shedding some of the many bananas we had been feeding him. After a somewhat prolonged tug-of-war and an immeasurable amount of feces he still would not let go. Finally one of the other Volunteers suggested he was scared to death from the way he was acting and maybe he was afraid of heights. So I bent over and put my head down as close to the ground as possible and he finally, traumatized and I am sure feeling quite relieved, let go of my hair and scampered away. Only later we found out from a Somali friend that these were ground monkeys and they were terrified of heights. They sure did not have those in West Virginia.

The Peace Corps had a policy of letting its volunteers off for a few weeks leave time during their tour of duty. The policy was in place to help build morale and to let the Volunteers become acquainted with a broader regional perspective of where they were serving. I decided to go to Djibouti and Addis Ababa in neighboring Ethiopia. So I took a trade truck from Hargeisa to Zeila near the Somali frontier and crossed over into Djibouti. At the time Djibouti was still under French administration and the French Foreign Legion had a large base in the town. A few pleasant days were spent there, after which plans called for going to Diredawa and Addis Ababa by train. Close to the hotel and the train station was a restaurant and bar. In the evening before boarding the train for Diredawa the next point on this excursion, I went in and sat at the bar to get something for supper. While eating I began talking with some Legionnaires who were also in the bar eating and drinking. Before long we ended up eating and drinking together. They were part of the Legionnaire unit that would be joining the train in Djibouti assigned to protect it for the trip across the arid hinterland of the colony to the Ethiopian frontier. They certainly were a mixed crew of different national origins and varying fluency in English, and it was interesting to be introduced, albeit a little inebriatedly, to this unique group of soldiers. They represented a wide frame of the world human community and many were in the Legion because of poverty or maltreatment or some other unfortunate abuse within the country from which they had originated. Many had been refugees and sought asylum in France through the Legion.

One of the Legionnaires' responsibilities was to guard the Franco-Ethiopian Railroad as the train passed through the rural countryside making its way from Djibouti to Diredawa and then on to Addis Ababa. The train was scheduled to leave Djibouti in the evening for its overnight trip to Diredawa. So I boarded it at its expected departure time of 6:00 p.m. and sat in the rear car with some of the French Legionnaires I had met in the restaurant and continued drinking with them. They had simply left the bar at their designated time to report and boarded the train for their assigned guard duty. The train had hardly left the station and the dinner I had consumed at the bar began to disagree with my stomach and it was churning away when I first began vomiting and this was soon followed with intense diarrhea. The toilet on the train was simply an open hole in the floor of the rail car through which everything passed onto the tracks and cross ties below. That in itself would have been a sufficiently obnoxious experience but a lot more was getting ready to ensue with it and would provide for one unforgettable experience. The meal had included steak and eggs which were apparently not too fresh and had spoiled somewhat. With this experience it would be years before I could eat that combination again.

As soon as the train moved into the open countryside it was attacked by *shifta* (bandits)[4] on horseback. They began shooting into the train with their rifles. This time it was the Legionnaires (who had been openly drinking even after boarding the train and I had joined in with them) shouting to the passengers in French and broken English and Italian to get on the floor which we did. Then the Legionnaires began returning fire out the window as the *shifta* on horseback rode alongside near the train firing shots into it. I crawled in and out of the latrine during this action. Fortunately no one on the train was injured or killed and the raid eventually ceased. After the incident was over one of the Legionnaires who spoke a little English pointed to the new holes in the rail car and then compared them to the holes that had been made in previous raids on the train. Before long the train was nearing the frontier to cross over into Ethiopia. The train stopped at the last station in French Somaliland and the Legionnaires disembarked and a different set of soldiers, this time Ethiopians, took over to escort it to its next stop in Diredawa where I was to get off. By the time we reached Diredawa I was thoroughly sick, exhausted, intoxicated, and shaken to the core from the experience.

When the train pulled up to the station I was so completely confused from drinking with the Legionnaires, being sick from the apparently spoiled food from the previous supper, getting virtually no sleep, and reverberating from the shock of the attack by the *shifta* that I drifted into what I thought was a hotel which was the nearest facility to the train station in which to crash. I stayed in there for a few days rejuvenating from this debauched emotional and physical state. Although not quite sure, I spent most of the time passed out and I think sleeping. Once recovering I linked up with some Ethiopian Peace Corps Volunteers stationed in Diredawa and it was then that I learned that where I had stayed was a bordello. At the end of the stay there, the madam said I had been in there for three days – at least that is what she charged me for. I have little legitimate memory of the experience or what kind of exciting time I may or may not have had at their business location.

After spending a few days visiting in Diredawa I again boarded the train this time for Addis Ababa. The train was packed with people and passengers were shoulder-to-shoulder and standing both in front and in back of each other as if on a crowded elevator. The Ethiopian soldiers were also on board as tightly packed as the rest of us. Suddenly, shortly before the train was to about to leave the station, the soldier who was on my right side began pummeling a young man with his fist immediately in front of me. The soldier yelled at both the young man and at me. I have no idea what he said although I suspected he was saying it in Amharic which was the principal and official language of Ethiopia. The soldier began slugging the young man so hard that blood splattered all over him and then on to me. But the soldier kept on beating him until he yanked the young man and dragged him off the train. None of the other passengers appeared to notice what was going on. At least, they seemed not particularly interested in the scuffle. As soon as they were off the train I said something in English wanting to know what was going on hoping someone would understand me. One of the other passengers several bodies away heard and he yelled back in English over the other passengers "He tried to sneak on the train without paying." Such was the manner of dealing with those persons who attempted to travel on the train without providing the requisite fare.

A first actual experience with war occurred in Aden which at the time was a part of the disintegrating British Empire but today is a part of Yemen. I had gotten a wisdom tooth infection while in Berbera teaching. Since there were no dentists in northern Somalia the Peace Corps sent me across the Gulf of Aden to a British dentist in the colony. The tooth was to be extracted in the medical complex there. Upon arrival I was directed to another building at some distance from the main complex. The dentist was located in a small wooden building with a wide porch on the front. As I walked up to it I was a little leery about what I might be getting into. A very corpulent Somali woman was sitting in a rocking chair on the porch amid a number of goats that ambled about. A slight wind was blowing sand across the wooden flooring. I spoke to the woman in Somali and she spoke back. Then I entered the door to an open waiting room with several wooden captain's chairs all covered with a light layer of dust. Wistfully, I sat down and lingered very much concerned about what was about to transpire. As doubt was about to get the best of the situation and I stood up and started to leave a British dentist opened the door in the back of the waiting room and said "Hello." An Arab teenage boy was with him. He introduced himself and the teenager whom he said would be helping him. The dentist asked if I had ever had the wisdom tooth x-rayed. I told him yes. He then explained he had no equipment for x-raying so he asked if I could remember what the x-ray had looked like. I sketched it out for him as best I could remember. He said he would have to extract the tooth. Then he proceeded to numb it. He directed the Arab teenager to hold my head in a hammerlock. The boy did so and the dentist commenced to work on the tooth extraction. It took some time, but he eventually was able to get it out with the Arab boy clasping my head the whole time as he worked. After he was finished he said he was pleased with the results and how it had come out and then sent me back to the hotel. Soon my jaw was pounding in pain and got very swollen, conditions which I tried to address by drinking as much beer as I could which was difficult because of a mouth that was so swollen.

That evening I decided to go walking just to get out of the hotel room for a while. Because of the intermittent attempts by some of the people in Aden to be rid of their colonial exploiters the British had placed an 8:00 p.m. curfew on the streets of Aden. Just as I was returning to the hotel shortly before the curfew time some British troops appeared on each side of the street. As they patrolled they got fairly close to the hotel and soon shots rang out. One of the soldiers told me to get in the hotel as quickly as possible which I did. As soon as entering several more shots rang out. I am not sure what happened after that but intermittent shots rang out the rest of the evening.

It would be on the return to Hargeisa from this leave time in Djibouti and Ethiopia that I would experience a second battle in Aden. I had had a flight from Addis Ababa to Aden with an overnight layover in Aden waiting for the return flight to Hargeisa the next day. During the overnight that I was there I stayed at a small hotel owned by a Jewish Arab inn keeper. It was a wooden building with a third floor lobby and in the evening since there was a curfew on I was sitting with others in the lobby and a fire fight erupted in front of the building between FLOSY (Federation for the Liberation of Occupied South Yemen) rebels and the British troops. It started with automatic weapons fire in the front of the building. The Jewish innkeeper came running into the lobby shouting for us to get down on the floor which we fortunately did in time to miss the rounds which penetrated the front wall of the hotel. The fire fight did not last long and no one in the hotel was injured but the attack left holes in the wall. After it was over the innkeeper talked with me for a while. He said he wanted to leave Aden and take his family to Israel because there was no future for Jews in Yemen. For some reason despite the live fire I was not particularly rankled by this experience with what would a few years later become common place in Vietnam. A letter home after returning to Hargeisa described it almost routinely in full detail. Here it is:

> The day before I came to Hargeisa a bomb exploded about a block from my hotel in Aden. One Arab was killed and some other people injured. The British had had enough of the terrorization so they suspended the Aden constitution and placed the government in the hands of the high commissioner. The[y] also put on an eight o'clock curfew. I went to my hotel about seven and about eight-thirty I heard a rat-tat-tat of a machine gun. I went to the window of the lobby to look out, but the manager shouted to get back and sit down. All the lights went

off in the hotel as another machine gun roared from the front door of the building. Soon the shots were coming from all directions. British troops swooped in to the area and the fighting spread to the top of the building across the street. A hand grenade blasted the opposite building. Flares went up. The battle lasted for about a half hour with occasional shots until ten o'clock. We were on the third floor of the hotel building and most of the fighting took place in the street below and on the top of a two story building across the street. We had an excellent view of it – it was like watching a war movie with cinemascope, panavision and all. The mop-up operation lasted till about midnight with helicopters and flood lights everywhere. BBC news from London broadcast the fight around the world at eleven as we watched the mop-up. It was interesting, but I don't think I would want to be in the middle of a battle. It got especially close when one British soldier stationed himself with his machine gun in the doorway of the hotel about thirty feet below us. Hand grenades put off quite a little explosion. We could feel the shock of it even though we were across the street. Something you don't get in the war movies. It had all been started when the British curfew patrol had spotted a couple of Arabs out after 8:00 o'clock. Turns out they had a couple of machine guns with them too. They never did catch the Arabs and supposedly nobody was killed in the fighting. It is a good thing to come in before a curfew I think. The ironic part is that if there is any trouble in Somalia the Peace Corps will be evacuated to Aden.[5]

The free spirit lifestyle of the Peace Corps experience in Somalia fit in fine with my own still libertarian view of the nature of life. The freedom and feeling of serenity was reflected in letters home as attested by the excerpt from the following while still in Berbera:

> There's one thing I've decided about being here and that is you're on your own, you don't have a boss, you can more or less do what you think is right without having someone constantly beside you watching. On my time, if I want to I can pick up and take off to just about anywhere in the country I want to go. I don't have to get approval from anyone. I don't have to worry about money because I can bum a ride or walk or thumb. And to top it off it's all pretty safe if you use your head. One of the five pillars of Islam is almsgiving and if you ever really needed anything you could stop at one of the nomad's and even though they probably wouldn't have much they would give you food and drink. When I come back to the U. S. I will tell you some of the true stories of the hospitality they have shown to lost Europeans on the desert.[6]

That is not to say that we were never being watched or that no one noticed our presence. On one occasion in Berbera we were put under house arrest and not permitted to leave our walled cottage. The Somalis had received a shipload of military equipment especially tanks and armored personnel carriers from the Soviets. They were being unloaded at the port in Berbera and they were destined for Hargeisa and other points in the interior. But as we sat in the house under confinement we could see them driving by on the street in front of us. We were not sure why they went past our place since we were not on the main road to Hargeisa. We think that it is possible that they could have driven around the block a few times so that we would see them more than once and conclude that the total number was far greater than what they actually got. Personally, I really did not care what kind of military equipment the Russians gave to the Somalis. It was between them. Once the armaments had passed through Berbera and on to Hargeisa we were released from house arrest.

Apparently, when the police had nothing better to do they would occasionally keep track of us. Here is a description of one occasion:

> He [the police chief] scolds us like a couple of naughty children. Kind of makes you feel wanted. They have taken to watching us. Yesterday we were at the beach and they came to make sure we were all right. [My roommate] left to come back to town and I stayed out there by myself soaking up the sun and reading. Back came [my roommate] in a couple of minutes saying we should stay together the police thought. I told him he would have to stay with me because I wasn't leaving. So he left. I was expecting the police to come back and scold me again. They're only trying to do their duty, I guess.[7]

Not all of the stay in Berbera was peaches and cream. Sometimes anger or maybe better called irateness would emerge:

> I think I was prepared for all the poverty, ignorance, anti-America, etc., that is around, but one thing I never thought about before I got here was the boredom....

I think it might be all right too if there was any appreciation of what we're doing. But when I go through Berbera and get stoned and people yell "Go home Merecan!" and then beg us for everything we own it gets kind of discouraging. I'm to the point now where I'm just waiting for one of the stones to hit me and I'm going to smash some SOB from here to Hell and back.[8]

Fortunately that event never happened. The development of this attitude was probably related to the boredom that was associated as much with the sleepy port city of Berbera and the relatively little there was to do there as anything else. However, there were a few events when we felt very unsafe in northern Somalia. One in particular is worth noting. One day when on a trade truck returning to Berbera after a few days visit to the Peace Corps hostel in Hargeisa, the driver stopped for a tea break in a small village whose name I do not recall. I was riding in the passenger seat. When the vehicle was parked and the villagers saw the driver had a "European" with him they began to surround the truck and soon the crowd scene started to take the form of an angry mob. I am not sure what they were so angry about but their animus was very definitely directed toward me. The only one who appeared to be on my side was the driver who was obviously trying to defend his passenger. As this unfolded, the driver told me to crouch down on the floor of the cab so I could not be seen. The mob shouted back and forth with each other for what seemed like an eternity as I crouched on the floor of the cab.

Slowly but surely the driver began inching his way toward the door of the cab as the crowd appeared to be splitting into two groups arguing back and forth. When the driver got close to the cab door he jumped in and immediately gunned the engine to get away from the crowd which was banging on the truck and shouting what I am sure were probably some kind of reproductive obscenities coupled with threats as the driver moved forward. He was able to break free from the crowd and get back on the main road which was only a dirt track. As we resumed our journey to Berbera he said that some of the angry crowd had wanted to kill me. He had risked his own life defending me which he felt was his duty as the driver. The event had been very scary and I was in a stunned state.

By the time I had gotten back to Berbera after this incident I was badly shaken and had decided to quit the Peace Corps and head back to West Virginia. However, because there was no telegraph communication with Hargeisa due to one of the many frequent equipment stoppages, it was not possible to immediately tell the Peace Corps regional representative that I was leaving. During the interim for several days before service was restored, I had the opportunity to cool off. Usually the only communication we had with the Peace Corps administration and other volunteers was through the telegraph. For whatever reason it was not functioning in the days following this event. That in and of itself was not unusual. By the time service was restored I had settled down and had a change of mind. I had actually written a letter home telling my parents of the decision. It was never mailed.

Despite the occasional challenges such as the above, self-confidence was becoming increasingly incorporated into these living conditions. This was especially true insofar as reliance on the need for material things for comfort and entertainment were concerned. Dealing with culture shock was also expressed in this letter while in Berbera.

> Physical hardships are almost nothing once you get accustomed to them. Now I use an outside john, eat goat meat (tough as shoe

leather), fight flies, ignore dirt, and become oblivious to poverty, ignorance, and disease. These are things that one becomes used to....

I am staying here by myself tonight since [my roommate] went to Sheikh and won't be back until tomorrow. I'm the only American within fifty miles.... This time last year if someone said I would be stuck in Africa by myself I would have said no, never. But it's not that bad, once you get used to it.... It kind of grows on you and it's not nearly so bad as it might sound....[9]

Besides the growing self-confidence we were also learning to deal with the unproven tales that so frequently circulated around as rumor. There are a lot of similarities about rural areas included in the following letter especially about the rumors of the grand and suspicious events that supposedly happened or were about to happen. Such similarly-themed stories could be found in rural areas of Appalachia, and probably in rural areas just about anywhere.

Big rumor in Berbera. Seems the military got all excited and said over their radio that three Peace Corps Volunteers in Berbera [there were actually only two of us stationed there] had been arrested for espionage. They sent the message and it was picked up by the Ethiopian Army who told the Americans there. I guess from there it went to the Ethiopian Ambassador [United States Ambassador to Ethiopia] who told the state department who told the Somali Ambassador [to Washington] who told the Peace Corps Rep here. Or some strange rumor like that. I just got odds and ends of it so I don't know how true it is or if that is exactly what happened. Did I tell you that our principal said that he heard we were arrested and that he called the District Commissioner who verified it and said we were awaiting trial. This all supposedly happened when actually we were spending a quiet Friday at the beach.

I am beginning to believe that these people would believe anything that they heard spoken on the radio in [the] Somali language. They say some of the strangest things that people have told them, these things being so obviously illogical yet they will not change their beliefs even when they can see the logic that something is false. [*Was this anticipating the development of social media here??*]

Around Hargeisa people are saying *Merican basass* [American spies]. They call it out as you walk on the streets. What I want to know is what do they have here for us to spy on. Besides it's an insult to think that I would be a spy for $130 a month. When people have seen only one thing in their life they come to believe that that is all that exists and they can fight what ever comes their way. They probably could on the same grounds. I would not want to fight anyone using their weapons and their abilities with them. However, they fail to realize that other people have other things and other ways which could completely obliterate them if they had the desire. This is why they think that we are spies because they have these new things and have no conception of what an arsenal the U. S. has with all its missls [*sic*] subs, jets, etc. I even had a boy in one breath say their army could whip anybody and in the next breath ask me what a submarine was.[10]

Toward the end of our first year of teaching at Berbera Elementary School some of the Volunteers and the Peace Corps In-Country Team at the behest of the Somali Department of Education looked at the possibility of a school construction program to be carried out by Volunteers. One of the most challenging problems facing the Somali Department of Education was that many schools were only a single classroom and an objective of state policy was to attempt to integrate the colonial era system that had been put in place as part of the different school systems that characterized the British and Italian colonial empires. In conjunction with that attempt to streamline and integrate the two systems the Somali government also hoped to expand the integration objective to include addressing the challenge of inadequate classroom space throughout the system and in the process make it possible for more young people to go to school. Toward this end they intended to double the existing one-room schools in rural areas by adding an additional classroom to as many of them as possible. This would give them more flexibility in aligning the two systems and expanding the number of young people enrolled.

During the summer break from teaching several of the volunteers had worked on an experimental project to expand a school in northern Somalia by adding some additional classrooms. The activity appeared to be quite a success. Eventually the Peace Corps In-Country Team, in cooperation with the Somali government and the United States Agency for International Development (USAID), decided to implement a plan which would set up an experimental project to determine the viability of building school additions in very rural and remote villages in different parts of the country. In effect, the conceptualized program envisioned a cooperative arrangement in which local districts would contribute what they could which was normally sand, labor, and water (a very important resource in the desert) and USAID would contribute the imported materials needed to complete the additions including windows, cement, hardware, and any other construction items that had to be brought in from industrialized areas of the world.

Working on the school building project was a lot of fun plus it was a good learning experience. So toward the end of the summer when the Peace Corps administration asked if anybody would like to volunteer to work on the experimental program to see if the school addition project could be expanded into other communities several of us volunteered. In this experimental pilot project a Volunteer would be assigned to a tiny village which had an existing school and his job would be to go to meet with the District Commissioner and the local elders to determine if the village wanted to expand its school and if it was willing to participate by coming up with its share of the match so it could be built. If they agreed then the Volunteer would arrange for the materials to be delivered to the sight and stay *in situ* while the addition to the school was being completed. Once the decision to proceed had been agreed upon, it usually took somewhere in duration from about a month to six weeks to be completed assuming all went according to plan. Before we had finished our committed tour of duty in the Peace Corps the administration was so satisfied about how it was working that the decision had been made in Washington to implement a full complement of volunteers to carry out this project with the next cycle of new volunteers coming to Somalia.

Getting involved in this arrangement led to a very profound experience and one which would provide an opportunity to visit many different areas in rural Somalia and to see how those mostly out of the mainstream communities could come together to achieve an objective. It had the added benefit of giving rural Somalis the opportunity to see an American for the first time. It would be a time of relative hardship for the Volunteer that occasionally bordered on the extreme, but also one for learning to appreciate a lot of things that had been taken for granted before to be able to function in the severe circumstances that working in such a materially challenged environment entailed. And it was also a tremendous learning experience to see and interact with people who lived in a very different and rural way from the more urbanized and relatively cosmopolitan people of Berbera.

So we loaded up for that first assignment in the bush. It was to be in a small village along the Somali-Ethiopian frontier. The road to the site followed exactly along the border between the two countries over a flat level plain that extended in an almost unbroken line for hundreds of miles. In fact, there were Ethiopian defensive bunkers scattered along the route we were to travel. We had to be careful when we came close to one – we could usually tell because they were frequently isolated and since the land was so flat and unobstructed they were usually in full view and, of course, they had the Ethiopian flag flying. As we neared them we made sure that we drove around on the Somali side of the border. We would spend about three months out in this section working on schools in two different villages. There was never an incident with the Ethiopian border patrol. The villages themselves were actually located in both countries with the dividing line usually running somewhere through the middle of the village. It was adjacent to an area of Ethiopia called the Haud which was inhabited primarily by Somalis and which was claimed by the Somali government.

It would have been impossible to complete any work in these villages without the assistance of a "houseboy" named Dahir. He was a fun-loving 15-year old who was from a different clan than the folks in the villages where we were going to build the school additions. His people were located in western

Somalia not far from Djibouti. This made him impartial in any discussions we carried out with the villagers in this area since he had no clanal relatives there. He was also married although I never met his wife who lived near Borama in western Somalia. He could speak passable English so we could communicate with each other. He frequently acted as interpreter when we were around other people in the village. However, in the negotiations with the village elders and developing the consensus necessary to move forward on a project it was usually the District Commissioner, virtually all of whom in this part of Somalia spoke English, who served in the position of interpreter.

The negotiations we carried out among us were limited only to men. And they could be somewhat prolonged. Frequently the Somalis would often talk among themselves and only in Somali, so I was never quite sure where their direction was going, but ultimately the various responsibilities got passed around and an agreement was reached to proceed along the general lines of the program as established in the Peace Corps' agreement with the Somali government. Dahir was never in on these discussions so I was usually not quite sure what kinds of trade-offs might have been made among the villagers and the District Commissioner to bring all this together. It just seemed to happen once we had all talked about it long enough.

On one such occasion the question of education for girls came up. The District Commissioner was translating and we were talking with an elderly sheikh. The old man looked at the District Commissioner and, speaking in Somali, it was obvious he wanted to ask a question. The District Commissioner said to me, "The sheikh wants you to tell him why we should educate girls." The question took me by surprise for a minute since it was totally unexpected, but I soon realized this was a golden opportunity to push for education of girls. I replied to him "If you educate a boy you only educate one person, but if you educate a girl that girl can teach all her children to read and write and as a result you can educate a lot more people that way with very limited resources." The old sheikh thought about it for a few minutes and then he said: "For such a young person you are very wise." Nonetheless all the schools that we worked on were boys' schools. It was inconceivable that boys and girls could attend the same institution.

Some really interesting experiences would come out of this venture. For the most part we had only a couple army cots, a few blankets, and a British Berkfield water filter which we took with us. There was so little water available in the villages that by and large we were lucky to get only a cup or two of water processed overnight. This I used to brush my teeth with or if possible to make a cup of instant coffee. Dahir got the murky stuff that we ran through the filter from somewhere around the village. I'm not sure where. There was a tea shop in the village and they made tea. Dahir cooked rice for us that we had brought to the site along with a few canned vegetables that we also were able to eat. I am not sure where the water for the rice and tea came from but maybe I probably would not want to know. Occasionally if the village butchered a goat we would get a few morsels of it. We stayed in what was the office of the one room school as we built the other room. Probably the roughest part of the stays in these villages was that there was no water for showering. So after about four weeks or so we would drive back to Hargeisa to the Peace Corps hostel to take a long-awaited shower. It certainly gave one a sense of the importance of water and showering in daily life.

Most of the time the attitude of the villagers in the rural countryside was generally one of curiosity. Many had never seen a European descended person before or at least not up close. Frequently, if I sat at the teahouse in the *megala*, people would come up as near as possible sometimes even feeling an arm or shoulder to see if it was real. On many occasions little kids would freak out when they saw you. Several times five or six year olds would didlybop down the main roadway of the village and, when they saw you, their facial expressions would burst out with terror, they would throw up their hands and scream for bloody murder, and they would run in the opposite direction. The villagers would often get a good laugh at the kids' expense over their response.

After completing school additions in two neighboring villages in this location on the Somali/Ethiopian border Dahir and I moved to another area of northern Somalia to a village located on the main road from Berbera to Hargeisa. It was named Redab Khartimo and the villagers and local administration were very friendly and receptive to what we proposed to do. Although it was very close to the village where the trade truck had stopped the previous year on the run from Hargeisa to Berbera and we had been surrounded by the mob, the experience in this community would prove to be very different. When we arrived we received an enthusiastic welcome from the villagers. Fortunately this village had access to more water and it even had a shower in the tiny one-room flat in which we stayed including a holding reservoir which was filled from the village well from time to time so we actually were able to stay relatively clean. We still labored under very difficult circumstances but this village was a real pleasure to work in. The people of the community were especially excited about getting an addition to their school. As the project progressed their attitude was so genuinely helpful and positive that we were able to add a number of ancillary facilities to the project as it came to fruition. Their eagerness to be involved was tremendous and they really pitched in to help.

The excitement about the reception we had received was so great that it led to a very expressive letter reflecting the enthusiasm that the villagers had inspired for making the project into a much larger facility:

> Sorry I haven't written for a while, but I've been kind of busy. I've got such a good response from these people [in Redab Khartimo] that we've decided to expand the school program. I've got quite a little operation going here. Besides the classroom, we're remodeling the present building. In addition, I talked the [Peace Corps] staff into letting me expand it into a sort of community center which will include a soccer field, volleyball-tennis combination court, basketball court, swings, a jungle jim apparatus, and an outdoor theatre for movies. It is mostly all my layout and design – I got one volunteer in Hargeisa to make the swings and jungle jim. The rest is mostly my ideas. I was glad to have some responsibility for a change. To top it off all the materials for this should run to less than $1000. It has kept me kind of busy doing it. I've been getting teaching materials, etc. from the American Consulate, banks, volunteers and Peace Corps, plus remodeling the present school. This project is sort of my "baby." I'm considering now whether to get some trees and set them out. Here is what it will look like:[11]

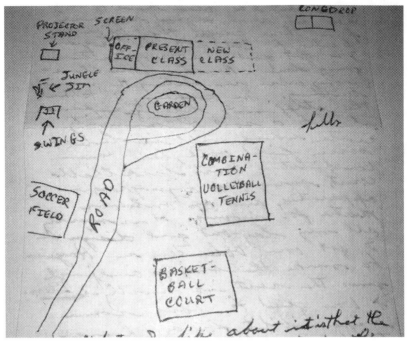

Illustration 2.1 – Layout of Ridab Khartimo school complex.

The interaction with the Somali community was a very real pleasure during the course of this project. We did indeed complete everything, except for the trees, and the villagers were as excited as we were. We built consensus and we all worked together very smoothly and it was probably a very positive reflection of what the Peace Corps and its philosophy were all about. People were coming together in mutual agreement to help each other. Later in the same letter the following observations were noted:

> I've been accepted by the other workmen as a qualified stone mason. It is a craft that should be useful in the future. It is not too difficult as far as skill goes after some practice, but working in the hot African sun takes some

endurance. USAID [United States Agency for International Development] sent up an inspector who came out to the project with the American consul in Hargeisa. From reports that reached me, he was duly impressed with the work on the school....[12]

The experience working with the people of Redab Khartimo is probably one of the most treasured events of my professional life. It certainly provided the opportunity to work in a totally foreign environment and to build consensus and accomplish goals with people who truly wanted to do something to improve their community. It is a memory too which reflects that we could all accomplish something working with others regardless of the degree to which the backgrounds and cultures varied among those involved. It also reflects the concept that rural people can work together to accomplish a goal which met their needs. So often rural people have been falsely accused of being too conservative and seeing no reason to take action to improve their lives hence they do not make the changes that are necessary to adapt to a continually altering reality. The actions of the people of Ridab Khartimo proved otherwise and indicate that rural people can and will change their conditions if the rationale for doing so meets their needs and is within the parameters of something they feel they can accomplish. Personally the whole very positive experience of the school construction program would also be a contributing factor toward acceptance of responsibility within the context of another culture and being able to produce results a few years later in Vietnam.

After finishing the complex at Redab Khartimo I was transferred down to the southern part of the country to work on schools in the Juba and Sciabelli Rivers area. The process was the same one we had used in northern Somalia, but there were a lot of different cultural and environmental factors at work. Southern Somalia had been an Italian colony and there were several Catholic Churches as well as a number of Italian settlers who still clung to the past. Because of the higher rainfall and passage of the two rivers bringing water from the Ethiopian highlands the vegetation and even the fauna were both different from the north. In the riverine area bananas were an important crop. The area also had a different variety of insects and related species as well as other animals.

One very unique experience was the invasion of the locusts. They swarmed. And did they swarm. Enormous numbers of them appeared virtually from nowhere one day. Locusts are essentially grasshoppers which grow to enormous size. Some of these reached at least six inches long and maybe five inches high and their trunks might be an inch or more in diameter. There were what seemed like literally thousands of them that descended upon us. They were unbelievably noisy and ate everything they could. Even the lizards which were usually always present in buildings and kept the other insects at bay disappeared in the face of the locusts. The locusts easily invaded the open air spaces in the little house in which we were staying. It was almost impossible to sleep because they would get caught under our cots and every time they jumped they would hit the bottom of the cot and thus could not hop away so they just continued trying to hop throughout the night banging their bodies against the bottom of the cot as we tried to sleep. Eventually, after a few days of intrusion, they disappeared just about as quickly as they had originally appeared.

Another set of pests – including one that was a dangerous threat – were the millipedes and centipedes. The millipedes, although not particularly comely to look at, were relatively harmless. The centipedes on the other hand, were very poisonous. They had, at least according to our Somali friends, a hundred legs that had poison ducts in them and if they got hold of you would empty all those poison ducts into you. They also had a red spiked tail that had a poison duct in it. One evening when we were allotted two hours of electricity for the house and we could use electric lights, I was sitting in a chair reading and I began to feel something crawling across the top of my right foot. I had on flipflops which were standard apparel. Looking down there was a centipede with its hundred legs and red spiked tail stuck up in the air walking leisurely across my foot. I froze. I did not want to move because to do so would have probably set off his poison ducts. So I sat frozen in place until he finally inched his (or maybe her) way across my foot. As soon as he had finally gotten back on the floor and off my foot I jumped up and landed with that right flipflop on top of him thus removing the threat. All in a day's work, but something to tell the other volunteers during story time.

One of the drawbacks of living in a culture such as Somalia's with a major dichotomy between men and women and with whom we could interact was the virtual total non-contact with women. The only exception to this was that we could and did have contact with sex workers and not only on a solely erotic basis. We could frequently talk with them and even discuss ideas and experiences especially in Mogadishu where virtually all of them spoke at least some English. It is truly with a feeling of missing out on a major part of the Somali culture that we had virtually no contact with women other than sex workers. Somali guys were frequently very friendly, helpful, and hospitable especially if you reciprocated in kind. But we had no way of learning about women other than seeing them in their daily activities of tending sheep and goats and taking care of children. Talking to them as independent human beings never happened.

As with most all things though there was one lone exception to this. There was a point in time when some Somali male friends and I were talking with each other while standing nearby a woman who was milking a goat. Generally-speaking in Somalia men milked camels and women milked goats. I inquired from the guys I was talking to about how it was done. They asked the woman if I could watch. Then they suggested that I should try it. The woman also invited me in Somali to do so. The woman then began actually showing and telling in Somali how to milk a goat. She let me try it but I could not get very much milk to come out. I am also certain the goat was as confused about all this as I was. Everybody involved, both men and women, had a good laugh, and I learned it took a lot more practice and skill than expected to milk a goat.

Women in Somalia as far as I could see never wore the burka or the hajib as in some other Muslim countries. Instead they wore a small skull cap sort of thing not too dissimilar to the headpiece worn by a lot of Mennonite women in West Virginia. They did wear long dresses but frequently their shoulders were not covered. In Mogadishu Somali women could sometimes be seen clothed in western dress.

Upon completion of the time in Somalia and returning home to the States from the Peace Corps I was on top of the world. Looking back, although I had tried the first narcotic drug in Somalia, the desire to get a buzz going was not a predominant factor in life. Alcohol consumption had the same pattern, though, since every time I took that first drink I wanted to keep on going until I got a buzz. But most of the time I was OK without drinking and drugging. The craving was not there. And, by my own rationalization, I really did not drink and drug any more than any other people at that stage of life. All was right in the world. I had acquired a set of skills that included especially the ability to live and operate effectively in a totally alien environment and I had a degree of self-confidence that just about anything was accomplishable if the proper effort and attitude were put into it. I had also gained a great respect for people of many different cultures and backgrounds and was beginning to comprehend the universality of all human beings. I had seen suffering and violence on a scale I had never seen before. All this added to a much broader acceptance of human beings for who they are and for whom they could become within their own conceptualization of humanity.

It was during the time in Somalia that I became very much opposed to capital punishment. I am not really sure what precipitated this – perhaps it was all the reading we had had the opportunity to do while teaching at the school in Berbera. At any rate by the time of returning to the States opposition to it had solidified and I had begun to believe in becoming actively involved in eliminating it especially in West Virginia. Such active opposition was not to lead to active participation in opposing it, however, at least not in West Virginia, because in 1965, unbeknownst because I was in Somalia, the Legislature of West Virginia had abolished capital punishment. And they had done it without my involvement.

❧ Chapter 3 ❧

Vietnam

Returning home from the Peace Corps and on top of the world and able to face any challenge, I thought it would be a good idea to go to graduate school. A bachelor's degree was simply not enough. Lots of people had them. Quite frankly, looking back, I think it was as much as anything a low self-esteem issue. In one way or another, I equated education – especially higher education – as somehow making the individual a little bit more morally superior to others. I had some money from an adjustment allowance provided by the Peace Corps for returned volunteers. Plus during the summer after returning from Somalia I worked some for the newspaper that I had formerly been employed by and saved a little money from that gig. So I headed off to graduate school hoping to be able to make it. The funding was quickly evaporated and, although I performed satisfactorily during the first semester, a couple of weeks after the start of the second semester I ran out of money and had to withdraw.

At the time the U.S. Census Bureau was beginning a survey in West Virginia and word spread that they were hiring people. One of the positions they were hiring for was a district manager (the exact job title no longer comes to mind) of a multi-county area that was being surveyed. It was during the height of the

Cold War and the federal government was measuring crawl spaces under houses, basements and similar areas around homes to be used for shelter in the event of a nuclear attack. The survey was intended to evaluate the available space that existed in a specific regional area and then an analysis of the data so collected would be forwarded the appropriate federal agencies for interpretation. I applied for the position and after a successful job interview got hired.

Although not seeing this as particularly what I wanted to do in life it paid well for the time being and after some adjustments and learning what was expected the Census Bureau Regional Director in Charlotte was happy with my performance. From the way they talked they were satisfied that I could be stereotyped as a capable West Virginia "good old boy" that they might utilize at a later date. They, in fact, advised that after finishing with whatever military commitment that might be coming my way to let them know because they always needed people to work both in West Virginia and at their Washington DC Headquarters in Suitland, Maryland.

They knew of the potential for military service because the Vietnam War was ratcheting up and so they had asked about completion of my obligation. Essentially all potential employers routinely asked young men what their draft status was since they had to factor that into any job package, and, of course, I had to tell them that the draft board was looking intently at me (since I did not have bone spurs). This was before the lottery system was put into place so it did not really matter what your birthday was. If the draft board thought you were eligible and available they would come looking for you. In fact, while working for the Census Bureau for that brief stretch of time, I was having lunch in a neighboring county and who should come walking into the restaurant but none other than "the draft board lady." She was so called because she had the authority to identify eligible young men to be drafted into the military. In actuality, she made a recommendation to the Local Draft Board which would then do the actual call up of the individual. She saw me sitting there eating lunch as she came in. Without hesitation she lifted up a long bony finger, pointed it at me, and said, "I'm gonna get you."

Alas, the handwriting was on the wall because if the draft board lady was going to get you she knew where to look and how to come after you. So I got in touch with the local recruiter, and because the employment with the Census Bureau was just about finished, we negotiated a voluntary decision to join the Army (hence, my serial number begins with RA rather than US which applied to draftees). And so I prepared to enter the military. The physical exam was at the same Induction Center where I had originally flunked the Peace Corps physical a few years before. This time I easily passed. Then I awaited orders to go to the initial assignment. The arrangement that had been worked out with the Army recruiter was that after Basic Training and Advanced Individual Training (AIT) I would go to Officer Candidate School (OCS) to be trained as a Second Lieutenant in the Transportation Corps. With all the interest in running around the world I figured the Transportation Corps was a good bet. And it had the added potential of being positive training and experience for a possible civilian job upon discharge from the Army. After completing OCS (within about a year of enlistment) I would sign on for another two years of active duty as a 2nd lieutenant in the Transportation Corps. If I did not complete OCS the total liability for service would be for only two years and I would be discharged with no further obligation.

So off I went to Basic Training and infantry Advanced Individual Training (AIT) at Fort Dix, New Jersey, in what seemed to be the coldest winter with the deepest snow that I had ever seen. Although I had not had a very high opinion of our expanding the war in Vietnam in a way I looked forward to seeing what indeed it was all about. I can remember sitting in our little Peace Corps house in Berbera, Somalia, in 1965 when the BBC news item about President Johnson dramatically increasing the troop level in Vietnam was announced. I can remember shaking my head and thinking what a major policy blunder that was. No foreign power was going to insert itself into another country's civil war successfully. All it could do would be to prolong the civil war with a lot more casualties and a lot more property damage which a poor Third World country could hardly absorb. And in this case it certainly turned out to be true.

After Basic and Advanced Individual Training (which was required for all new recruits) at Fort Dix it was off to Officer Candidate School at the Fort Benning, Georgia, infantry training facility. From the beginning I was not particularly excited about it. It was not that I could not really handle it. It was challenging but not unduly so. However, it did not take long to decide that this was not a good path for me. It came to a head when the people in charge (whoever they were) decided they were not going to honor the promises of assignment that had been agreed upon before enlistment. There was not going to be any going to the Transportation Corps as an officer. Everybody was going into Infantry and would be assigned to an infantry platoon in Vietnam. To me this simply voided any agreement we had especially since it would mean another two years of military service after finishing OCS. By then it was widely known that a young lieutenant would have to spend 18 months rather than a year in Vietnam if he wanted to get an early out instead of being reassigned for the full extra year when he returned to the States. The alternative to eighteen months was to return for a one-year assignment stateside after a year in Vietnam. By this time if I just stayed in as an enlisted personnel it would be possible to get out in a year at the end of the regular enlisted tour-of-duty in Vietnam. After talking to the company commander about it we pretty much agreed that we should part company from Officer Candidate School. He said he thought he could get me a Specialist 4th class ranking, which he did, and I was sent to a holding company for a few weeks prior to some home leave and shipment to Vietnam.

After a couple of weeks leave back in West Virginia I left for Vietnam. The journey there went first to visit relatives in New Mexico then to some friends in California who had been in OCS at Fort Benning. They were among the several others who had taken the same path I did once the post-OCS assignment that had been agreed upon with the recruiters was voided. We drove up the Pacific Coast Highway from Los Angeles to San Francisco where we went to Chinatown. From there it was on to Fort Lewis in Washington State and a couple days later a flight from Seattle to Cam Ranh Bay. After a few days adjustment in Cam Ranh Bay we were split up and I was sent to the American Division Headquarters at Chu Lai in the southern part of I Corps. I had a good friend from Puerto Rico I had met at Fort Benning. We were actually put on the same flight from Seattle to Vietnam. I had hoped we might be assigned to the same unit since we both arrived in-country on the same flight, but that was not to be. We each were sent to separate units when we left Cam Ranh Bay. I was assigned to the American Division in the northern part of South Vietnam. My Puerto Rican buddy went somewhere in the Mekong Delta. Fortunately, I learned later he made it through the experience and back home.

For several days after arriving at the American Division Headquarters we spent a week or two in a holding company getting acclimated to Vietnam, the war, and military action. While there, we performed various routine maintenance functions, after which GI's were assigned to the different units that they would actually serve in. Having an infantry MOS (military occupational specialty) I was assigned to an infantry battalion of the 11th Light Infantry Brigade based at LZ (Landing Zone) Bronco located adjacent to the village of Duc Pho in Quang Ngai Province in southern I Corps. A group of us were flown to brigade headquarters there where we were briefed for a few minutes by some of the officers in charge. At the end of the briefing we were to go to our actual units of assignment. Before standing down, however, a captain asked the group "Is anyone here a college graduate who knows how to type?" Two or three people came forward and the captain asked us what our majors were. I told him mine was economics.

He said they needed a typist to work on a project for a few days and to come inside the S-1 hootch[1] for a typing test. I followed him in and he gave me something to type (on a manual typewriter which was basically all that was used then). I typed out the paragraph or so that he handed me. He looked at it and said that I was going to be working with him for a few days. He then sent me to drop my gear in a billets hootch and get a bunk. There were only a couple of bunks in the hootch and obviously somebody had already staked out a claim on one of them so I picked the other one. This was the start of what would be a very different war zone assignment from what most infantry GI's experienced. As it unfolded over the next several weeks the adjutant and his assistant would see that I could function in a non-western society under war zone pressure and that would lead to a lot of different assignments based out of the adjutant's office which would be unlike those that most new 'grunts'[2] experienced on their initial assignments to Vietnam.

Most newly-enlisted GI's sent into combat in Vietnam were young and inexperienced. They had enlisted or been drafted or joined the army under pressure of their local draft board. It was not unusual to see 18 and 19 year old kids operating M-16's and M-60's or whatever other weapon they had been assigned. They had been trained to be killers and now they were actually getting the opportunity for doing it. They worked in a situation and under conditions they did not really understand or have the background to deal with. Much has been written about the effects of the violence of war on these young people. Probably as important was the "culture shock" they were totally unprepared to deal with. And culture shock was something the Army left virtually untouched during their training. They were terrified – not only with the brutal pragmatism of armed combat but also with an alien culture that was totally confusing to most of them. This was even more so for infantry soldiers coming from an urban background especially those from the inner city thrust into a rural village society that they had no way of comprehending. Yet they were expected to function satisfactorily to accomplish any mission they were assigned.

The officers who were supposed to lead them were by and large as equally inexperienced and ill-equipped to handle their responsibilities as the new recruits were. Although many of the young officers were highly motivated and competent, a lot of them were straight out of OCS with no prior experience in a war zone and who also had no training about how to operate in a rural area with no understanding of the cultural challenges they faced. Some were frequently very "gung-ho" types and ready to brashly assert their courage and capabilities. Many were as inadequately trained as some of the troops they hoped to lead. Sometimes they tended to be very overconfident in their abilities as officers. This could and frequently did change radically once they were on assignment in the field. Most of them soon learned it was not quite the optimistic adventure story they had pre-supposed it to be. They were only marginally more capable of completing war time tasks than the men they were assigned to lead and, for the most part, just as naïve and ill-equipped in dealing with different cultures. In some cases their maturity level often failed to surpass that of their troops. This was a perfect set-up for developing a prejudicial attitude toward the Vietnamese regardless of what ethnic American background the individual soldier happened to represent. I have tremendous respect for all these young men who were trying to do the best they could under very trying circumstances and with substantively inadequate training for what they were supposed to be doing. Many were thrown into circumstances of war that would lead to an indelible and lasting emotional impact with which they would have significant challenges dealing upon their return home. In light of the untenable situations in which so many of these GIs were placed it is not hard to grasp the readjustment difficulties large numbers of them faced when they returned to the States. In a country where returning veterans from past wars had traditionally been greeted with a great deal of patriotic fervor from a grateful public, they were now only to be frequently scorned as somehow "less than" upon their return.

The experience of having been a Peace Corps Volunteer in Somalia was to prove very useful in adapting to Vietnam. As Volunteers who were to be working with indigenous societies we had been trained thoroughly with what to expect and how to deal with the culture shock associated with operating in a very different society. The actual experience of working and living with non-western peoples during service as a volunteer provided a comfort zone with others that very few newly arrived infantry GI's had ever experienced. The prior participation as a Peace Corps Volunteer would make it possible to adjust rapidly to the challenges of war-zone Vietnam and to function effectively with little direct supervision and frequently under very abnormal and difficult circumstances. There was no new overwhelming cultural adjustment required.

Once having been pulled off to type for a few days I put a stringent effort into doing the best job possible. The long hours working 12 hours a day seven days a week were just part of the opportunity for getting the job done. The result was that it was not long before the officers in the adjutant's shop realized that I could readily function under the challenging conditions of a war zone and in a different cultural milieu. It was not a big deal to go into the village of Duc Pho or to do any other assignment that required thinking or acting outside the box in a non-Western society or in a combat situation. So during the course of the deployment in Vietnam I had the opportunity to do a lot of different assignments working through the adjutant's office as a sort of special assistant or low-key trouble shooter in an infantry brigade headquarters. The result was that unlike most infantry GI's I was not "humping."[3] Although our brigade headquarters was constantly under attack during that time, in part because it was only a few kilometers away from Ho Chi Minh's birthplace and it was one of the few LZ's that had never been overrun, the challenges we faced were very different from those faced by most grunts. As personnel in a brigade headquarters operation we were mostly involved in defensive activities although on many occasions the assignments were outside the LZ's perimeter and sometimes in villages and under more diverse combat conditions.

Instead of humping I ended up being essentially a problem-solver for the brigade adjutant. If something was not working right as frequently happens in a war zone, or if there was some special project that needed attention, I was assigned to do it. The experience would provide exposure to a lot of military life and to the atrocities of war that would generate an internal moral quandary that I would soon turn to alcohol and other drugs to resolve after returning to the United States. It would also mean getting promoted to a hard-stripe buck sergeant (E-5) with only a total of thirteen months in the US Army. Such accomplishments are often readily possible in a war zone.

One of the first temporary assignments was presiding briefly over a Courts and Boards section which had become seriously backlogged with cases and could probably best be described as chaotic. Some apparently higher military authority had insisted that the cases be moved forward more quickly. In administratively sorting out those cases a pattern readily emerged. The cases were what the Uniform Code of Military Justice (UCMJ) refers to as special courts-martial. Virtually all of the cases were against young African-American soldiers many of whom had come from relatively poverty-stricken urban neighborhoods. Of over a hundred cases that I became familiar with only one defendant was white. And, as well as I am aware, he was acquitted although his case was resolved after leaving for a different assignment and no longer working in the Courts and Boards section. As well as I recall from this distant point virtually every single African-American was convicted.

The cases usually all revolved around a couple of issues. One was smoking marijuana which was illegal under the UCMJ and the other was refusal to be point man which is the most dangerous position on an infantry patrol. Asking around as we cleared out these cases it became readily apparent that white kids who were doing the same things were getting Article 15's (a lesser offense) under the Uniform Code of Military Justice for their offenses and black kids were getting special courts-martial for committing similar actions. This was one of the many moral quandaries that contributed to tearing me apart as a human being during participation in the Vietnam War.

Excerpts from the following letters, the first dated 25 Oct 68 pretty well sums up the experience:.

> I got appointed NCOIC of the legal section and message center. The people I got appointed over are bitter because they didn't get the job. I don't know anything about either job, so I don't really know what I'm doing, yet the results could

send somebody to LBJ prison [Long Binh Jail] (probably the most inhumane place anywhere in the world right now – witness the recent riot which the Army brushed over as a racial riot – what hog rot). Since I've been working in the legal section we have not had one Court-Martial returned as not guilty. In fact, I know of none in the records. I really don't like to be a part of a kangaroo court that commits people before they are tried. Would you believe the legal section actually types up court reports before the trial? It is true. We've even cut the orders sentencing someone to prison before the trial. I haven't really decided that I can be a part of something like this. Perhaps all the persons tried are in fact guilty, but it's all such a farce. My own Christian values can't really let me think all this is right. I wish so much that I had stayed in the Peace Corps until I was past 26. [The age at which one would have been exempted from the draft.] I am certain now that I'll spend two years in purgatory for the two I've spent in the Army.

I hope this doesn't sound too bad, but this is such a horrible experience to me that men could do such evil to each other. I've almost become convinced that the supposed savages in Africa are typical of us all.[4] Everywhere I go everyone seems to be viciously fighting with someone he should be sitting down with and drinking a beer.[5]

Later the letter continues:

Last night we got hit by the Viet Cong. There is something in that scream "Get up! They're hitting us!" that sends cold chills down your spine. I was the last one to get out to the bunker. I actually got up as soon as the alarm went off and everybody except two guys went running out to the bunker. They had been drinking so were deeply asleep. I grabbed one guy and hit another in the stomach to get them up. Maybe it was silly on my part, but I just couldn't let them lay there in open exposure to the attacks.

In another letter a few days later dated 5 Nov 68 a similar stream of thought continued:

> I realize one thing now. If anyone ever received a court-martial or a Dishonorable Discharge from the Army I would take it with a grain of salt. They have abused their privilege of judging so much that it is little more than the Catholic Inquisition of the Middle Ages.[6]

This experience would be one of many in the Vietnam adventure that would contribute to the moral quandary within my own personal value system that would be troubling for many years to come.

On another special assignment I was charged with escorting a Vietnamese woman, her mother, and her two infant children to Division Headquarters in Chu Lai. The woman had been a witness in an alleged case of murder of an ARVN soldier by an American GI. She was to testify for the prosecution in a general court martial trial of the American soldier who had been accused of murdering the soldier to steal his watch. Once I had gotten them to Division Headquarters I had to accompany them through her appearance before the court. As part of the assignment I had to be present while the prosecutors called her to the stand and through an interpreter took her testimony in which she described what she had seen of the murder for which the defendant was on trial.

During the course of the trial the defendant was also called to the stand to testify. As part of his testimony he kept using the words 'gook' and 'dink'. Toward the end of his time on the witness stand the prosecutor asked, "Private, you keep using the words 'gook' and 'dink' in your testimony. What do you mean by those terms?" The witness answered simply and without any hesitation or appearance of feelings or emotion, "Dinks are for you and Gooks are against you." Such is the way of putting people into a box. The defendant was acquitted by the jury which was composed of officers from the Division. After the acquittal the presiding officer (I can no longer remember if he was a Colonel or a General) came up to the soldier, put his arm around him, and said "You're a good man, Private. You can work for me any time." When I reported this comment to the adjutant he immediately directed the clerk in charge to cut orders reassigning the acquitted soldier to the unit of the General Court's Martial Presiding Officer.

Perhaps the single most demoralizing event, however, occurred in a few brief minutes on an otherwise uneventful day on the LZ. Taking a short cut to get from one assignment location to another I passed by what appeared to be a new barn like structure which I had not remembered ever seeing on the LZ before. The door was partially opened and I was curious what was inside. Being a buck sergeant by this time I could stumble into just about anything with curiosity and get away with it. Generally, no one was going to say anything about anywhere I went or what I did.

Inside was a sight I will never forget. Human beings were locked in bamboo cages. (It is hard even now to write about this.) The cages were similar to what a large dog is put into for transport. The human beings locked inside the cages had no clothes on. The cages were so small the prisoners could not stand up in them. They could only remain in some sort of fetal position. I will never forget the anguish and dissonance I felt as I turned to walk out and one of the two or three GIs on duty in the building and standing nearby said flatly and almost benignly in the context of you really probably don't want to see this, "You'd better get out of here." The revulsion, the dismay, and the sadness were almost unbearable. It was like being zapped by a stun gun. Several more concrete blocks were added that day to the wall I was building around myself.

One evening I was working late and returned to the hootch about 10:00 p.m. There were a couple of people in the hootch I did not know and one I had only briefly met before. One of them was a sergeant and near him naked and curled up in a fetal position was a young guy who was sobbing quietly to himself. The sergeant said that the young man was from West Virginia and since I was from West Virginia they thought maybe I could talk to him and establish some sort of rapport with him. They thought he could be helped out by talking to a fellow West Virginian for a while. That is why they had brought him to the hootch. I tried to talk to him but he was trembling and barely audible. After a few attempts to help him it became apparent that he needed much more than I could give by talking to him even though I was familiar with the city he was from and tried to bring his home town into the conversation. Later, after the sergeant took him away, I wrote a letter home about it. But because of its disturbing content I was afraid to mail it. It was dated 22 Apr 1969. It was finally included with a second letter posted on 30 April 1969.

> Dear Mom and Dad,
> Hope this letter doesn't disturb you too much. I've seen a lot of things over five continents, but tonight I saw something that was probably more tragic than I've ever seen

before. Don't read the rest of this letter if you don't want to hear what war really is.

Tonight I worked until about 10 o'clock. I came back to the hootch and my roommate brought in a couple of people with him. They had been to see a movie. One of the guys had just been evacuated from the field for combat fatigue. I've never seen anything so tragic in my life. The kid was from [West Virginia][7] and he was pathetic. An M-79[8] round was fired nearby (we're real close the perimeter) and he almost went wild. His eyes went into a wild trance and he shook. We calmed him down and then the electricity went off because the generator ran out of gasoline. I've never seen anything like it. He jumped up and said they're after us. They're going to get us. His platoon sergeant was here and he tried to quite him down. I'd always thought I'd had it bad here but this kid had been out in the field and had drug his friend (whom he'd known since grade school) blood soaked thru a rice paddy and his friend had been dead all the time he'd drug him. The fear in this guys [sic] eyes when he was here was tragic and pathetic. During one time when the M-79 rounds were going off I just reached out and held his hand. He was trembling and shaking and seemed to be without hope of any kind. Finally we got him back to his unit, but I don't know what happened after that. I've seen a lot of war in Africa, the Middle East, and Vietnam but this is the first time I've seen what it is in people. I hope I can help him somehow.

Will write later letting you know the outcome of this. Please pray for this guy and the thousands of others like him here.[9]

The experience of that evening was so unsettling that I was afraid to mail the letter home. Eventually there was some good news with this situation and so I decided to send it with another letter which said:

> Didn't know whether to send you the inclosed [sic] letter so I held off for a little while. However, it appears to be having a good ending. Several people from his company all the way up to division are trying to help him. I think we can get him a job at the USO beach in Chu Lai as a life guard. He has shaped up some since I wrote the other letter. Hopefully he will be okey by the time he goes home.[10]

And in June, after taking care of something at Division Headquarters, I wrote in a letter which looking back on it must have been an incredibly naïve view of the tragedy of combat on the soldier. It seems so innocent and unwarrantedly devoid of any concept of the lifelong impact such trauma has on the individual.

> I went to Chu Lai a few days ago. I ran into ... [the guy from West Virginia] that the clerks Mafia got a job for as a life guard – remember he had combat fatigue? I stayed with him. He is doing real well. He has a shack on the beach with three other life guards. They have a club and USO right behind them. No "lifers"[11] ever come down to hassle them. He works for two hours a day on the stand and is off. He can wear civilian clothes to the Mess Hall (I've never heard of it in Vietnam). I'm happy to say that he has very much recovered from his experiences in the field although he is still nervous and he drinks a bit too much. But with the progress he

is making I think he should be in good shape by
the time he returns to the States....[12]

Several years later when teaching at West Virginia
University, I had a student with the same last name as that
soldier who was also from the same general area of West
Virginia. I asked her if she knew him and she replied, "Yes, he
is my first cousin." So we followed up with a conversation. He
had returned safely from Vietnam having completed his tour
as a lifeguard on the USO beach in Chu Lai and was employed
at an industrial establishment in his hometown area.

One day toward the end of the temporary assignment in
the Courts and Boards section a young buck sergeant named
Ridenhour came to the S-1 shop and said he wanted to press
charges against an officer. The Master Sergeant sent him back
to see me. He began his discussion with an incredible tale about
widespread and senseless killing in a small village that a unit
attached to his battalion had allegedly carried out. He said he
wanted to find justice under the UCMJ in the case of the officer
in charge of this incident whom he accused of directing the
murder of a number of Vietnamese civilians who were mostly
women and children. He understood he had the right to do so.

When asked to provide some details he related the terrible
events of how an officer had ordered his men into the village
of My Lai and begun killing off women and children at will.
He went into a great deal of specifics about the incident and
the gory details of the tragedy. He insisted that he wanted
to bring charges against this officer. He had heard from his
fellow soldiers that he could do that which legally under the
UCMJ he could. My reaction was at first disbelief that what
he had described could have actually even happened, but
he continued with such heart-rending and blood-soaked
descriptions of this heinous affair that I soon came to believe

that what he portrayed as having occurred in this small village was true at least in some part.

When he kept talking of pressing charges he said he wanted to do so as soon possible because he was about to DEROS (that is, leave Vietnam and return to the United States) and be discharged from military service. He said he wanted to see some kind of justice before he was out and everything was forgotten. He also related there had been an investigation but nothing had come out of it. When he said he was about to be released from the Army I told him that if what he had presented was true it was way bigger than anything he could handle individually by himself. I also suggested that if he did file charges he would get tangled up in the Army's bureaucracy and maybe never be discharged at least not in the foreseeable future. Under army regulations he could not receive his discharge until all pending legal actions including any he had initiated were settled and there was nothing left to be adjudicated under the UCMJ. Instead, because of the enormity of the accusations, I recommended that he get his discharge first and then take action after he returned home. That way he would not have the enormous preponderance of the Army bureaucracy with which to interface pending any action.

He had said during the course of our conversation that he was from Arizona. After we had discussed several options available to him I suggested that when he got back to Arizona that he should write letters to Senator Fannin or Senator Goldwater, at that time the state's two senators, and tell them exactly everything that he just told me and include all the details as succinctly as possible. It took some convincing but he left the S-1 shop rather reluctantly. He did not file charges. He indicated that he really wanted to but that he would think it over. He did stop by the adjutant's shop one more time very briefly just to inform us that he was leaving the country and he would be following up with what we had talked about. Apparently, when he did return to Arizona he wrote to lots of senators besides those from his own home state. Eventually, of course, the details of this atrocity would be brought before the American public.

By and large even though very disturbed by the incident and the stories he told about it there was little I could do and so pretty much chalked it up as one more heinous event in the course of an even more heinous war. But that was not to be the end of it for the S-1 shop. A few months after SGT Ridenhour's last visit to advise us he was returning to the States some top brass showed up at the S-1 shop totally unexpected. By this time I was working on other projects for the adjutant. But the officers who had arrived without notice demanded an Article 32[13] investigation about an "incident." They insisted that we had it. I got called off whatever it was I was working on at the time and was thoroughly grilled over something I knew absolutely nothing about. They ransacked the Courts and Boards section going through all the files and leaving them in total disarray. They raked me personally over the coals demanding that I find it for them. But at the time I had no idea that what they were talking about was related to what SGT Ridenhour had described nor did I have any idea where the Article 32 investigation report was or for that matter even what it had involved. This was the first mention that I had received of any Article 32 investigation although SGT Ridenhour on his initial visit had said that an investigation had been carried out shortly after the My Lai incident happened. At the time I did not realize he was referring to an Article 32 investigation.

When they had come in demanding it I had no idea what they were talking about or what they were even looking for. It would be some time before I could connect the discussion with SGT Ridenhour with what they were so diligently trying to find. They gave few details concerning what it was about but they became highly agitated over their failure to find whatever it was they were looking for and thought they should find in our operation. They even berated the adjutant and assistant adjutant in front of the other GIs for it not being there which in and of itself was an almost unprecedented behavior in a military war zone. After they finally left in an agitated state and without the report they were seeking, several officers had a very unsettling discussion off to themselves at the brigade headquarters. I was shuttled away which was somewhat unusual when officers needed something done in a hurry. Generally, they encouraged me to hang around in such an event in case they required supporting help, but this time it was obvious they did not want anyone to hear what they were talking about or what their response to the visiting division officers' requests should be.

Apparently, looking back in retrospect, there had been an Article 32 investigation completed about the "incident," but in light of the totally inadequate record keeping system (or, perhaps more precisely, no record keeping system in the Courts and Boards section) it is not surprising that they found nothing. It is also very possible that it had been trashed by somebody who did not want its contents discovered. I personally had no knowledge of the investigation or any of the paperwork associated with it. The only knowledge I had of the affair came from the two or three hours I had spent that afternoon with SGT Ridenour and his brief later visit before departing from Vietnam. It would be shortly after this ransacking of the Courts and Boards section and the attempts to badger the officers and men in the S-1 shop into producing some sort of documentation that the massacre would be brought to public light by the media back in the States. SGT Ridenour had indeed followed up with his intentions and relayed the story of the My Lai Massacre to the Senate of the United States and to the American people.

Occasionally it was possible for GI's to wangle a three-day pass to some location that was considered relatively safe and unaffected by the war. Nha Trang on the South China Sea was one of these locations. So a couple of other guys and I sort of conspired together and eventually got a pass. We headed for the supposedly safe city of Nha Trang to have some fun. It was not quite as pleasant as we had hoped. I wrote home about it, and then followed up with another letter later. The first read:

> Dear Mom and Dad
> I'm in Nha Trang on a 3-day pass. The city is only a few miles from Cam Ranh. It has all the exotic pleasures of the east. It is located on the ocean and is surrounded on three sides by mountains. Right now I'm in the restaurant on the top of the Nha Trang hotel seven floors up. The scenery is just fantastic – a combination of French and oriental architecture including a cathedral and a huge Buddha at least 100 feet high in shining white alabaster.
> Looking at the city on the ocean side it could be on the Riviera, while on the other side are the mountains and the endless miles of tropical rain forest.
> The streets have the same excitement of the Middle East or Africa. Nha Trang appears to be about the size of Mogadishu. The only change is the color of the people. The dust, the garbage thrown in the street, the thousands of children running and screaming, the cripples begging for food or money from their filthy hovels layed out along the sidewalks. Mixed among all this are the prostitutes with their expensive clothes showing the latest fashions

of Paris and New York. Tinkers cry their wares from stalls swarming with flies and strewn with trash. Hundreds of motor scooters speed through the streets barely missing the beggars and children who pay no attention to their carelessness.

Then to leave the streets and to come up to the top of the hotel is a complete change. The panorama shows all the beauty and none of the poverty and misery strewn thru the streets below. I've seen enough of it that I've decided to stay in the hotel for the rest of my pass.

I walked up the hill to see the Buddha. It is about a mile from the hotel. At the bottom of the hill is an oriental temple with dragons and ugly creatures done in a fantastic display of colors. Steep stone steps lead up to the Buddha who sits in stately majesty the symbol of eternal peace and perfect wisdom. Huge dragons also stand in front of him lining the walkway leading to the temple inside his belly.

As I looked at the symbol of eternal peace the echo of bullets rang out. I ignored it for a minute until a couple rounds ricocheted off the hill top and I decided someone was shooting at me. So I quickly descended from the symbol of peace for more secure cover. I had left my pistol at the USO since weapons are not supposed to be carried in the city. However, if I decide to go out again it will be carried under my shirt with magazine chambered.

Sometimes I feel like Humphrey Bogart wondering around the tropics....[14]

This was only the beginning of a series of actions that were to reflect a bunch of close calls encapsulated in a very short period of time that helped to cement the already growing insularity developing within my sub-consciousness. The letter after the previous one talked about the intensity of the experiences.

> Dear Mom and Dad
>
> Usually I don't write because I don't have anything to write about. Well, for the past couple weeks things have been poppin'.
>
> Guess I told you about the assassination attempt at the Buddha. Well, since that happened my life has been a series of close scrapes.
>
> While I was still in Nha Trang a fire fight broke out about 4 a.m. I was sleeping with loaded pistol under my pillow. I jumped up and grabbed the pistol, then I got down on the floor and waited as machine gun bullets smacked against the side of the room. It was a great fire fight and being on the receiving end of a machine [gun] in a small concrete and brick room is deafening.
>
> So after that I decided I should return to Duc Pho. We had a stop in Qui Nhon. As the plane approached the runway the wheels went out on it and we crash landed. Only a miracle kept the plane from smashing off the runway and into the nearby buildings. It was a big C130.
>
> Both of these were harrowing experiences especially when added to the events at the Nha Trang Buddha. However, when I got to Duc Pho two Vietnamese witnesses were needed in Chu Lai to testify at a premeditated murder trial at a General Court-Martial. I was detailed to take them up. They were both women and they decided to bring their two children. So I

loaded them all up on a chopper and took them to Chu Lai.[15]

After being at the Brigade headquarters where incoming mortars and rocket attacks or attacks on our perimeter were practically an every day or two occurrence I thought people stationed at the Division Headquarters in Chu Lai were pretty much safe and out of harm's way. At the Division level GI's did not even carry M-16s. At the brigade level we were mandated to carry the rifle at all times along with several dozen rounds of ammunition. We never knew when we were going to be hit or what kind of precarious position we might find ourselves in.

Thus it was a little surprising on the escort duty taking the Vietnamese witnesses and their kids to Chu Lai that on the overnight stay in the billets that we got hit. It was one of the most vicious attacks on unsuspecting GI's that I have ever witnessed. The following was in a letter describing the event:

> That night the VC decided to hit about 3 a.m. It wasn't too bad and everybody went back to bed. At 7 am an explosion sounded that about knocked me out of bed. All HELL broke loose. It was the most unreal experience I've ever seen in in my life. They were sending rockets into division headquarters billets area. It was so vicious in its initial phases that nobody grabbed anything let alone a weapon. Guys jumped out of bed and ran to the bunkers naked and in their scivies [sic]. I didn't even want to hesitate long enough to grab my glasses.
>
> It was so bad in the initial attack nobody bothered to scream "Incoming rounds" as usually happens. It was right on top of us. They began to bracket by firing one shot, then

another, and then dropping everything else between these two points.

I actually felt for the first time in my life that I would meet my God in only seconds. I was past panic stage and I was in a daze expecting that I only had moments to go. I really believe that I was closer to my Creator than I have ever been.

Guys were running around with blood streaming from their heads and bodies. It was a moment of terror.

But then it ended as quickly as it started. Fifteen minutes later it was all over. It wasn't quite [sic - quiet] however as the fighters and gunships went into action against the enemy.

Since then I have been shell shocked. Every time I hear artillery go off I want to run to a bunker....

We had eight people killed in the attack and some 80 more wounded. I didn't get a scratch.[16] The war was all encompassing. It went wherever you went. The futility of bombing to bring about objectives was evident throughout the war. It failed to accomplish any sort of successful outcomes by contributing little if anything to achieving the war's aims. The following excerpt from a letter home blithely illustrates the situation:

Things have returned to normal here. The VC have interrupted their more than week of silence with mortar barrages night before last and again tonight. The other night I got to see my first B-52 strike. The big bombers came from Guam and the whole earth shook as they poured thousands of pounds of bombs on an enemy entrenchment about four kilometers from here. Bellowing flames leaped into the air in complete silence until the rumbling blasts and tremors could reach our area. Then it sounded like an earthquake. Those things could level a city, but against a guerilla force they do little or nothing. The VC just to prove it threw in a few mortar rounds not long after the B-52 strikes. It was millions of dollars gone in a gigantic display of fireworks and trembling.[17]

What I did not comment on in this letter was that this was a relatively densely populated province in an essentially rural part of Vietnam. The bombs, besides creating the air and ground show described above, would have resulted in hundreds of innocent people killed or wounded, people who wanted only to be left alone to farm and to raise their families. The tragedy of the war was felt most intensely by those most innocent of being a part of the cause of it. Only a veteran who has actually been in combat and on the receiving end of somebody else's weapons can truly understand what "incoming rounds" screamed to immediately terminate any sort of other activity means. It seems, too, that only those who have never been on the receiving end of bombing raids can say "Bomb the Hell out of 'em." Although not aimed at us the Air Force flew B-52 bombers over our area and were so close to the LZ in their targets that the very ground quivered and shook much as if there had been an earthquake.

Attacks on American air facilities by the Viet Cong were in part a retaliation for such air strikes. In fact, LZ Bronco where our brigade was located, was the air strip where many fixed wing air craft took off and landed. On the tarmac you were an open target where there was literally no place to hide. Once, when leaving to go to an assignment at some place that I can no longer remember, there were two fixed wing C-130s on the tarmac which were there for boarding troops. They were loaded from the rear. Just as we began loading, Charlie[18] began pouring munitions into the landing strip. I had been among the first to board and so was in the front of the cabin. The pilots immediately began to taxi down the runway to take off with GIs still trying to board and dangling out of the open tail of the aircraft as it began to taxi. We were trying to pull in the ones who were half way in when the pilot started to move. Our plane was the first to make it off the ground with some GIs who were not yet boarded hitting the tarmac spread eagled. Shrapnel pelted the side of our plane and punched a bunch of holes in it. Fortunately no one was hit. The other plane immediately began to taxi for take-off right behind us. Once we were airborne we were so close to the other plane that we could see flames coming from its side where it had apparently been hit. The flames were soon extinguished, and both planes landed safely in Chu Lai. No one on either of the planes was a casualty. We did not know what happened to the GIs who were left spread eagled on the tarmac and had not been able to board the planes.

Only a few weeks before DEROSing (returning to the States) I was Sergeant-of-the-Guard a perimeter defense duty that was assigned by rotation among various troops at the LZ. Shortly after locating in place in the bunker the Vietcong began a ground attack on our section of the LZ perimeter. Normally two soldiers were stationed in each of the perimeter bunkers but for some reason we were shorthanded that evening. When there were not enough troops to fully man all the bunkers a second soldier was not stationed in the sergeant's bunker. Alone I was armed with both an M-16 and an M-60 machine gun which was pretty normal for each bunker. Generally each of the soldiers would operate one or another of the two weapons. For the most part, however, the M-60 was operated most efficiently when it had two persons firing it. One person would shoot the weapon while the other trained ammunition into it so that it could be fired more quickly.

As the attack progressed word came down from the central command center to open with all the fire power we could. Only rarely had I used an M-60 machine gun but that night I fired it as quickly as I could muster the strength and coordination to operate it by myself. It was much easier to operate if two guys manned it. By myself I pumped out as many rounds as I could. When it was red hot from firing so many rounds and could no longer be held, I would put it down for a few minutes and begin firing the M-16 which had to be reloaded after every magazine had been expended.

Soon some additional messages from central command started to come down. That first alert from the operation's post had said that the next bunker adjacent to mine had been overrun. It was only about a hundred feet or so away. Then came the jolt that would send cold chills down my spine. The order "Prepare for hand-to-hand combat" was directed over the radio for the sergeant's bunker. It had an unbelievably chilling effect. The perimeter had already been penetrated at the adjacent bunker. Alone in the bunker without any back up was almost surreal in its tumultuous impact on the psyche. This was probably the most fear I have ever experienced at any one time in life.

Alone I was turning out as much fire power as I possibly could but with that message of terror a moment of clarity came over me. The thoughts that ran through my mind I shall never forget. What the hell am I doing here? I'm on these peoples' land. All they want is to get their land back which belongs to them anyway, and I'm here trying to kill them for what reason? There was no reason whatsoever for doing what I was doing. That was the beginning of a long and emotional hard road toward a philosophical belief that people should be left alone to solve their own problems. It was not my job as a soldier and as an American to tell them how they should organize their society. It was theirs and theirs alone to determine their own future. This was something in which I should never have become involved. It was insane and I had become a part of the insanity.

Eventually the attack would be repulsed with help coming in from our M-50 machine guns emplaced on the mesa behind the perimeter and with fire power coming from the bunker on the left side which had not been overrun and was fully manned. The sergeant's bunker would not be penetrated, and I did not have to engage in hand-to-hand combat. The bunker which had been overrun was reclaimed. The relief was enormous. But the process of believing that another society's land and values was theirs to decide what to do with had begun and how other people handled that decision was none of my concern. That concept firmed itself solidly with the action that had taken place in that fire fight. To this day I do not know why that bunker was not overrun. The Viet Cong surely had to know that there was only one person in it since only one weapon was being fired at a time rather than two as would normally have been the case in a fully manned bunker.

Throughout the assignment at LZ Bronco it was not unusual to have the Viet Cong lob single mortars or rockets into the facility. These were usually for terrorist purposes to let the GIs know there was always someone waiting to cause damage to them. It was especially common for these rounds to come at chow times when they would lob them into the mess hall. As a result, frequently we would go to the mess hall, get some food, and take it someplace else to eat it hoping to avoid any unwanted guest for dinner. The Viet Cong knew precisely where all the facilities were on the LZ and also what time meals were served because of all the Vietnamese employees who worked there and took the information back to them. The incoming rounds could come at any time during the day or night. Usually there would just be one, but you never knew when there might be a couple more following the first one. The result was that always after a single incoming round there would be a tense period of inaction while awaiting to see if another were to follow. Ocassionally this might be repeated several times a day.

Probably the closest call I had in the war was a direct hit on the hootch I was staying in a few days before leaving Vietnam. It occurred shortly after the attack on the bunker when I was sergeant-of-the-guard. It was one of those lone shot attacks for the sole purpose of terrorism. In the mid-afternoon a rocket made a direct hit on the hootch I was in. I was so "short" with only a couple of days to go that I was not even working. In fact, I had been carrying a "short stick" for several days by this time. A short stick was a baton sort of instrument that was totally worthless for anything. It could not really be used to strike anything with because it was too short and unwieldy. It had an ornately decorated brass knob head that was totally useless connected to a short piece of wood about a foot long. I'm not sure where the custom originated but the little one-room PX operated by the Koreans in which GIs could buy gum, candy, insignia, and other miscellaneous items not usually supplied by the military sold short sticks. When I got within a few days of DEROSing I had, like so many other GIs, purchased one. Most officers and NCOs knew that if a GI carried a short stick that it was useless to ask him to do anything that was much more than perfunctory because it would be to no avail. Our attitude was pretty much "What are they going to do – send us to Vietnam?"

The attack occurred as I was getting gear together and processing the paperwork that comes at the end of a tour. The rocket hit the opposite end of the hootch from where I was sitting on the edge of the bunk bent over lacing up my boots[19] which was a very fortunate position to be in in such an event.

The impact of the rocket knocked me to the floor and sent a piece of shrapnel through my watch. The canvas of the hootch and some of its rib structure came tumbling down and the end which had received the direct hit by the rocket caught on fire. I crawled out from under the rubble with only a few bangs and bruises but otherwise unhurt. I remember thinking in an almost sardonic nonchalant sort of way "What the hell – all in a day's work. I'm out of here soon." Looking back I think God was saving me for some other purpose because if whoever had fired that rocket had been even a hair's width on a different angle when he fired it I would have been blown to pieces. It was a lone shot meant primarily for terrorism and it was not followed by any others.

Shortly before the hit on the hootch I had been sent to Sa Hyen to negotiate with the local port authorities to let some provisions into the country. They were refusing for some reason to let them in and I was dispatched in a low key effort to get them to change their minds. I went to Sa Hyen in an Armored Personnel Carrier (APC) with a convoy which was going to pick up the provisions and bring them back to Duc Pho. By the time I got there the issue in question had already been resolved and the Vietnamese authorities had decided to let the provisions in. It would take two trips of the convoy to get all the provisions back to the LZ. I was riding on an APC on the way back to the LZ and was scheduled to ride on the same APC again when we made the return trip to pick up the second load of materials. However, when I got back to base the captain told me to go be sergeant of the guard that night because we were short-handed again on the perimeter and he did not have anyone else to do it. It was a little bit annoying because being sergeant of the guard was usually a bit ho-hum when there was no action and also because it was more interesting being on the convoy. The APC, of course, accompanied the convoy back to Sa Hyen without me. On its return to the LZ the convoy was attacked and the APC I would have been riding in was hit by a rocket and one of the GIs on it was killed and several more were wounded. Again I think God must have been saving me for some other purpose.

It was in Vietnam that I had the first major experimentation with marijuana. Actually I had initially tried it before joining the Army in Webster Springs a small town in one of the rural mountainous counties of West Virginia with a couple of cousins of mine that I was visiting. It really did not cause much of a buzz and basically thought no more about it. Although it was not very common stateside then, by the time of arrival in Vietnam pot had become almost universal in the country among GIs although not all soldiers smoked it. Interestingly there was a concept that was prevalent that you could not smoke pot and drink beer at the same time because the impact of one would neutralize the effect of the other. Regardless, I tried mixing the two and got good effects from both. At LZ Bronco soldiers were basically split between "juice freaks" and "pot heads." For many GIs the two groups did not mix but I could go either way and so mixed in pretty well with both groups. One reason for the split into two groups was that beer was legal and pot was illegal. It seems that GIs who did not mind breaking the law were potheads while those who were pretty strict and conscientious about following the rules were juice freaks.

At first I was a little leery of using marijuana because it was illegal and I had seen so many courts martial for its possession, but it was not long until coming to appreciate the effects of it and unlike beer it tended not to have the negative next day hangover consequences of alcohol. Both were readily available. GIs could buy beer for a dime at the little bar they had for enlisted personnel at the LZ. Anything stronger could only be bought at the Officers Club and so was not generally available for enlisted personnel. Another hallucinatory item that was available at least for a while was what we believed to be the original darvons. These were the ones that had a center to them which made the pill into a much stronger narcotic. I don't think they are made anymore. The S-5 shop had an industrial kitchen size jar of them sitting out where they were readily accessible. The shop rarely had anybody in it because they were in charge of community development and were usually out in the field. Any GIs close to the S-5 shop soon learned they could slip into the shop and grab a handful of them and they would keep you going for the rest of the day until it was break-out time for beer and marijuana. Eventually the Army caught on to what was happening and the darvon jar disappeared. So it was in this situation that I first learned to mix alcohol, grass, and pills for maximum effect.

Although readily availing myself to marijuana and pills in Vietnam when I returned to the States I pretty much let them go by the wayside. The principal reason was the paranoia I developed about the possibility of going to jail especially for marijuana. For the free spirit that I was that would be an almost intolerably unacceptable construct. It was hardly worth doing anyway since Stateside marijuana had been cut to the point it almost had no real effect especially compared to the very high quality stuff that we got in 'Nam. It simply was not worth it. There was plenty of alcohol which was legal. Later I would renew the use of pills to supplement the alcohol. Both of these were legal and, if properly handled, jail became less and less of a relevant factor with their use. All this, of course, was designed to protect the ego incubating within the wall I was rapidly continuing to build.

Returning from the Peace Corps stint in Somalia had been a very happy time and one in which Volunteers could talk freely about the various events both pleasant and unpleasant that had characterized their experience. Although there was some disbelief that physical and cultural conditions could exist as they did in that part of Africa by and large it had been a reception of warmth, acceptance, and a welcoming attitude. People were also very open and receptive to talking about the experience and learning about the African continent and its people and their ways of life. And I enjoyed talking to them about it. There were many invitations to speak about the Peace Corps and about Africa.

All this would begin changing significantly after induction into the army, military training, and shipment to the war zone. Slowly as events began to unfold especially with the incessant attacks on the LZ and virtually anywhere else I was in Vietnam (with the exception of Cam Ranh Bay) looking back I was slowly developing a wall around myself – a wall that would insulate the ego from any feelings or emotions regarding the war and its inhumanity. It was a necessary defense mechanism much as an abused child develops those lack of true feelings and emotions as a means of self-preservation. It was a matter of becoming numb to the events, actions and people involved because there was no internal mechanism for processing the unwieldy experiences and emotions that had become so much a part of life.

In going through the letters to family this pattern of becoming numb to surroundings slowly emerges. The Peace Corps letters, although they are sometimes characterized by whining about boredom and inadequate nutrition are by and large vibrant and full of excitement and interesting things going on. In many respects the initial letters from Vietnam are similar. They were very reflective and descriptive of the actions that were taking place.

Gradually, over time the wall around feelings and emotions grew much more formidable. It was about the time I was a "two digit midget"[20] that it was definitely noticeable. The following letter dated 15 May 69 is indicative of the emergence of that wall. It was descriptive of the attack on Duc Pho and LZ Bronco on Ho Chi Minh's birthday. We were

only a few kilometers from his birthplace in Quang Ngai
Province. LZ Bronco was one of the few LZ's that had never
been overrun. I was in the vicinity of the beer and soda yard
when the attack began.

> Well, I think Ho Chi Minh's Birth Day Party is
> over. It was a bit nasty as I'm sure you've read in
> the papers. Personally he [the Viet Cong] sent at
> least 20 rocket, RPG, and mortar rounds within
> 200 meters of my hootch. On one occasion he
> sent a round direct to the hootch but a pallet
> of soda blocked it – I can now say Pepsi Cola
> saved my life – of course it blew hell out of 80
> cases of pop. They were about 20 meters from
> the hootch.
> The devastation on other areas however
> was pretty bad. I saw it on the morning the
> 12th of May. It brought war about as close to
> home as I've seen it. **However it's good not to
> talk about it,** [emphasis added] since I've made
> it thru the worst of things and that I'll be home
> in a 100 days.
> I understand that the Americal Division (of
> which the 11th Brigade is a part) was the hardest
> hit during the party. However, Duc Pho (also
> called LZ Bronco) remains the only major fire
> base in Vietnam that has not been overrun.
> I'm sure newspaper reports by now must have
> something in them about us. We're still very
> hale and hearty altho [sic] a bit haggard by
> Charlie's latest offensive.[21]

What I did not mention in the letter was that the beer
pallets had also been hit. And, indicative of what was going
to come in life I took advantage of it. GIs were instructed to
hit the ground in place when strikes came in and they could

not readily get to a bunker. I hit the ground in place and since beer was spewing forth from the warm beer cans that had received shrapnel hits I rolled closer to be able to catch the spewing beer ostensibly so it would not be wasted but also because I could imbibe it. What a way to endure an incoming attack, drinking warm beer spewing from a shrapnel-pierced can while the rockets and mortars blow up around you! Only a true addict could do that.

Shortly after this letter another dated 21 May 69 added more detail. It stated that 31 were killed and 128 wounded (there were approximately 300 men based on the LZ). The letter continued:

> The next day Charlie put in some rounds on the hillside and started a grass fire. The hill was mined and all the mines started going off. We finally got the fire out.... Our casualty clerks were working 30 and 40 hour shifts without sleep trying to keep up with the casualty reports. I know I will never forget 12 May 69.[22]

And forget it I did not. Instead I wrapped it tightly within the wall I was building around myself including it along with the fear, mistrust, anger, doubt, self-loathing and a million other feelings and emotions that would not be dealt with for many years. Contributing to this was a letter from a sibling suggesting not write in such detail because it was upsetting our parents to read the letters. So after about this time there is very little discussion of what was happening; instead letters were mostly chit-chat stuff about life in the military and how it would be great to get out of Vietnam and back to the States. Very few feelings and emotions about the trauma of the war went back to West Virginia after this.

Although there was a lot of tragedy and sadness during the conflict that is not to say, however, that there were not some touching moments in Vietnam -- moments that I still cherish. One revolved around a "hootch girl" who took care of the GIs in our hootch. It was common practice in Vietnam to have what were called hootch girls whose job it was to keep the hootch in order and to generally keep the place clean and neat. These young women were permitted to be there by the Army and were paid by the GIs. They also took care of the GIs clothes especially doing the washing of uniforms and polishing of boots. The Army seemed to feel that it would improve morale the less grunge work their soldiers had to do. Most of the hootch girls resided in the local community and many were married sometimes to ARVN soldiers. American soldiers were under strict orders to treat the women with respect and there was under no circumstances to be any sort of sexual interaction or overt intimidation whatsoever. To my knowledge this generally held true at least at LZ Bronco. When there were other activities going on such as the rice harvest when they were expected to work in the patties or when we were under prolonged attack they were not permitted on the LZ. There was some controversy among the Army brass about the wisdom of this policy because it was thought and probably appropriately so that these women were ready intelligence sources for the Viet Cong. But there were other Vietnamese employees at the LZ as well. Among these were the people who worked in the mess hall and the men who emptied the short-drop latrines[23]which were different from the long-drop latrines used in Somalia. Short-drops had to be serviced on a regular basis. These men were also a ready source of information for the Viet Cong.

In one of the hootches I stayed in – I was actually in four different ones over the year in 'Nam – we had a hootch girl named Thu. She was married to an ARVN soldier and she was a very serious and hardworking young lady. I treated her with respect and dignity as a human being. Some of the GIs who were in the hootch whether because of racism, misogyny, feelings of cultural superiority or whatever often talked to her like she was some kind of servant or even a dog. To me she was a hardworking employee who did what she could do under such very adverse circumstances and in the totally different cultural milieus in which she worked and in which she lived.

One day as I was about to relocate to another hootch and she knew I would be leaving she came up and handed me an embroidered handkerchief which she had made by hand. It had TALBOTT and THU written on it. She knew my name, of course, from the Army fatigue shirts which had our last names stitched onto them. She also had two flowers on it and had trimmed it in gold. In addition, it had the word SOUVONIE which was a pigeon corruption used in Vietnam of the French word souvenir. When she handed it to me she said simply in her broken English, "You are different from the others." It was a moment of mutual respect between two human beings who had been caught up in life's events over which neither had any control. It was a very touching gesture and brings warmth to my heart even writing about it today. But as with Dahir, the young man who worked with me in Somalia, I have no knowledge of what kind of future they both had in their very tragic national experiences.

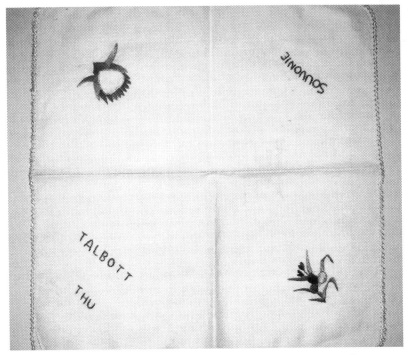

Illustration 3.1. Thu's embroidered handkerchief.

Not long before leaving Vietnam and being discharged from the Army the Master Sergeant of the S-1 shop said there were a couple of guys who wanted to talk to me and they would be coming around shortly. He did not say what it was about, but just that they wanted to discuss some things. A day or two later two individuals, supposedly army personnel, showed up. They were not dressed in normal work fatigues and had, as well as I can remember, no insignia indicating what they were about – no rank, no MOS, just a patch saying US Army and nothing else. Their appearance belied anything I had seen in the Army before and when I first met them they seemed sort of surreal compared with the rest of the military experience I had had with other personnel in Vietnam over the preceding year.

They asked if they could talk privately with me. I said yes, and we went outside the S-1 hootch to the piss tube[24] to talk. They introduced themselves by name but not really by what they were affiliated with or any other indication that might put them into a distinct group or for that matter what they were about. In a vague sort of way they inquired about plans after being discharged which would happen soon after I returned to the States. They made some comments that they had heard from the officers and NCOs that I had done a good job during in-country service and that there might be interest in an organization they were associated with which did work from time to time for the military.

Quite frankly I felt a little uncomfortable talking with these two men. Their evasiveness and lack of clarity when I asked them some questions concerning what they were all about left me with a real feeling of uneasiness. They were pleasant and polite enough and almost friendly but they were not being as direct as I usually like to be when talking to people about business and career moves. They were "just exploring some options." After our discussions which lasted for some time they asked that I not disclose any of our conversation to anyone or that I had even talked to them at all. It was a request to which I agreed essentially because I was not sure what they were all about. They also indicated that they would like to meet again soon and talk some more before I returned to the States. This I also agreed to.

Several days later one of them showed up with another fellow who was a little more dour looking and less talkative than the first two men had been, but he also seemed to be the person in charge. We had generally the same sort of conversation that occurred during the first meeting. However, they did expand somewhat on the information they had provided initially. There was some mention of needing reliable people who could operate under pressure in a war zone and that they required responsible individuals for their activities. They also alluded to the pay being very competitive and that costs for additional training, travel and other expenditures would be covered. Although they made no formal offer, they strongly indicated that they would like for me to agree to become a part of their operation. They indicated that they would prefer that I begin a paid association with them before leaving Vietnam. They said it was important that we agree to a relationship with them as soon as possible.

The more I heard of it the more it seemed that these people were recruiting mercenaries or involved in some other sort of clandestine or covert operations. I was a little leery of what they were suggesting and also not sure how these men, which by this time it had become apparent were private individuals operating through some kind of unofficial arrangement with the military, were going to have me involved in their operation. We talked quite extensively although they were still fairly evasive with direct questions especially the new man who was there for the first time. It was also a little confusing that it had been the S-1 Sergeant who had originally said they wanted to talk to me. This surely meant that they must have had some sort of legitimate association with the army although not through normal official channels. Usually if something were done through such channels as one's sergeant it would be on some kind of official business associated with the Army or another service branch. It also became abundantly clear that they had had some extensive communications with the officers and NCOs in the S-1 shop out of which I worked and maybe even with a few Division personnel who were familiar with my work. They seemed to know a significant amount about my background and previous experience. It all seemed relatively hush-hush and not through ordinary ways of communication for military discussions. Quite frankly, the whole interview process, and that is what I had come to believe it was, seemed very much out of the ordinary and it had an almost unreal atmosphere to it.

At the conclusion of our second meeting they made it clear they would like to have an upfront commitment at the time. Pressing for an answer they indicated that it was essential that some arrangement be agreed to. When I refused to do so they obviously were not very happy about it because I put off any agreement with them until after leaving Vietnam and returning to the States. They finally in a reluctant sort of way said a decision did not have to be made at that point. During our conversation I had told them that I would like to visit with family for a while after returning to the States although their demeanor indicated they were not very empathetic with that idea. In fact, they wanted a commitment to something right then and there, what specifically was uncertain, before leaving 'Nam. I refused. They seemed a bit annoyed at the decision not to commit to them at the time. They asked how they could get in touch in the near future after I had returned to the States. I gave them my parents' telephone number and said I would be there for several days visiting and if I went somewhere else my parents would be able to put them in touch with me wherever I might happen to be.

A couple of weeks after returning stateside I got a telephone call from the one individual I had met with both times at the LZ and who had done most of the talking. He began to inquire about interest in our previous discussions and that he would like to follow up. From the tenor of his initial discussion he seemed certain that I was going to give him an affirmative commitment at that time to something and even to sign a contract for future employment. However, by this point in the few short weeks after returning home I had become angrily and almost rabidly anti-war. After an initial polite discussion of a several minutes duration, I can remember I told him forcefully and distinctly that we did not have anything in common and I did not wish to have any further contact with him. We had nothing between us to talk about. He became very abrasive thereafter, and before we hung up the phone he adamantly and directly ordered me not to talk to anyone at any time about any of our discussions because there might be unpredictable and reprehensible consequences. He even went so far as to threaten me with bodily harm. After a few more minutes of diatribe he apparently felt this was not enough of an intimidation and to further assure confidentiality he added a special threat of injury or death to my parents. This latter part of the conversation I would completely obliterate from memory for several decades. It would only emerge to be revisited after many years into recovery.

At the time, considering the nature our discussions had taken, I thought I might actually be put on a hit list of some sort for refusing to follow up with him. I am not sure if that was a part of the paranoia of returning to civilian life in the extreme anti-military, anti-soldier, anti-Vietnam Veteran milieu of 1969 or if I was actually losing my mind. For many years I harbored a concern about our discussions with him and refusing to become a part of the operations that he and the others had proposed. To date I have heard nothing further from him or either of the other two and eventually our interaction would pass into relative oblivion. It would be years before I would ever be able to talk about this episode, and I never ever spoke to anybody about the physical threat to my parents. However, that, as we shall see later, would change on May 27, 2016.

Looking back at that incident I am still a little puzzled about what their objectives were especially about the kind of job responsibilities that would be involved. However, I am certain that it included some sort of covert military or related activity somewhere in the world probably in Southeast Asia. At the end of the tour in Vietnam, my mind and soul had become so jaded that I actually gave some serious consideration while still in Vietnam to following up with their proposals. And I had indicated that to them. After returning to the States, my mixed up befuddled moral quandary was grinding away at the very essence of my soul to think that I had actually given even minimal consideration to becoming a professional killer, but such was the insanity of the person that I had become and now no longer understood. It would be a rocky road for many years to come.

This chapter should be ended on a lighter note. It was with a sense of real pleasure and joy to leave LZ Bronco for the last time at the end of in-country duty. It was then when I was handed orders to go back to the States that I learned I had been awarded the Army Commendation Metal and the Bronze Star. In the orders we were directed to go to Cam Ranh Bay where we would get on a plane back to Fort Lewis, Washington. The time was late August 1969 and it was in the aftermath of when President Nixon had ordered a significant reduction in military forces in Vietnam. As a result, the base at Cam Ranh was trying to process way more homebound soldiers than it was capable of handling efficiently. The consequence, of course, was that the facility especially the mess hall could not readily accommodate the number of troops passing through it. By this time I knew that it was not mandatory to eat at an Army mess and with buck sergeant stripes I did not have to ask for permission for much of anything. I was pretty much free to do what I wanted within reason. So each mealtime rather than wait in a long line for Army chow several like-minded GIs walked the less than half a mile or so with some fellow soldiers about to be discharged and not wishing to stand in line, and we all ate at the Air Force mess hall. No problem, we didn't have to wait in line and nobody questioned what we had done. We did this for lunch and supper both. The way troops were boarded was that your name was called out, they gave you a boarding pass, and you immediately picked up your gear and got on the plane. We thought because of the sheer number of troops present it would be a long time before our names would be called. It is noteworthy to mention that missing shipment in a war zone is a court-martialable offense. Finally when my name was called I went up to get the boarding pass and the crusty old sergeant giving them out yelled at me: "Where the hell have you been? This is the third time I've called your name. I ought to make you stay here!" Of course, being a buck sergeant heading home there were no consequences and as I smiled at him and said "It's a really nice day," he handed over the boarding pass and said "Get the hell out of here." It was with a great deal of gratitude and relief that I boarded the plane for Yakota Air Force Base in Japan and onward to Anchorage and Seattle.

CHAPTER 4

PTSD, Addiction, and a Professional Life

Returning from the Vietnam War soon became an experience of feeling totally alienated from that conflict and not even wishing to be identified with the events that had happened there. Becoming very self-conscious I was reluctant to even admit to being a Vietnam veteran. There was an isolation in my emotions from the rest of the American people and whether consciously or unconsciously my soul rejected having been a part of it in any way. I was in a moral quandary of immense proportions – I had come to staunchly oppose the war after I had seen what was going on. When the United States had first gotten involved with the introduction of massive numbers of combat troops I had thought the expansion of the war a foolish public policy move. It came in full force in 1965 with the Gulf of Tonkin resolution and President Johnson's announcement that he was sending substantial additional numbers of combat troops to Vietnam to support those who were already there.

A Peace Corps Volunteer at the time, I was in Berbera in Somalia teaching English and history at the Intermediate School when I learned about it. It was in the evening and I was sitting at home in the little house allocated to Peace

Corps teachers listening to the evening BBC news when the announcement came across the air. I can remember shaking my head and thinking that was downright stupid. Ground forces were not going to change people's minds. All they were going to do was lead to a bunch of killing especially of women and children. By the time of returning home from the Peace Corps and the local draft board catching up with me I had more or less, even though still holding some reservations about it, come to believe that I could enter the military and serve in Vietnam with a somewhat open mind. (Or maybe it was just a case of resigning myself to fate and rationalized it by thinking I was going to go and see for myself what was happening there.)

The course of the war and participation in it led me, especially after the events at the bunker while sergeant-of-the-guard at the very end of the tour of duty in Vietnam, to turn adamantly against the war. It was a moment of clarity that would have a lasting impact on my attitude toward both the war and eventually toward any action that involved violence in the name of peace. On discharge I became part of the growing number of people including former soldiers in the conflict who actively opposed the war. I attended many of the emerging anti-war gatherings and participated as a demonstrator in several of them. Although never very active in it, I joined Vietnam Veterans Against the War. In part, I think, all this participation in anti-war activities stemmed from dealing with the moral quandary I faced as an individual who had been an actual participant in the war and who now had no way for addressing the emotional and spiritual trauma and tragedy of what had been experienced. Now I was adamantly opposed to it because in part it seemed to be the only recourse available inwardly for dealing with it. I was having real emotional and spiritual problems resulting from involvement in it. They were tossing and turning in my mind constantly. I loathed myself for having been a part of it. I felt dirty and ashamed and somehow violated for the role I had had in it. It was a feeling that would be retained for a long time and at least some of that reticence in dealing with it would linger significantly in my psyche even until after I had come into the rooms of recovery.

At that time in our country's history there was no real process in place for addressing matters of Post-Traumatic Stress Disorder not even in the Veterans' Administration. The federal government, which had been the cause of the veterans returning with the moral and emotional challenges they had, simply refused to acknowledge that they had a problem; their attitude was basically "suck it up" and get on with life.

By and large, apart from academic and anti-war activities and a minimal involvement in Vietnam Veterans Against the War, I did not even want people to know I was a Vietnam veteran. Even on those few occasions when talking about involvement I pretended that I had only been a lowly clerk. I do not ever remember before coming into the rooms of recovery ever telling anyone about the medals I had received. For years I would not volunteer that information in any sort of conversation with people who had not been associated with the war. The violence and tragedy encountered as a soldier was best left in the dark never to be revealed. Rarely or never did I talk about feelings or emotions that had resulted from the experience. It was particularly grueling to encounter the animosity and outright antagonism of returned Vietnam veterans who supported the war. They seemed to have a unique singleness of purpose in antagonism toward those few veterans who were able to openly oppose the tragedy of which we had all been so much of a part. We incurred their wrath probably more so than any other anti-war demonstrators.

It was especially stinging in this attitude of antagonism to be called a "traitor" by other Vietnam veterans and even more so by those who had never served. The animosity toward the war that had grown from participation in it was because of love for country and the belief that we had been led astray by politicians who were either ignorant of what was truly happening or were simply trying to cover their tails for the erroneous decisions they had made earlier. I was then and still remain a loyal and proud American. The exercise of First Amendment rights in opposing the war, and for that matter other policy decisions that led to improper and unnecessary violence, was a responsibility as a citizen. And I took that responsibility seriously.

Many years later and dealing with a different era of wars and veterans David Brooks writing for the **New York Times** succinctly codified the process in an article entitled *The Moral Injury*:

> The victims of PTSD often feel morally tainted by their experiences, unable to recover confidence in their own goodness, trapped in a sort of spiritual solitary confinement, looking back at the rest of the world from beyond the barrier of what happened. They find themselves unable to communicate their condition to those who remained at home, resenting civilians for their blind innocence.[1]

That spiritual solitary confinement would follow me for a very long time and would not change until becoming actively involved in my own spiritual recovery many years later. It was virtually impossible to communicate this condition to others who had not served in the war and who had no idea of its physical, moral, emotional, and spiritual consequences.

Even though very much a part of the anti-war movement I wanted any participation in it to be confined to speaking (or perhaps better referred to as yelling), picketing, and other peaceful activities. Violence to protest the war simply was not acceptable. I was at many demonstrations including the enormous one in Washington DC following the Kent State

University killings. But I could not bring myself to continue involvement in a demonstration if the action turned into violence or destruction of property. That was no different from what had been left behind in Southeast Asia. And if a protest turned into physical attacks and destruction of property as actually happened at one I was involved with in the DuPont Circle area of Washington DC, I would separate from it. Violence was self-defeating because after everything was said and done we were all supposedly objecting to violence. To respond to it with more violence was simply untenable. Early on in graduate school I had taken a course in Governments of Asia. For the research paper requirement I had written about Mahatma Gandhi's philosophy of *Satyagraha*. I identified closely with this radical yet peaceful approach to bringing about change. It seemed an appropriate mechanism for ending this insane conflict. Later, in recovery, striving to find that power greater than myself and beginning to study especially Buddhist and Taoist literature it would become clear that I was not alone in the concept that we cannot find peace through greater violence and retaliation.

Although becoming adamantly opposed to the war, I could also not see throwing away military decorations as some anti-war protesting veterans did. I had been awarded the Combat Infantry Badge (CIB), the Army Commendation Medal, and the Bronze Star. Medals were awarded for accepting responsibility and doing what we were supposed to do and not for assuming the onus for making inappropriate and self-defeating political and military decisions originating in the Pentagon or the White House. As I saw it, I had done what was required as a citizen and an American and that is what I had carried out to the best of my ability throughout the service assignment in Vietnam. Now that requirement was to oppose as a loyal American citizen what I increasingly viewed as insane public policy decision-making in Washington by those who were physically, emotionally, and spiritually detached from the personal tragedies that were occurring on a daily basis in Vietnam and other parts of Southeast Asia.

The isolation from the rest of society and the view that other Americans looked down on participation in the war and wanted nothing to do with me as a fellow human being was brought abundantly to life in that first civilian job after returning from Vietnam. Shortly after coming back from the war, I had gone to work for the US Census Bureau in Washington DC at its Suitland, Maryland, Federal Center operation. The job had resulted from the brief work done for the Census Bureau earlier in West Virginia. After returning from Vietnam and looking for employment I had contacted the folks at the Census Bureau to inquire about a position. They had remembered the earlier period of working for them in the state and so when I asked for a job after being discharged they hired me starting out as a GS-9 writer of training materials in their Washington central office.

Shortly after reporting to work it soon became evident, however, that many co-workers wanted to have little or nothing to do with me. They easily made their distaste for my presence readily noticeable. It was as if I was being shunned for having some communicable disease or that somehow I had to be evaded at all cost. I was not quite sure why they had the attitude they had, but they did. During a coffee break discussion one morning the subject of some recent events in Southeast Asia came up. I voiced an opinion of how I thought the war was wrong and we should not be involved with it. It was not particularly confrontational nor did it stir up much other discussion. I had simply just made a statement of opinion as often happens in coffee breaks. No one commented or particularly seemed to care about what had been said, and we all went back to work following the break.

Later that morning, however, shortly before lunch, one of the other writers who had strenuously avoided me those first few weeks on the job came by my cubicle and asked if I would like to go to lunch with her and some of our other colleagues. I agreed although I was a little surprised at this unexpected invitation especially in light of their initial coldness. We went to lunch, and it did not take long to realize that they were all strongly opposed to the war. We now had a major commonality. Later, in private, the writer who had extended the invitation to join them for lunch told me that being a Vietnam veteran with an Appalachian accent that they from the beginning thought I had just been brought on board as an in-office proponent of the war – a war that was becoming increasingly unpopular – and for that reason they had wanted nothing to do with me. Looking back at that, the experience reflects its own peculiar brand of regionalism and insularity on behalf of the other writers, but we did have a good relationship from that point on and we all got along well with each other. Reflecting on the incident illustrates the growing division at the time within the United States about the war policy and how it was beginning to tear America apart at our workplace and at home.

As with so many families in America the war began to take a toll on the solidarity of the relationships with various members within the family unit. Probably no war since the Civil War had put such a strain on our basic unit of social organization. Our own family was not that much different from so many others. At family gatherings and meals, which while growing up had been such congenial affairs, now for the first time began to become occasions for arguing and shouting back and forth about involvement in the war and what our country should be doing. Always before while growing up meals had been tranquil and sometimes educational and frequently fun opportunities. Now they were not. The bickering and uncomely behavior got so bad that Mom put the topic of the Vietnam

War off-limits during meal time. It was not to be discussed. Stick to sports, the weather or some other less controversial mundane topic. Such was the agony to the family and to the community of the impolitic results of this foreign policy imbroglio and its implementation that our federal government had so ignominiously come to pursue in the previous decade.

During that time frame it was also not unusual to hear increasingly in both public and private about "those crazy Vietnam veterans." The references could be heard in casual conversations on the street or in parks, at public gatherings, even at social functions. This seemed to expand rapidly after news of the My Lai Massacre became public. The dissatisfaction with the policy being pursued by the bureaucrats in Washington increasingly came to be directed toward the veterans who had been ordered, most against their will, to be the physical players in this destructive and failing operation. As that happened, increasingly I turned inward and shut myself off from the rest of society especially anything that would have identified me as having been a participant in the killing. Subconsciously I tried to pretend that the war had not existed. The wall I was building was becoming bigger and bigger. In particular, as the full realization of the atrocities of the My Lai Massacre began to emerge, I became even more mute about having participated in the war and about association with the unit that had been the involved party in the tragedy. I do believe that this rejection by society at large and the animosity and almost antagonism shown toward Vietnam veterans on their return significantly intensified the degree of suffering from PTSD for almost all of us who had served and returned.

It was an almost conscious decision to drown this moral quandary from Vietnam in alcohol and other drugs. Shortly after returning home and going to work for the Census Bureau at its headquarters in Suitland, the solution of choice for this demoralization surfaced. Day time work if I kept busy was generally OK and I could function fairly well in society and on the job without too many thoughts of the war. However, the night time fears experienced by so many war veterans rapidly became a part of life. The change was very evident when compared to one of the letters that had been sent home from the Peace Corps. During the two-week leave period visiting Djibouti and Ethiopia, I had to utilize traditional Somali transportation. To get to Djibouti I had to take a "trade truck" which was simply a deuce and a half with a driver and passengers in the front cab and commodities, livestock, and people in the back. I nonchalantly noted in a letter home "It took three days to get to Djibouti by truck. I spent one night with some Volunteers and the next night slept out in the bush."[2] There were no qualms about sleeping alone in the rural Somali countryside before we travelled the following day for the last segment of the trip. After Vietnam sleep would not come so readily. Now I became afraid to go to sleep even in my own bed. I would become fearful at night especially after the sun had gone down. I could not explain it, but it very much became a non-understandable part of life, and it would significantly influence any actions trying to deal with it. No matter how hard I tried, it seemed that sleep would not come of its own at night. It became increasingly necessary to have something else that would allay this chronic sleeplessness. As with so many others I turned to various chemicals to assuage the condition.

Claude Thomas, a youthful helicopter gunner in Vietnam who eventually found serenity and peace in the practice of Buddhism, writing in later life about his military experiences and recovery, aptly summed up this phenomenon that had also become so much a characteristic of my own life:

> Part of the reason I had difficulty sleeping
> was because of my night terrors: the sound of

artillery (that isn't there) firing in the distance, of helicopters on assault, that special look of everything illuminated by artificial light, the sounds of small arms fire.... For me, this is what rises up out of the silence that is special to night. I hated the sun going down. I fought and struggled with my inability to sleep, and the more I fought, the more difficult the nights became. So I turned to alcohol and other drugs (legal and illegal) for relief, but my suffering just got worse.[3]

Fear of going to sleep would become a major contributing factor to the progressive daily alcoholic and drugging behavior and dependence that was rapidly developing in the aftermath of returning from the conflict in Vietnam.

In an almost rash decision, I can remember sitting in my apartment shortly after starting to work for the Census Bureau and thinking "I'll just drink every night before I go to bed." And so I began drinking until ready to pass out before crashing into bed. It was a pattern that would last for sixteen years without interruption. During that time I got drunk virtually every night to be able to go to sleep. It was the only way I could deal with the night terrors. Even that occasionally did not work and I would still have nightmares about the war and events related to it and toss and turn throughout the night long after coming back to the States. Periods of sleeplessness and insomnia had become an integral part of life.

Usually I did not have problems during the daytime because if I kept busy enough my mind would not return to thinking about the war and the moral quandary associated with it. Part of the reason, too, that I did not usually drink or drug during the daytime was that once I took the first drink it set off a compulsion and I could not stop. If I was in a situation where I could not continue until passing out I would be absolutely miserable. A few times at the Census Bureau when we went out to lunch I had tried having just one or two drinks, but I would be in such bad shape throughout the rest of the afternoon that I did not see the advantage of drinking at lunch. I even went so far on those few occasions when I did drink at lunch to try to keep the buzz going by sniffing the government's glue throughout the afternoon in hopes that the withdrawal from those few lunch time drinks would be lessened. It did not really work all that well though in assuaging the effects of the alcohol. So I developed another pattern that would last for a long time and that was simply not drinking anything with alcohol before quitting time when on the job. Weekends and holidays, however, when there was no concern about quitting and the buzz wearing off were different. I could and would occasionally drink during the day whenever being able to finish the job.

The effects of the war still lingered as our immediate family began to grow. Only a few years ago my daughter reminded me, "Daddy, do you remember that when we were kids we could never go to fireworks like the other kids did?" As a parent there were still many of those inbred fears from the war. I had forgotten about the fireworks but certainly do remember the sirens – whether they be police cars, fire trucks, or ambulances. I would always jump for cover, or an inward and unsettling fear would come over me. I also had trouble being in lines or crowds of people. They were too close and I thought I would be smothered. Some of these external triggers seem to last forever. As recently as a few months before this writing and long after becoming clean and sober I was walking through a parking lot and the tailgate of a large truck parked nearby suddenly and unexpectedly dropped down beside me making a loud crashing noise, and I jumped as if it were incoming rounds with immediate flashback of yesteryear. Then I gently smiled to myself knowing that I was in God's care and walked gently on

The time at the Census Bureau would be short lived. Although the work was easy enough writing training materials for the many temporary employees that the Census Bureau used around the country for its various censuses and surveys, I was not particularly interested in it. I became so radicalized during this year immediately after returning from Vietnam that I wanted something else out of life. Besides the Census Bureau had taken a dim view of some of its employees running off anti-war materials on the government print shop's copying machines. (I don't know why they would take such a view.) The longer I was at the Census Bureau the more I kept thinking of the possibility of going to graduate school. This time the GI bill would provide a source of income and if I worked a little it would be possible to get by. So I made a decision to leave the Bureau and return to my undergraduate alma mater. Initially in the application process for graduate schools I had been accepted to Howard University to attend on a part time basis, but the idea of full-time graduate study became more appealing especially as increased radicalization took over. And I did not think it would be possible to make it financially with the cost of living in Washington DC going full time to Howard University on the GI bill. The decision to return to West Virginia University was based on its cost (in-state tuition was still possible) and they had recruited a professor of African history and now offered coursework dealing with the continent in both history and political science plus they taught Swahili to support the linguistic requirements for students of Africa. Interest in Africa had in no way been diluted by the sojourn in Vietnam or by participation in the war.

It was to be in the Ivory Tower that I would turn for the solace from the conflict of the spiritual wounds of the experience in Vietnam. Claude Thomas so forthrightly presents the dilemma of the veteran especially one who has not been physically wounded. He writes:

The physical wounds of war and violence, although significant, are less significant than the wounds that cannot be seen. The wounds of the soul, the spiritual wounds, the psychological wounds, are far deeper. You can treat physical wounds; you can manage them. People can see them and acknowledge them. The wounds of the spirit, the wounds of the soul, the wounds of the psyche – these can't be seen as clearly. For example, people say that Vietnam veterans exhibit antisocial behavior. But it's just that there is no way for us to relate in a traditional social way after our experiences in war. That was taken away from us.[4]

For my part disappearing into academia would be the initial respite. That would become the remedy for relating to the traditional social way after the experiences of the war. Getting absorbed in graduate school would create the path for dealing with the trauma and the tragedy. It would be a respite filled with the chemicals needed to accommodate it but also one that would keep me enraptured in academic challenges and accomplishments and thus devoid of satisfactorily facing and dealing with the moral dilemmas that had sprung from involvement in the war. It was impossible to escape from the dilemma that would doggedly follow for many years to come, but I could avoid addressing the issues of its cause.

Entering graduate school and with a lifelong interest in history and an acquired interest in Africa I became submerged in academia. Rapidly I found the escape that I yearned for through a combination of booze, drugs, and hiding out in the Ivory Tower. At first, that same leeriness toward me of being a Vietnam veteran was present on campus as it had been at the Census Bureau but that attitude soon disintegrated when people found out how strongly I was opposed to the war.

As a result, I felt very comfortable in graduate school. The professors I met and studied under were all very understanding and accepting of the negativity of the Vietnam military experience. The dissertation director in particular would provide a substantial amount of support and encouragement for moving forward in graduate school. This was a world apart from the reception Vietnam veterans were getting on Main Street from the general public where they were so frequently viewed as some sort of pariahs in the humanity of mankind and were banished into the annals of the socially disinherited because of their involvement in the conflict. It was a result of this faculty and fellow students' acceptance and interaction that I soon became a straight "A" student totally different from the "Gentlemen's C" of undergraduate days. I participated in academic extracurricular activities and loved research and writing. By losing myself in them, both provided easy escapes for dealing with the torment of the war which continued to drag on seemingly forever, and with the news media reminding all of America and the world on a daily basis that Southeast Asia was still a very lively hot spot for American GIs.

The experience in graduate school was a time of joy accompanied by a sense of accomplishment as well as an academic and practical learning experience. The university community itself was very cosmopolitan offering a diversity of opportunities for interaction with people from all over the planet. During the first semester back at graduate school the opportunity for some campus activism soon emerged. One of the courses that had been listed in the schedule of courses and that I had planned to take as one of the language requirements for graduate study was Elementary Swahili. It was rightly an appropriate language for any student interested in Africa. However, since it had not made the ten student enrollment cut-off in the pre-registration period it had been cancelled from the listing of courses before the regular registration day. This did not stop three of us from visiting the academic provost in the heyday of campus protests and telling him about our need for it in our programs and with a vague sort of intimidation that we could take some radical action if it were not rescheduled. He was actually kind of empathetic, or at least acted that way, and said he would talk to the dean of the college about reinstating it the following semester.[5] Shortly thereafter it appeared on the new schedule of courses for the Spring Semester, and we all three were able to complete both Elementary and Intermediate Swahili as part of our graduate programs along with several other students who simply wished to expand their horizons.

It was also during this period that I began to become more intimately involved with political campaigns and the election process. Almost by accident I met a political activist who would soon become a good friend. In fact, our wives would also become good friends and so we did a lot of things together. It was with this friend, who was from a working class Italian background, that I began learning to thoroughly appreciate the challenges facing working people in everyday American life. He himself had come from an immigrant family and he was an active participant in the local municipal and county political scene. His political involvement included not only the large number of second generation eastern and southern European people who lived and worked in the area but he also was closely aligned with many individuals associated with the university. It was a somewhat unusual combination but he made it work to get elected to several different offices over the years.

This became a very real opportunity to appreciate the significantly diverse multicultural background of working people in Appalachia. It was from this diversity of groups within the political process that the stereotype of the supposed Scots-Irish Appalachian was blown apart. There were especially in this jurisdiction, as there are in so many other parts of West Virginia, people of Italian, Hungarian, Greek, Slovak, Polish, Russian, African-American, Serbian, Austrian, and many other backgrounds that when they came together politically, which they could and often did, realized victories at the ballot box. This was also the opportunity to understand the purpose and comprehend the utility and role of "slates" in which specific individuals had been endorsed particularly by organizations that had similar political objectives. It sure made a believer out of me when first serving as an observer during a recount for one of his elections when literally hundreds of ballots were marked exactly the same. People could and did join together in their common interest to accomplish political goals and to force the polity to provide for their legitimate concerns of everyday living in their community. It was a system that worked.

This friend himself was often an active candidate for local office and like so many who have stood for election sometimes he convinced the voters and sometimes he did not. By working in his many contests I became aware of the multitude of different nuances that can be articulated in a campaign. It was a great learning experience too for meeting many other candidates and elected officials at the state and local level and beginning to feel comfortable working with them. This would be an especially useful advantage in a later college career when many job assignments would include cooperating with local elected officials to accomplish common higher education and community development goals. It would also have the effect of making me very pro-working people and pro-union as I had never been before. That political orientation has remained to this day.

Although not feeling totally belonging in God's world as I would find it later in recovery this experience in higher education was probably the closest that I came to it before that recovery commenced. In fact, I did not want to leave graduate research and writing. To do so would have required relocating in another world without the security that had been found in graduate school. It also permitted me to continue travelling the world running away from myself. I had become so accepted in graduate school and graduate research that resources could easily be identified to pay for international travel for research and conference participation. With the GI bill and a wife who worked and also took graduate classes we had a pretty comfortable life unlike many other students who had to struggle significantly for graduate degrees and frequently ended up with enormous debt that they carried into their working careers.

After passing the initial comprehensive exams to begin researching and writing the dissertation, with the encouragement of a dissertation director who had identified a source of potential funding, I applied for and received financial support for archival research in Britain and field research in Kenya the area of specialization. The funding paid for virtually all the costs for the overseas research for the doctoral degree. In the following year, again with the encouragement and assistance of my dissertation director, funding became available to present some of the research findings in a paper to be delivered at a conference on Kenya at Trinity College, Cambridge University, in England. Shortly after completing the field research I was appointed a teaching fellow in the history department while writing the dissertation. This had the added advantage of a living stipend and probably more importantly a tuition waiver for being enrolled. In all, because it was possible to lose myself and not have to face the real world of jobs and life, I ended up with a Master's degree and a Ph.D. in History. And as a result of an interest in working in international economic development I also completed the M.S. in Agricultural Economics with an emphasis on rural economic development. I was giving serious consideration to going for a law degree and staying a few years longer in this ivory tower realm of acceptance and unreality. However, when telling my wife what I was considering she curtly informed me "You're going to get a job because I'm pregnant."

Before finding a job, however, there was still one last call from Vietnam. One day in the College of Agricultural building while working on that second master's degree, a senior professor who had also been a long time administrator at the university and had been involved in the institution's diversified and long standing international programs especially in Africa, asked me to step into his office. I did so, and he soon began to express the possibilities of undertaking what, looking back on it, was a pretty insane idea. The Agricultural Economics department, as with so many other departments across higher education research institutions throughout America, had enrolled international students, especially graduate students, in all kinds of academic programs. West Virginia University was no exception. The professor expressed concern about a particular Vietnamese student – the student was actually an office mate at the time – and the uncertain future that the student had. This was in the aftermath of the fall of Saigon. The student himself had become a good friend. He was an especially talented and congenial person and an excellent student.

The professor's concern was that the student's wife was still in Vietnam. There was a period in the aftermath of the North Vietnamese victory in which some Vietnam veterans who had married Vietnamese women were permitted to return to get their wives and children. The professor suggested – he knew that the student and I were friends – that I should pose as the student's wife's husband and return to Vietnam to get her and bring her back to the United States. At first, I could not really believe what he was proposing, but I thought about it – in a way it appeared to be my kind of challenge – and was seriously considering how that might be pulled off. I was not quite sure how to do it especially never having met his wife and having no idea what she looked like. And, of course, she had no idea what I looked like either. We also did not know for sure where she was in Vietnam. The plan was that somehow or another I would link up with her – the professor felt certain she could be located – and she would pose as my wife and I would bring her safely back to the States. The professor said he could probably arrange for a marriage certificate which would validate all this.

After a couple of discussions with the professor I finally decided it would be a good idea to discuss it with my wife. This occurred shortly after she had informed me that she was pregnant. The dismay on her face when I mentioned it to her was pretty profound. It was kind of like I was abandoning her just as she had found out we were about to create a new life. Although she empathized with the student, whom she also knew and liked, she frowned on the idea as way too risky especially in light of the turmoil that was currently underway in Vietnam. After some serious consideration of the many different variables in the proposal over which I had little or no control and the fact that I was soon to be a father which in and of itself was a very exciting event that I looked forward to, I reluctantly told the professor I would not do it. I very much regretted not being able to help out my friend whose plight I certainly empathized with. He soon finished his Master's degree and moved to another part of the country where more Vietnamese had relocated in the aftermath of the war. Looking back at that incident I wonder if part of the concern for this friend was somehow or another reflective of the guilt and shame I so wholeheartedly felt about involvement in the war. Maybe this was an early subconscious consideration of an attempt to make amends somehow and to come to terms with it psychologically. A spiritual inquiry of looking inwardly for redemption and reconciliation was not yet a part of life's equation.

So it was with a good deal of reluctance that I started looking for work in academia. Original intentions and academic preparation were all geared toward international economic development in the less developed world. With a Ph.D. in history and a primary specialization in African history and a Master's degree in agricultural economics coupled with the experiences in Africa and Asia I thought there was a great opportunity to hide out in the Third World. There I did not have to conform to normal standards and face the reality of dealing with people in a developed society where there was no place for people with addictive habits to hide out and where the standards required a conformity to one's own culture. However, my wife informed me that she did not want to raise kids overseas (in an ironic twist of fate our daughter is raising our grandchildren in England). So with my background I turned to higher education. At least that would probably be within an acceptable comfort zone and I was relatively certain I could continue the drinking and drugging life style relatively unabated.

One day I got a call from a friend in graduate school who said there was an opening in one of the state colleges for an administrative position, and he further said that I was the person they wanted. Although vaguely familiar with the institution which was located in central West Virginia I did not know much about it and certainly did not know about a vacant position there, and of course had not applied for it. He was from the area where the institution was located and when he was on a home visit he had heard from a friend who they were considering for the position. I would have the opportunity to become very familiar with it over the next twenty-seven years.

Apparently someone had nominated me for the position (probably one of the agricultural economics professors) although to this day I do not know who it was. The graduate school friend suggested writing a letter letting them know I was interested which I did. A resume was included with the letter. Shortly afterwards I received a call from the President's administrative assistant with an invitation to come for an interview. I went for the interview which went well and within a few days they called me to report for work. When I accepted the position it was at the highest salary (although paltry by today's standards) of any Ph.D. in history that a graduate from my institution had received for an entry level opening. I would remain at that institution for 27 years. PTSD and its associated addiction would insure that for most of that time there would be only lateral changes at the institution never really advancement in any significant way.

When beginning the job I actually felt more comfortable than I thought. It involved primarily working with a rural constituency and, although hard ball politics characterized it as with so many institutions of higher education and perhaps as much or more than with corporate America, by and large it was a comfortable situation to be in. It was easy to relate to the small town venue and the very pleasant but sometimes very provincial town folk. And the acceptance by the constituency I worked with was ambient enough. This was in spite of the daily evening drinking which continued unabated. That void, that hole in the center, that lack of whatever it was that was needed to feel complete and released from the bonds of war, was always present. And it never seemed to be filled no matter what had been accomplished or what successes came about in life. Mostly, without realizing it, the unaddressed PTSD issues from Vietnam always cast a pall over my very existence and participation in life.

One of the greatest pleasures during that time was having kids. I loved to hold them when they were infants and to play and wrestle around with them when they were toddlers. Even the changing of the diapers and the occasional tantrums and sicknesses that normal kids have were all an acceptable part of life. As they got older both of them were involved in extracurricular activities. Our daughter was always a cheerleader and our son was in whatever sport was in season. We spent countless hours going to their events and by-and-large enjoying being the parental spectators. But I rarely got involved with the other parents – I did not feel acceptance and thus could not be a part of it. Being a big collegiate football fan for years we had season tickets at WVU first going with my wife and then for many seasons taking our son until he got old enough that it was not cool to be seen with dad anymore at football games. I guess a lot of parents go through that phase of life but for me there was always the exception, the uniqueness after the day was done and dealing with what would be the night terrors and the solution for them – drinking until passing out to be able to go to sleep.

Because of the nature of the work I was doing there were frequently people from other countries at our home. For the most part these were undergraduate students from the institution where I worked but sometimes faculty or graduate students from other institutions either in the United States or abroad. A diverse range of countries around the world were represented in this medley of people from all over the globe. Our daughter became good friends with a Japanese student and our son did the same with a Dutch student who was on a basketball scholarship. The international dimension of our family activities was a good experience for both of them and gave them an opportunity to know people of diverse nationalities, races, and religions.

That same process of participation but not heartfelt involvement characterized much of my working career. By and large I could function – and sometimes did function very effectively and with high quality results – but I never really felt that I fit in. I was never truly a part of. I usually felt shy and not quite as good as peers or, alternatively, far wiser and more capable than they. I could sometimes build consensus and get people working together frequently with some very positive results, but I never really felt a part of the institution. I emotionally conceived myself as an outsider who believed he was never accepted. Later in recovery I would find out that acceptance was not possible as long as I could not accept myself as the creation of God that we all are.

The result on the job promotion factor was that even though new and more responsible positions opened up from time-to-time even though having the qualifications and applying for them usually I was passed over, or as occasionally occurred, selected only for a temporary appointment to fill the position or the responsibilities until a permanent replacement could be found. Apparently, I had a unique capacity for researching and developing projects and finding the resources to pay for them. I think this is what kept me on the payroll. During the entire time at the institution no one ever criticized the quality of my work and on many occasions they offered praise for a job well done. Looking back from the hindsight of recovery I know now that the lack of acceptability of myself undermined any significant upward movement because I was so ill at ease that I could not function in a role that involved extensive management of other professionals since alcohol and sometimes other drugs prevented finding that acceptance within myself. Because of the low self-esteem that had become so thoroughly imbued in my character over the years of hiding from the real traumatized person I had become from the experiences of Vietnam and its aftermath of drinking and drugs, I never once was able to lobby the administration for more responsibility or a promotion. I would occasionally write a letter of application when something became open but to actually let it be known that I very much felt I could make a contribution in the position I could not seem to do it. Numerous changes in responsibilities occurred over the years but they always came from the top down and were usually unexpected. With recovery would come a new and comfortable acceptance that I was a part of God's world and could function effectively with a great variety of others.

In 1983 there would be a dramatic although not totally sobering change in this lifestyle. The film producer Stanley Karnow brought out his thirteen week series about Vietnam. Beginning with French Indochina in the aftermath of World War II it used actual news and video footage as well as commentary to examine the causes, the progress, and the results of American involvement. Starting with the first segment I stayed glued to every minute of it. I was actually finding a little bit of myself through each presentation. For the first time I began to feel a small degree of comfort with looking at myself through the series. On many occasions tears would stream down my cheeks, but I stayed glued to it. It was as if I was beginning an understanding of myself through the process of healing. Although having reflected on Vietnam on a few occasions it was always from the point of view of an outsider trying to find himself and usually drunk or high in the process. My wife when she saw the emotional turmoil produced through watching the series advised me to stop and not think about it. But I continued to be entranced by each episode, and faithfully followed every installment to the very end.

It was about a year after that series was broadcast that the substantive change in this drinking pattern came about. For sixteen years I had been drunk virtually every night usually beginning about 9:00 or 10:00 p.m. and passing out about

1:00 a.m. The result, of course, was numerous hangovers. But in January 1985 I went to work one morning hung over as usual. Generally, I stayed in the office gulping down coffee until about 10:00 or 10:30 trying to cure the hangover. But that particular morning it was necessary to go to another building across campus for some reason and in the process I encountered the President of the institution whom I rarely saw in the morning. He spoke casually and then struck up a congenial conversation about something. I was so hung over that I could barely respond.

Walking away from our encounter I thought to myself, "Why do I have to be this way? Maybe, just maybe, I could go to bed tonight without getting drunk." I went home that evening and made it to the normal drinking time but somehow managed to get through the rest of the evening and go to bed without having anything. There was some trouble getting to sleep but I finally did. The next morning there was a wonderful feeling. It felt great! Although skittish and uncomfortable going to bed sober I did not have to get drunk to get to sleep. That began a stretch of not drinking at all that lasted until March of 1986 – a period of 14 months. That's a long time for an addict to go without drinking or drugging.

The end of the dry period would come as the result of arranging a travel/study program in Western Europe. It was the first of several such educational experiences that we put together for students at the college. At a restaurant in Paris the sobriety suddenly fell apart. I pick up that first glass of good French wine and boom it was gone. I drank until nearly collapsing. Although the same thing happened as always happened when picking up that first drink, the lengthy period of sobriety that ended in Paris that evening brought about a permanent change and that change was that I never had to go back to daily drinking. It was possible to skip a few days between drunks. However, the same consumption pattern still continued. Each time I picked up that first drink a similar result occurred. I drank until passing out. I could not stop after consuming the first one. The old fabric of the drinking bouts was back. It would last for another sixteen years but just not on a daily basis. Nonetheless, I now knew it was possible to go for a few days without drinking if necessary and this would later play a role in recovery. It was also a part of the rationale and pretense that I could control my drinking – I had proven it. I'll go for a couple of days without anything to drink. "See, I can do it, I'm not addicted to anything!" (To which I would say today, "Dream on Alice, Wonderland's on the Third Floor!")

Occasionally, although it was pretty rarely, I would let God help out with some challenge in life. Normally, I felt I was in charge and could handle any problem on my own. I really did not need help from God or anybody else for that matter. In mid-life and with a life-style that shall we say was less than the healthiest possible, I realized there was a need to make some permanent changes. I looked at the options of quitting smoking or quitting drinking. One of them had to go because slowly but surely a healthy lifestyle was going downhill perhaps irreparably. This is the age, of course, when we start seeing our friends and family members sometimes becoming terminally ill and we have no capacity to be able to do anything about it. It is also the age where we begin to understand that we are not going to live forever.

The answer seemed to lie in quitting smoking. I certainly could not imagine life without alcohol and the other drugs that contributed to its effectiveness so it would have to be the tobacco. My wife would not allow smoking in the house. The obnoxious habit had to be undertaken outside or in the garage. The garage, of course, as for so many men, was the husband's domain. It was set up to be able to easily smoke and get rid of the trash that goes with smoking. One evening, after having pondered the thought for a few weeks, I decided it was time to do it. In the garage I had a beer in one hand and a cigarette in the other. Jesus had said "If you ask you shall receive." I knew that from the lengthy early exposure to a loving, caring and forgiving God in childhood. Still holding the beer in my left hand I snuffed out the cigarette and in a true prayer said, "God I can't do this by myself. You're going to have to help." Still holding the mug of beer I threw the snuffed out cigarette into the garbage and walked back into the house. To this day there has never been a craving for a cigarette or any other form of tobacco after that prayer. The compulsion to use tobacco was totally removed and has never returned. That experience had shown that, although not realizing it at the time, God could and would work in dealing with life's problems if we just genuinely surrendered and asked for help. Without understanding what was going on, as coming to understand it after entering that first Twelve Step program, I had genuinely admitted to God a powerlessness over the addiction to nicotine and asked for his help with eliminating it. He removed the desire totally without any adverse consequences whatsoever. There has never been any inward compulsion to return to that habit. It was totally taken away and not replaced by another negative trait. If we truly surrender something to God he will not replace it with some other bad habit.

However, I did not know at the time it happened that God had totally removed the craving for tobacco, so for the next eight days after snuffing out that last cigarette, I was afraid to drink a beer least the desire to smoke would return. Smoking and drinking went hand-in-hand. You could not have one without the other. But, quite frankly, folks, eight days is a very long time for an addict to go without a beer or some other chemical. I was really afraid that since smoking and drinking did in fact go hand-in-hand that as soon as the first beer was sipped there would be a craving to smoke. But after eight days had passed I said, "I cannot take this anymore. I've got to have a beer." I opened that first one and as was the usual pattern a whole bunch more were opened, enough to get a good buzz going until about to pass out and then went to bed. But I did not crave a cigarette. The desire was simply not there. I would drink lots of alcohol and pop lots of pills in the aftermath of the experience in the garage but not once since that time has there ever been a craving for a cigarette or any other form of tobacco, and I had smoked for more than thirty years. In fact, it soon became totally repulsive to even smell the smoke. It was so much so that in self-righteous contempt I became opposed to anybody smoking around me and even threw a young couple who were out walking off my land one day when they sat down to rest for a moment and lit up. That action was literally "my way or the highway" as ego took control of the situation.

The college that employed me was small and in an especially rural location. It was very much a traditional baccalaureate institution in the sense of having been a teacher preparatory school that emerged into a state college over the years. In many ways it was provincial but that very provinciality was what gave it its meaningful role in West Virginia higher education. By percentage of enrollment, it had the largest proportion of first generation college students of any public institution in the state. Although very much respecting its ability to bring in students whose families had not previously experienced an education beyond high school, the insularity from its relative isolation was something that needed to be cracked just a bit. No major changes which would turn it into a more cosmopolitan and diverse institution were going to be forthcoming from the administration but there were a few opportunities to crack a dent in the provinciality and to bring the school into a tad more of a wider world perspective.

And some of these opportunities soon presented themselves. The travel/study programs in Europe were chances for seeing a different way of life for students who by and large had not been out of West Virginia except maybe to Virginia Beach or the Outer Banks or to visit relatives in Ohio or Baltimore. They also had tremendous support from non-traditional students who saw them as an opportunity to live and learn and get college credit. They were very personally satisfying professional experiences, and they were one of those few opportunities to see students actually growing in their experiences. So much of education shows results only after a lengthy period of time. But to see students from a county that might have only one stop light in the entire county trying to navigate through London or Paris or Amsterdam and feeling comfortable to be able to do so was enormously satisfying. We did several such travel/study programs over the years including also a couple of field trips to Toronto which was only a day's drive from central West Virginia. Both of these permitted a lot of students to get an international experience at a relatively low cost. In the case of Toronto, this also had the added dimension of permitting students to know that the international arena was within driving distance.

One international travel/study program also provided another early chance for dealing with the negative factors of post-traumatic stress from Vietnam. That opportunity came on a London program when a British friend was able to secure a ticket to see the play Miss Saigon. I had told him about wanting to go and see it. I also told him I wanted to see it alone mainly because of not being sure what the reaction to it would be. After explaining the wartime experience to him he was able to arrange for a box seat that only had one other couple in it. As it turned out they were more interested in each other than in the play. That would help a lot. There was very much an element of fear and anxiety about seeing the play, but for some subconscious reason I had to do it. The play was incredibly realistic and it was not long into it that tears were streaming down my face. It was both fascinating in the sense of the realism that it portrayed and it was similar to the Stanley Karnow series in that it meant facing the memories of the war. It is noteworthy that although the play takes place mostly in Saigon, and I was never in Saigon, that it could be extrapolated to other parts of the country where I had served. Whenever it was over I had taken one more step, however tiny, toward dealing with the moral conflicts that had been inherited from the war experience.

It was by chance that we learned from another institution in West Virginia that a school in Japan was looking for a more rural location to place students for an intensive English program to prepare them for effective participation in higher education academic institutions in the United States. So we contacted the institution in Japan and through a series of communications over a fairly long period of time and a couple of visits by Japanese counterparts to our campus we were able to develop an Intensive English program which was open for all international students. We retained a TESL specialist professional coordinator for the program. And, by state law as a non-credit program it had to be self-supporting, we developed a fee structure that made it so. The program was open to any student whose first language was not English and we were able to attract many students from various parts of the world over the years although the majority were always from Japan. The result was that we did significantly increase the international presence on campus.

One of the outcomes of our travel/study programs was an interest in the development of a course in international marketing. No one on the business faculty had any experience in that area; however, I had taken a course in the subject as part of the master's degree in agricultural economics. So with the consent of the division chair and the dean we developed the course. The course permitted students to know that there was a much wider opportunity to engage in a global marketing scenario than what one might find aiming a product solely at the United States. It is still a part of the curriculum today.

Probably the most challenging course that we were able to develop while at the institution though was African American History. Much of my graduate work had been involved with Africa including the dissertation, and with doctorial fields in American history there were several courses which related directly and indirectly to the African American experience. As with the International Marketing course no other instructor on campus had any experience in this area. So with the approval of the Chair of the Social Sciences division we developed the course and introduced it to satisfy an elective requirement in history and social sciences.

On the first day of class an interesting question came up. Although the class always had a majority of white students there were usually a significant number of African American students. The college, and indeed the area it served, had very few resident African Americans. Most of the African American students were athletes who had been recruited from other parts of the country to play on the college's sports teams. On the first day of class and beginning to introduce the subject and discuss the course requirements listed in the syllabus and the various expectations, one of the African American students asked the question, "Just exactly what are **your** qualifications for teaching this course?" He was the one who put the emphasis on the **your**. For a moment I was taken aback having never quite been asked such a question before. So I outlined some of the more relevant academic qualifications such as having a doctorate in history and having done graduate course work in the subject matter. But I could immediately sense that there was a real plausibility question inherent within his inquiry. After a little discussion which was obviously unconvincing, I finally took a line from the old civil rights movement and said, "Will you just give me a chance?" It is a pleasure to note that the African American students did give me a chance and having taught that class for many years afterward always got good feedback on evaluations of it from both white and African American students. At retirement the advertisement for a replacement had the course listed as one of the candidate's responsibilities in the position. It is still being taught at the institution today. And the student who posed the question about qualifications went on to become my student assistant as an upperclassman and now has a successful career of his own.

Another class that I never expected to teach was West Virginia History. This came about quite by chance. The course had been scheduled as an off-campus staff development offering at the request of a non-educational state institution. The adjunct instructor who was retained to cover it upon closer review of credentials by the department chair did not meet the necessary qualifications. I was working in administration at the time and since it was a fully enrolled evening class she pleaded with me to cover it. As an undergraduate I had had the course but that had been many years before. Finally I agreed teach it and with a great deal of rapid research and last minute preparation was able to teach it keeping just one lecture ahead of the students throughout the course. It was fascinating and it endeared an interest in the subject that I have retained. This was especially so because with the experience in politics and working people participation in the electoral process I knew there were many different cultural inputs into the state besides the stereotypical Scot-Irish who have been glorified (or demeaned depending on perspective) as the basic constituency of the state. Not only were there numerous other European immigrants into the Appalachians there has also been a significant African American contribution. Beginning with the 1890s West Virginia has had a number African

Americans elected to public office all of whom were elected by predominantly white constituencies. That favorite of the national media McDowell County (sometimes referred to as the "Free State of McDowell" by fellow West Virginians) has a vibrant history of blacks in the political system including the first African American woman ever to sit in a state legislature in the United States. She was appointed in 1928 by the governor to fill the seat of her deceased husband who had won the position in the 1926 election and subsequently passed away unexpectedly. Her name was Minnie Buckingham Harper. Another very prominent African American woman from McDowell County was Memphis Tennessee Garrison who was active in the Civil Rights Movement and served on the United States Commission on Civil Rights. A more contemporary Appalachian who does not reflect the Scots-Irish model is Henry Louis Gates, Jr., who grew up in Mineral County, West Virginia.[6]

Many descendants of the numerous early eastern and southern European workers who came to the state in the late 19th and early 20th centuries have also played significant roles in West Virginia politics. This includes our current senator Joe Manchin. Grandfather Mancini was brought to Appalachia from Italy as an orphaned child and as with so many other immigrants benefitted from the opportunity and his own hard work. Somewhere along the line the name got anglicized to Manchin. Many of his descendants have been involved in the state's politics including especially his uncle, A. James Manchin, who coordinated John F. Kennedy's contest with Hubert Humphrey in the 1960 West Virginia presidential primary election and proved a Catholic could win in an overwhelmingly Protestant State. He later went on to become Secretary of State and Treasurer for West Virginia.[7]

Although never feeling a part of the mainstream I did feel that the time was well spent making a contribution to the people of the central section of West Virginia that the institution served. This was especially so in that such a large proportion of the students were first generation college students and also because particularly later in my career the institution increasingly reached out to non-traditional students and gave them a path for achieving some educational fulfillment in life. Many of these students, both traditional and non-traditional, remained in West Virginia to make vibrant contributions to the state.

The outreach to non-traditional students became increasingly to mean that we had to take education to the student rather than expecting the student to come to campus. West Virginia had long lagged behind other states in establishing an effective and efficient system of community colleges which has been one of the factors contributing to the slow adaptability of its citizens to an increasingly technological and diverse world. In an administrative reorganization later in my career I was asked to take over responsibility for outreach and extension classes. It was a real opportunity because I could link up with genuine West Virginians who would otherwise never have had the opportunity to develop their thought processes outside traditional culture. The response was nothing short of spectacular in the number of people who recognized and welcomed the opportunity to grow. It very much reflected the optimism of our Appalachian character that when we had genuine chances to improve our conditions and to grow as individuals we took advantage of them.

One such opportunity for doing this came upon a visit to see the principal of a new high school in one of the college's service area counties that was currently under construction but had not yet been completed. The purpose of the visit was to request classroom space in the new structure for extension classes to be taught in the evening. He proposed that to do it right the college should set up a higher education center as an integral part of the new high school. I jumped at the opportunity. He himself had been a person who had pretty much pulled himself up by the bootstraps. We discussed this opportunity with the Dean and the President. They were very interested and gave the go ahead although none of us had really figured out how or who was going to pay for it. Certainly nothing of this nature had been placed in the college's current budget upon which we could draw down. But as it's said, "If the project is right the money will follow." So we opened that center on a shoestring. I could spend part of my time on it and a student assistant was authorized for it as well. We also got significant assistance from some of the public and private agencies which had staff development funds in their own internal budgets and were located in the service area. Under West Virginia Higher Education policy staff development classes could be opened to the general public if the contracting agency agreed. It was an easy sales job because the agency directors we worked with all understood the true value of education for the general public and, in fact, they often looked toward recruiting potential employees from non-agency participants in the professional development classes which they sponsored.

The response was overwhelming. Enrollment sky rocketed in a couple of semesters. The interest was intense. And the primary source of students came from women who were outside the age cohort of traditional college students and who by and large, because of family responsibilities, could not otherwise have had access to higher education. Many of them were scared to death about going to college but they came nonetheless. One particular instance comes to mind. A woman called the center and told me about an extended family member who had graduated from high school, got married, and was the stay-at-home mom of three kids. One day her husband came in from work and announced that he no longer wanted to be a husband and father. He walked out taking the pick-up truck which was their only transportation with him. She was desperate. Friends had managed to get her on public assistance and food stamps, but she wanted to do something to be able to raise her kids. We gave the family member the contact number of our center which was being established at the time and suggested that she call it. She did. We asked her to come in. She said she had no transportation so I told her if she would provide directions I would come to her house which was way out in the country. I went out and we had a long conversation at her kitchen table. She knew nothing about college but a spark of hope slowly emerged in her demeanor as we talked. Because of her extreme situation she was eligible for need-based student assistance and we worked things out. She was able to arrange for temporary transportation from neighbors and extended family who knew her situation. And once the other students got to know her and the situation she faced, they began helping as well.

On the first day of class she came in frightened as she could be at the starting of her new life as a college student. We talked for a while and I did something never done before or since. She said she felt very intimidated by what was about to happen. I volunteered to go to her first class with her. We asked the instructor and she said it was OK, so we went in and sat down together beside each other. The instructor began to organize the class as is normal during the first meeting. After about fifteen minutes or so I looked over at the student and she gave me a smile that said, "It's OK for you to leave now." That student went on to make the Dean's List and she became a great outreach and role model for others who were uncertain in their venture outside the box. If someone came in and felt overwhelmed by the circumstances of life or unsure of success in college we connected them with this student. Looking back now I think God was putting this together and using her to help other unsure and doubtful Appalachian women to have the opportunity and support that they needed to change their life circumstances. She helped many women especially who never would have had such a chance without her involvement as a mentor, because whatever they had as a challenge to furthering their education she could relate something probably more challenging. After graduation, she went on to become employed in a professional position and raised her children in the process.

That center reached literally hundreds of students over the years that could not have had the opportunity for a higher education experience before it was established. Today the center is a part of the state's relatively recently developed community college system. I firmly believe that in Appalachia just as was the case with the elementary school and recreational facilities in Ridab Khartimo in Somalia that given the opportunity rural people will jump at the possibility to make the changes that will improve their lives. This is especially true if they can visualize a path to move forward in the accomplishment of their goals, and that path is within the parameters of their ability to make things happen. They will also help each other out as was shown both in the new Somali school complex in Ridab Khartimo as well as this higher education center in the heart of Appalachia 9,000 miles and more than three decades away.

One of the biggest drawbacks to working at this institution was that because of the administrative and teaching load there was virtually no time or funds or encouragement for research and writing which were activities that I had become very much involved with and enjoyed in graduate school. The institution viewed itself as a deliverer of higher education access and not for the most part a creator of new research outcomes. However, a few opportunities presented themselves from time to time and when possible, I took advantage of them

Perhaps the most important and personally fulfilling came from my earlier doctoral dissertation director at West Virginia University. In concert with Kenyan professors both in Kenya and those working in the United States he and a colleague in Kenya decided to compile an Afrocentric economic history of the country. Much of the research and publications about Kenya stemmed from non-Kenya scholars particularly researchers at leading institutions with an international reputation and they by-and-large tended to take a Eurocentric or sometimes even a Marxist approach to Kenya's history. It was very pleasing to be offered the opportunity to prepare the chapter on "African Agriculture".[8] For the most part this publication was to be primarily interpretive not including a significant amount of new original research which would have been difficult given the institutional situation. But it was a real pleasure to have the chapter accepted for inclusion in the work and to have it well-received by other scholars when the book was published. In addition, it was possible to get my dissertation published in book form, but this was based, of course, on research and writing that had all previously been carried out in graduate school.

There were also a few occasions when articles would be produced on college academic activities particularly in international education. And there were occasional opportunities for conference participation and paper presentation. Writing book revues and a few West Virginia Encyclopedia articles could also be added to the list. But for the most part it was not possible to develop a lengthy or substantive publication list based on new research given the circumstances. Looking back I am not quite sure what God intended but whatever it was, it could not be accomplished until some initiative had been taken in dealing with the ever-present addiction problem which characterized so much of the time at the institution. Eventually that would be addressed and a whole new outlook on life would emerge.

CHAPTER 5

Recovery

Over time alcohol and other drugs brought fewer and fewer feelings of relief. Even though continuing to drink every few days and to pop pills to add to the kick the sensation of getting high simply was no longer there. I tried topping off the alcohol especially with anti-depressants to get it to work better. It didn't. It was not long until reaching the point that I could not get a buzz going and yet I could not stay sober. I was in the depths of hell. I could not understand why the chemicals that had been consumed over the years would not work anymore. They always had. The resulting quandary was almost similar to the stages of grief. Initially it was a state of disbelief, then a state of self-pity, then lost with nowhere to go. Feelings and emotions were only on what was I to do. There was no place for me, yet there was nothing that could be done about it. Hopelessness and despair characterized life. There was really no one to reach out to because nobody really understood. I certainly did not understand. I did not know why I was different. It was an untenable situation that could not last.

Toward the end of active addiction, the only people I maintained any sort of real relationship with were family. And in the case of a former son-in-law who was also a practicing alcoholic and addict we maintained a close drinking affinity often to the detriment of other members of the family. One special event that would influence the beginning of the surrender which is so necessary for recovery occurred at the start of Thanksgiving Break in 2001. I had been scheduled to go to my daughter's home for the holiday. But when preparing to leave an inner voice said to call her. I did and she very discreetly but succinctly let it be known that I was not welcome because we both knew what would happen. I would arrive and ensure that there was an adequate beer and wine supply for her husband and me both to stay virtually totally plastered for the duration of the visit. In about as perplexing a moment as there ever was in life I slumped down in a chair and in a prayer of total surrender whimpered out to God: "God show me how to do right by my kids when it comes to alcohol." Later I would learn that there is only one way an addict can do right by their kids when it comes to alcohol and that is not to take that first drink or drug. This was the beginning of the first stage of the total surrender which is required to be able to receive the gift of recovery. Initially I did not understand that popping pills was a part of that pattern of addictive behavior.

And this would also be the beginning of a several month journey that would eventually lead me into the rooms of a Twelve-Step recovery program. Quite unexpectedly one evening I got a call from a former student living in Oklahoma. He said that he wanted to return to campus and finish his degree. He had had to leave school before graduating due to family responsibilities. He had been my advisee when he was previously enrolled as an undergraduate. He had also taken some of my classes and was an excellent student. He was calling regarding information on how to go about being readmitted so that he could complete his last semester. In the course of our discussion he indicated that he intended to live on campus in one of the residence halls. He was an older student who had been married for several years and had three kids. I advised him not to live in the residence hall which would be composed primarily of a bunch of young people only recently graduated from high school many of whom would have far more diverse interests than their own immediate academic achievement and advancement. I offered for him to live at my house for the semester. This was not an altogether altruistic measure since I was scheduled for hand surgery in the near future and would not have full use of it for about six weeks. I suggested it would be a good trade off for both of us if he lived at my house while I recuperated from the surgery and he could complete the semester staying there. He concurred and at the beginning of the semester he moved in. I had the hand surgery and he very much helped out around the house and doing the chores I could not do during recovery from the surgery. It was a good experience for both of us.

In one of our many discussions over those next few months we talked about fishing and boats. I loved fishing either river bank or lakeside, but had rarely been out on a boat to fish. I mentioned about always wanting to buy one but never had the knowledge background (or the inclination to spend the money) to get one. He had been raised in Louisiana and grew up around people who had had a great deal of experience with boats and fishing in the bayous. He said to let him browse around on-line and see what he could locate. It was not long until he found what he thought would be an appropriate boat for the lakes in our vicinity. Although hating to spend the money it was easily within an affordable budget.

We went to the dealer and checked it out and test drove it. He approved of it and suggested buying it. I did. The first Saturday morning that we took it out I was hung over from drinking the night before. It soon became readily apparent that it would not be possible to enjoy the boat on the lake if hung over. I vowed not to drink the night before if I wanted to take it out the next day. And I kept that promise. By the time the semester ended the student had imparted quite a bit of knowledge to me about boats and boating. Fishing and boating on the many lakes and rivers within a day's drive would become a major pass time over the next several years. For the first time in life I had spent money on something just for fun the sole purpose of which was not in any way dedicated to fulfilling an addiction. A major manifestation of drinking and drugging expressed itself in being a miserly tightwad especially when it came to buying consumer goods. At the end of the semester the student graduated and eventually moved his family back to West Virginia where they live today.

Following that semester during the interim term in May before the regular summer school session started I taught a class which straddled the Memorial Day weekend. By this time my daughter had relented about coming to visit. I very much wanted to bring the new boat and aquatic skill set to her part of Virginia and have fun with her and her husband and the grandkids on Lake Anna a very large lake located fairly close to their home. My daughter informed me that it would be okay but only if I would not drink with her husband who had started a 28-day out-patient recovery program. I figured I could go for a few days without drinking and the fun of having family and kids on the boat would be well worth it. It was a pause in active addiction that could be handled.

In preparation for several nights before going to Virginia I got plastered. On the last evening before leaving Weston I remember finishing that final beer before going upstairs to pass out. The unusual arc that it took as it was pitched into the trash can is still a vivid memory. As it turned out, it would be the last drink or drug as I write this narrative many years later.

After arriving in her part of Virginia we did take the boat out on Lake Anna. We had a great time including the grand kids who were very much into water recreational activities. Prior to arrival my son-in-law and I had planned on going fishing each evening after we had spent the day on the lake with the kids. However, as soon as supper was over every evening he would say quickly "I have to go to a meeting" and off he would take. We never did go out to any of the smaller streams or lakes to go fishing.

On the last day there, which was Memorial Day itself, we had planned on taking the grand kids to the local swimming pool after which I would return to West Virginia and to the relief of several cold ones both along the way and after getting home. But a few minutes before noon when we were about ready to load up and leave for the pool he suddenly said again "I have to go to a meeting," but this time it was different. He added, "Would you like to go with me?" I can remember being both startled and terrified when he said that, but was able to mumble out a yes. Little was said when we got into the car except that I can remember blubbering something like "I'm scared shitless." Little did I know that this was about to be the biggest turning point in my life.

When we got to the meeting people were milling around talking and seemingly very happy. I am not sure quite what I expected, but whatever it was, happiness and congeniality were certainly not be a part of it. As the meeting opened the guy who was leading it had some people do some readings. He then asked for folks to introduce themselves by their first name. Most of them said I'm so-and-so and I'm an alcoholic or addict. When it came to my son-in-law's turn, he said "I'm so-and-so and I'm an alcoholic." I shivered in some kind of opaque trance when he uttered those words. If he was an alcoholic and I could drink him under the table, and had done so on many occasions, what did that make me? When the introductions got to me about all I could muster to introduce myself was to say "I'm Duke, and I have a drinking problem." At least it was possible to get that out.

It was during the meeting that I began to hear words and concepts with which I could identify. These people actually when they spoke sounded like the way I felt when there was any kind of addictive activity going on in life. The dependence on alcohol and drugs served as a recourse for dealing with everything that had ever happened. And the same was apparently true for most of these people. Moreover, these people were not drunks or bums laying under the bridge – low bottom people who could not handle their booze or dope. They sounded like responsible individuals dealing with the everyday challenges of life. However, when it came to drinking and drugging they all did exactly the same kind of thing. When they picked up that first one they could not stop until they were totally bombed and passed out somewhere. They could not stop on their own. It was a concept that reverberated throughout my persona as each of these individuals explained the challenges they had had with drugs and alcohol in their lives and their inability to control what happened as soon as they started using them.

Perhaps the main attention grabber though was a lady sharing her experience drinking and driving and staying under the legal limit that it took to be charged with a DUI. Over the years thanks to a novelty item to gauge one's alcohol content provided by Student Services at the institution where I was employed, I had learned to drink and generally stay under the legal limit. It was a device that looked somewhat like a kid's whistle which you blew into and it would give you a reasonable estimate of the alcohol content of your blood. I practiced and practiced on it until getting pretty good at estimating if the consumption level was within the legal limit which at that time was higher than it is today. This device, of course, would not hold up as evidence in a court of law, but it was certainly ideal for getting a decent and practicable estimate of what your blood alcohol level actually was and whether or not you should be behind the wheel.

The original plan was that after we took the grandchildren to the pool and I was to return to West Virginia, I would stop at the beer cave in a large convenience store (there was one close by), load up, and, knowing from previous experience, precisely where along the nine mountains separating Charlottesville from Weston, the town where living at the time, that I could pop a beer can and reasonably expect to stay under the legal limit. I had done it several times before. Then after getting home there was a refrigerator full of cold ones and a well-stocked wine rack to finish the job. This coupled with the pills that were also stashed at home would make it possible to pass out and crash into bed. But the lady who began sharing about drinking and staying under the legal limit was about to blow these active addiction plans away far more than she probably expected.

First of all, she stood up which is somewhat unusual at a meeting unless someone's back is bothering them or there aren't enough seats to go around. I have been to thousands of meetings since that time and have never quite seen anybody stand up to share the way she did. I have even been to meetings at that specific location since then and no one ever stood up. After standing, she looked directly at me and without taking her eyes off me related her story of how she had learned to stay under the legal limit and drive and she had done this on many occasions. Why was she looking at me? Why was she standing up almost pointing at me? I was getting ready to do exactly what she was talking about. She was giving me the creeps with her sharing. Hopefully, I would soon be out of this mob of sober people all looking at me. I would soon have the brief relief that drinking that first beer brings and would be able to mellow for a while driving back to West Virginia. After she had vicariously worked me over with her own experience staying under the legal limit and driving she sat down. And somehow the meeting came to an end and I was in an emoitional shambles.

Sometime toward the end of the meeting one of the participants had given out desire tokens for anybody who wanted to start a new way of life. Not really sure what I was doing, I had taken one. As soon as the meeting was over one of the guys who had been in attendance came over and said something like could we step aside and talk. I said sure. He introduced himself as an MD and said he was an alcoholic and addict. He began to talk about how he was powerless over alcohol and drugs and that once he took the first drink or drug he could not stop. That was me, I thought. He said I might want to consider that there was another way and that we did not have to drink or drug. It was during our brief discussion that, for the first time, as he described what alcohol and drugs did to him that I said: "I'm an alcoholic." I was shaking and ensconced in a kind of fear I had never felt before. But it was to be the beginning of a new life that I never knew was possible or even existed.

After the conclusion of that first meeting and the discussion that followed it, we returned to the swimming pool. I said goodbye to the grandkids and my daughter and left to go back to West Virginia. I did not stop at the convenience store beer cave. I did not pop any beer cans along the way and try to drive and stay under the legal limit. Instead, I arrived home totally sober and, even though there was a refrigerator filled with cold beer and a wine rack replete with many bottles and several containers of pills awaiting me, I went to the computer to see where recovery meetings were located in our area of West Virginia. Soon I was able to find a meeting location in nearby Buckhannon. I went to bed totally sober and to work the next day without a hangover. After returning from work on Tuesday afternoon I set out to find that meeting.

It would not be as easy as I thought. I actually got to the church where the meetings were held but no one was there. Finally locating a custodian he told me that there was no meeting that evening but there was one the following evening which was Wednesday. So after work I again scurried over to the location – at least now I knew where it was. Upon getting to the meeting the people in it said it was a closed dual recovery meeting. I had no idea what that was but, although I was informed that I was not allowed to attend it, the people were very friendly and helpful. The meeting was closed to people who were only addicts. They said a participant needed another mental or emotional problem besides addiction. They added that if I hurried it would be possible to get to the recovery meeting in Jane Lew which was close to Weston and it was for alcoholics and other chemically addicted people.

So speeding as quickly as possible I arrived at the location they described, but nobody was there. I know I was in the right place having been to numerous meetings at that site since then. However, for some reason there was no meeting there on that particular night. This was becoming frustrating because, even though not wanting to drink or drug, by this time I was in a sort of 'la-la-land' with not being able to do anything about the addiction but equally unsettled because there was no meeting or anybody else in recovery with whom to talk. All I knew was that I did not want to drink or drug any more.

On Thursday I made another attempt. The folks from the Wednesday closed dual recovery meeting had also mentioned a Thursday meeting nearby. It was located on the campus of the college in Buckhannon. I made it to the building where the meeting was held and walked up the stairs not knowing what to expect. Having found the room I ventured in and although small it had several people in it. I was not sure what to do. I just walked in and sat down at that first meeting in West

Virginia. Several people spoke and although very wary again of being part of the group I identified with them just as with the folks in the Charlottesville meeting. They talked about their powerlessness and how they had no control over their use of addictive substances. After the meeting was over a few of them came over to talk. They made sure I got a current schedule of meeting locations in the surrounding area. And one of them, a short lady with the widest-brimmed hat I had ever seen, came over to me. She didn't say a word but she put her arms around me and gave me a big hug and then she said simply, "We're glad you're here." It was like going from a black-and-white movie to a technicolor movie!

The next night was Friday and after work I went to a speaker meeting at the church I had originally been turned away from because it was a closed dual recovery meeting. By this time I was so confused I do not remember to this day whether it was a man or a woman who spoke let alone what they said. But what I do remember is meeting some of the folks in attendance. I also remember leaving the meeting. Walking out the door I asked God to keep me sober because it was not possible to do it by myself – it was a prayer of desperation and surrender. Although frequently staying sober for several days at a time Friday night was usually not one of them. Getting into the car and heading toward the freeway I was still praying. Driving down Main Street the prayers continued. Just as I was getting into the lane to go onto the expressway back to Weston something somehow, a hidden directive coming from somewhere, said to go into a nearby Wal-Mart. I quickly swung across a couple of lanes of traffic – fortunately no vehicles were in those lanes – and got on the street leading into the Wal-Mart.

Parking in front of the grocery entrance I went inside and walked over to the produce section. There was nothing that I knew that I needed and was not quite sure why I was in there, but something inside said that that was exactly where I needed to be at that time. I like fresh fruits and vegetables a lot and so started just browsing around to see if anything looked particularly good. I roamed around the produce section for a few minutes. Little did I know at the time but God was at work in my life. Soon one of the guys whom I had met at the end of the meeting a few minutes earlier came in through the door on the far side of the building. I later found out he had come in to look for tires for his truck. He saw me and walked all the way across the store to the produce section and started talking to me. Confused as I was, I listened intently as he explained what recovery was all about, the Twelve Steps, the surrender required, and that we could live one day at a time without drinking and drugging. We essentially had a meeting of our own right there in the produce section. With this assistance from another addicted person an understanding of powerlessness was reinforced and I knew there was a friend I could talk to. Going home when the store closed, I did not get drunk or high even though there was still that refrigerator full of beer and that well-stocked wine rack along with the assortment of pills. At least, so far in recovery I had learned that we only had to get through that one day without drinking or drugging. The discussion with the new found friend and what little I had grasped of recovery so far made it possible to get through that first Friday home alone. God had provided just enough to get through that one day. The expansive booze supply would stay intact and untouched until August when I took all that could be found at the time as a contribution to a family gathering.

It was with a great deal of eagerness that I embraced the aura of the fellowship and all that it extended to the addict. I started going to as many meetings as possible. I devoured the literature. Somewhere during those first few weeks of sobriety someone had suggested it was necessary to get a sponsor to help take one through the Twelve Steps and find a way for living without succumbing to your addiction. This would be the second hardest thing I was to do on the path to recovery. The hardest, of course, had been admitting that initial powerlessness over chemicals that had occurred in Charlottesville. The low self-esteem carried within me, however, would be the protective shield for this endeavor, or so I thought. I decided to ask the man who had befriended me in Wal-Mart. He had made me feel really comfortable when we were talking originally, and we had talked several times since that first encounter. Although afraid to ask him – somehow inwardly I perceived I was not worthy enough for him to help me – I finally rationalized through that low self-esteem that he would not really agree and would say no. Then there would be no need to worry about finding a sponsor the concept of which was very troubling – having another man to talk to about one's inner most self and what had occurred during an active addiction career. However, because of that unworthiness and lack of self-esteem I was absolutely certain that he would deny the request and this challenge would be over and there would no longer be a need to be concerned about it. So after fidgeting around about this for a while I finally got up the courage to ask him. To my surprise he replied with an affirmative yes. Today I know why he said yes.

The immediate thoughts that came to mind were, "Oh God, what do I do now?" Getting help from other people in dealing with personal problems was not something I could easily do. But since becoming one with the fellowship of recovery over the years it is increasingly evident that God puts the right people in our lives for whatever our needs are at that particular juncture in life. So it was to be with this. It makes no difference who or what God puts together, if we have truly surrendered the right people, places and things will be there. I was an ivory-tower academic and this new sponsor was a coal miner. But I really believe the arrangement was ordained by

God. He had about four and a half years of sobriety at the time. More importantly, he somehow knew just the right thing to say and how to say it. As temperamental as I had been toward the end of active addition and as emotionally unstable as I was in early sobriety, he seemed to be able to get through as nobody else before had done.

We started discussing the steps and on a couple of occasions we went out on the boat, moored it, and listened to and discussed the recordings of people telling their stories and talking about dealing with their addictions and other personal problems by taking the Twelve Steps and making them a way of life. Like so many newcomers I thought I was unique and everything adverse that happened was somebody else's fault. He taught me that I was responsible for my own recovery and that I was also responsible for my own feelings and emotions and happiness. Other people were not. I do not know how many times he said, "Now Duke, we're only looking at ourselves...." Like so many others in the rooms of recovery I would say "Yes, but..." and get all pissed off every time he said it, and it seemed like he always said it every time we talked. But he was right. In reality if we are truly going to be happy we are only looking at ourselves. It is an inside job. Eventually recovery would lead to the Gnostic, Buddhist, and Taoist literature that would serve to help become one with this concept.

The First Step had been the hardest. It took forty years to accept the concept of powerless. The second part of this step admitting "that our lives had become unmanageable," I could only skimp over by acknowledging that a life based on drinking and drugging had become unmanageable because it no longer worked anymore (if it ever did). It would take a few years to realize that throughout a life of addiction there had been some unbelievable unmanageability which I was unable to comprehend at the time. Until having been clean and sober for a while and having grown spiritually enough to accept it and understand it as unmanageability was I able to comprehend it. Eventually though the realization crept in that I had undertaken all kinds of crazy actions many of them in the mad pursuit for more money which I viewed as security, a security, however, which was never found no matter how many insane activities might be attempted and subsequently disposed of. The same had been true of chasing around the world in the mad pursuit of finding someone else, somewhere else, who was me.

The Second and Third Steps were relatively easy. Having grown up with a loving, caring, and forgiving God during childhood it was easy to readily accept that God would help if asked. During my drinking and drugging career I had believed in God but my attitude was one of God you go do your thing and I'll go do mine. My interpretation of God had been basically that I was tough and could handle whatever came down the pike, and I surrendered to no one. I could take care of everything and really did not need the active involvement of a higher power. Moreover, I had proven it with the experiences in Africa and Asia and other parts of the world. I could control my own destiny. In the long run, when it failed to work out that way, it was the beginning of the end. I finally had to surrender. In looking back, however, even though hating the word surrender – it was not even in my vocabulary – every time I picked up a stimulant whether I wanted to admit it or not I surrendered to the alcohol and other drugs because they took control of life. The Second and Third Steps are really yes or no questions. And, yes, I came to believe that I was ready for God to come actively into my life in a way that I had never let him before. And yes, I made the decision to let him do so. I did not know at the time how or in what manner he would come into my life. I don't think I really even cared. I had not grown spiritually enough to conceptualize that. But it did not matter. All that had to do done was to become willing. With that willingness and a decision to let him take control of my life at some future date I could move forward in God's time to a greater spiritual oneness with him. And that, in desperation, I chose to do.

As we approached the Fourth Step, like so many other newcomers who confronted this step for the first time, there was some serious apprehension and stubbornness about carrying it out as suggested. That reticence, of course, as with so many of us in initial recovery, involved a great deal of self will run rampant. I would do it but would just not write anything down. I did not want any incriminating evidence of any kind of failure or other unresolved challenges in life to be confessed in writing. My sponsor had other ideas. Slowly but surely he convinced me that writing everything down was the only way to go. So finally despite significant forebodings I reluctantly began to write and eventually committed a number of shortcomings to pen and ink on a paper tablet. Looking back it was a relatively feeble list of character challenges compared to what would be found in later years. Conspicuously missing in the list were any references to the experiences in Somalia and Vietnam. Even though PTSD had characterized so many of my addictive thoughts and actions throughout post-service life, it was a deeply buried trait that I had strongly and unwittingly tried to sub-consciously camouflage as something that was non-existent or insignificant. Also missing was any recognition of the extreme codependency that had been an integral part of life over the years of addiction. Codependency was a concept which at the time I was not even able to recognize the terminology for let alone commit to writing it down on paper and then doing something about it.

The Fourth Step is where we begin to find out who and what we really are. Because of our addiction most of us have built a wall around our true selves and thus we failed to recognize our genuine strengths and weaknesses. Though it has a foreboding all its own for some, it is the opportunity to begin to find that lost soul who drowned his or her life's challenges in alcohol and other drugs. It is the beginning of the examination of ourselves as human beings created by God that helps us to be able to identify who we really are and, in many respects, to understand that God had been with us all along. We had somehow survived our addiction and were now prepared to do something about it. The Fourth Step is the opportunity to grow spiritually and to begin to become one with God's world and the rest of our fellows. As that happy and spiritually upbeat Franciscan teacher and scholar Richard Rohr describes it "Step 4 is about creating a good and trustworthy lamp inside of us that reflects and reveals what is really there, knowing that 'anything exposed to the light will itself become light' (Ephesians 5:14)."[1]

Today I know this relative lack of unwittingly not putting some of the more serious emotional challenges on that initial Fourth Step list was a reflection of God's wisdom working in recovery. It is a certainty that I was not ready to deal with anything like the effects of Vietnam or of codependency at that stage of spiritual growth. Indeed, if someone had said I was going to be dealing with the moral morass of the events involved in Vietnam when I first came into the rooms of recovery, I would have turned around and walked right back out into an almost certain crisis of self-destruction. Spiritual preparedness was simply not advanced enough to reach that deeply within the walls I had built around myself to be able to liberate the soul at that point in recovery. The same was true of the codependency issues of which I was not even aware. Later, after some few years of recovery and spiritual growth, God would hit me over the head with both of these and say now is the time for you to address these issues. God never gives us more to deal with than we can handle at any specific juncture of our lives. And he certainly did not expect too much from me at the time of that first Fourth Step even though thinking when it was finished that it was indeed a thorough, far-reaching, and insightful character examination. It was only the beginning of learning a way to uncover our own true inner selves and the value we hold within those selves.

The Fifth Step "Admitted to God, to ourselves, and to another human being the exact nature of our wrongs," is an opportunity to connect with spiritual reality possibly for the first time in our lives. By admitting to ourselves we recognize our humanity. By admitting to God we connect with the spiritual universe. We may say that God already knows. Yes, he does but in this action we commit ours selves to that God. And the third part of this step, admitting to another human being, is the mechanism by which we connect to the rest of humanity because we have shared our intimate selves with a representative of that humanity. We have begun a true relationship with God, with ourselves, and with our fellows.

To take that part of the Fifth Step about sharing with another human being my sponsor came over to the house and we sat down at the dining room table. Of course, I was very apprehensive as most all of us are when we are about to take this step. Inwardly, I thought I sure do not want to do this. We chatted for a few minutes and then I shared with him the written list. Oh God, I thought, he is really going to think that I am some kind of chump. Apparently he did not. We talked about some of the points on the list and he shared some of the character traits that he had had to deal with on his Fourth and Fifth Steps. In actuality it turned out to be a very pleasant give-and-take experience. For some reason after getting over that initial fear of talking to him about what was on the list, I wanted to talk about everything I had ever done. And we did. During our conversation we even added a few more things to the list. Finally, when we had finished going over all the items and spent some time discussing each of them he rose to leave.

As he was going out he gave me a big hug. It was the first time that I could remember ever having been hugged by another guy who was not a family member. It was kind of an unusual experience, but since that time in the rooms of recovery and outside of them it has become a much more commonplace part of life without chemicals.

After my sponsor left I went outside on the back deck. The sun was shining. It was a beautiful day. The quite stillness around the house reflected the calmness within. For the first time in life I felt I was a part of God's world. I belonged. The feeling of serenity and peace were all encompassing. I felt closer to God than I had ever felt before – that I had become one with his world. It was a oneness of simplicity and tranquility. It was the beauty of the acceptance of the self as belonging to the world that God had created. There was a calmness and sense of being never felt before. I was no longer apart.

My sponsor suggested going somewhere alone to take the Sixth and Seventh Steps. Step Six is "We were entirely ready to have God remove all these defects of character," and Step Seven is, "We humbly asked him to remove our shortcomings." These are steps that only take place between the individual and his or her God. So the next day I took the boat and went out on the lake. I found a quite spot in a cove, spent some time in prayer and meditation and then asked God to help me become totally willing to have all the garbage listed in the Fourth Step list removed and taken away. Then I relinquished to Him everything on that inventory. It was a time of serenity and peace. Fellowship with God and with the environment had become one. Ego was disappearing. It was okay to let go. No longer did I need to control the universe and what I found in it while trying to make the changes to it that ego said should be made. All was well. It was possible to live in the moment and this moment was a time of closeness to God. There was a spiritual emolument in the solitude of the lake in summer surrounded by God's beauty which reflected itself in the greenery and splendor of the deciduous woodlands encompassing the cove with the sun shining brightly overhead with its refreshing air and the water lapping slowly against the shore. The hole in the center that I had so assiduously tried to fill with a multitude of various chemicals over the years began to start filling with the love of God. It was a love that knew no bounds, and that love radiated through the natural environment in peace and acceptance. God became a love never experienced before.

As my sponsor had also suggested I pulled out the charcoal lighter kept on the boat and lit fire to the list. I held it as long as possible before letting go of it when the flames were licking my fingertips. The ashes fell from the burning paper sifting themselves gradually into the water and disappearing into the depths of the lake. So did everything that was on that list. I was free. Slowly but surely the wall I had built around myself over the decades was crumbling away. This became a major first step of the spiritual journey that was going to lead to a happiness, serenity, and internal peace never known before. It would become a spirituality that had never even been conceptualized simply because I had never before known anything like it. It had been impossible to know such an experience as long as the chemicals of substance abuse blocked me from the sunlight of the spirit. Hence there was no way to have envisioned it, but now I was becoming one with it. It was a unity with God's world and a freedom that had never been known before.

After spending some time in prayer and meditation and relishing the new spirituality that had just resonated from the experience, I transcended into a more mundane practice that I had often come to the lake before to do. It was time to go fishing for a while. It was an activity that had been planned even before leaving home for the lake. Staying at the same spot in which the boat had been moored to take the Sixth and

Seventh Steps I rigged up a bottom feeder line with chicken livers. It was something that had been done many times before. Set up a bottom feeder line and then rig up another pole to fish for something that fed on top of the water. And so I did. As soon as casting the bottom feeder line into the water I picked up the other pole and began to thread a lure that would work top water. Before completing it, however, the bottom feeder pole began quickly wriggling across the deck of the boat and would have plunged into the water had I not jumped up and grabbed it just in time as it was about to go overboard. With some effort I began to work it in and soon pulled in the biggest catfish I had ever caught. It seems God has a way of combining spiritual growth with a little fun!

Returning from the lake I continued to work on moving forward. I read the literature about the Eighth and Ninth Steps and reviewed what needed to be done next. I asked my sponsor for guidelines on developing the Eighth Step list. After reflecting for a while on them I began making a list of all the individuals who had been harmed during a career of substance abuse. Family members were first and foremost on the list especially my children. There were others as well. Perhaps the most troubling were the ones I did not know about. The licentious behavior in Africa and Asia as a youth had led to liaisons with women usually sex workers who may or may not have become pregnant. There was no way of knowing. It had long been a concern that there might be children of these encounters who were unknown to me. It would be an egregious sin to create a biracial and culturally distinct child and abandon it in a society which could not accept it. The anguish of thinking of that possibility would frequently be an excuse for drinking and drugging in earlier days. It was conceptually unbearable to have created a life and then not taken responsibility for caring for it.

There were others on this list. As folks in the fellowship advised do not worry about how amends will be made at this time – just complete the list to the best of your ability. That I tried to do. When finished with the list I went over it with my sponsor. He made suggestions about changing the list. Then he provided some advice about making the amends as part of Step Nine. It was time to take responsibility for past actions. With a little bit of trepidation I initiated the process and began to try to mend some of the damage caused in the past. Although none of the amends quite worked out as expected they were underway. A new way of relating to other people had been introduced by Steps Eight and Nine.

In the case of some – such as the possibility of mixed race abandoned children in the Third World – I could only ask for God's forgiveness. It is always possible that the opportunity might present itself and who knows with modern DNA testing all that might change, but what is important today is that we recognize the past and become willing to make it right if there is any possible way of doing so.

It was during the process of taking these early steps that for the first time I heard, "Welcome home, Soldier!" It came very suddenly and very genuinely while in a group of people I had just met. It was, of course, totally unexpected since it had been over thirty years since leaving combat. To the extent possible I had buried the Vietnam past as deeply as it could go into my psyche. Somehow or another, I do not even remember for sure how the conversation led to it, but it was with other more recent combat veterans. As soon as they learned I was a Vietnam veteran, one of them extended his hand and said it. I was stunned not knowing quite what to say. It certainly was a heartfelt and very much appreciated gesture. I think I mumbled "Thanks" or something like that. But the feeling within was one of the most unusual I have ever had. A sense of acceptance welled up inside. It was a gesture truly intimate and compatible with early recovery from chemicals. It embodied the spoken inclusiveness of society as never before. It has happened several times since then and it still rings sweetly in my psyche every time I hear it.

The continuing practice of taking a personal inventory has led to a great deal of identifying and addressing of issues that it was not possible to deal with when initially coming into the rooms of recovery. Probably first and foremost were matters related to Post-Traumatic Stress Disorder (PTSD) from the war in Vietnam. As mentioned earlier, there was nothing on that first Fourth Step list that related to the war. However, after a few years into recovery all that would change. Initial recovery was pretty much limited to those mundane, run of the mill, dramatic challenges that interfered with personal growth. After the fog had lifted and I was no longer in the la-la-land of initial recovery some spiritual change and acceptance began to blossom in life.

The immediate source of this concern about what had happened in Vietnam came with the beginning of the Second Iraq War. With the initiation of the war there was full discussion of it in the all media. Television especially would be a major point of implosion because my mind and soul returned quickly to Vietnam every time a war news item came on, which was virtually every time the news was broadcast. It was kind of like God had hit me over the head with it and said "Now is the time for you to address the issues of Vietnam." I became majorly restive, irritable and discontent. I talked to my sponsor about it. He was curious as to why I had never mentioned it before. I told him it was hidden in the background of the soul and there was no way it could be dealt with when first coming into the rooms of recovery. Looking back I had subconsciously tried to cover up the past by forgetting about it and pushing it further and further into the dark recesses of the mind. As this new awareness emerged, initially I went to a psychologist (one who was in recovery himself). After meeting and talking with him a few times suddenly I had to talk about it. I had to talk about it to anybody and everybody who would listen. And I did. It was as if a flood of feelings and emotions about everything that had happened during the war and its aftermath suddenly had to be discussed and openly addressed.

At length, I talked with all kinds of people both inside and outside the rooms of recovery. Many, of course, had never been into a war zone and had no first-hand knowledge of what I was talking about, but by and large they listened and I desperately needed a sounding board. With the suggestion of the psychologist and with the encouragement and direction of my sponsor and others in the rooms of recovery accompanied by much prayer and meditation it soon became evident that it was necessary to let go of this whole debilitating trauma of the war and its aftermath through the Sixth and Seventh Steps. We talked at length about it in the recovery rooms. And in what was to become a glowing incident of God at work the place for that Sixth and Seventh Step was identified as the Vietnam Veterans Memorial in Washington DC. It would become an act that would help enormously in dealing with the tenuous emotional instability that surrounded the events of the war and that had so dominated the post-war experience and its aftermath of addictive behavior.

Once the decision was made others helped me to take action. One friend in recovery who lived in the northern Virginia area drove me to the Vietnam Veteran's Memorial and left me there at the entrance. It was emotional and traumatizing thinking of the experience that was about to ensue. The weather was overcast with clouds suggesting the possibility of rain. Walking over toward the memorial the feeling of disrespect and indifference of the people in the vicinity of the monument overwhelmed and annoyed me. Children were playing noisily and obnoxiously on the grass.

Someone should keep them under control. People were talking loudly and unceremoniously to each other oblivious to the immense spiritual nature of this place. A rock band was blasting its reckless energy incoherently nearby casting a pale of dishonor throughout what should be a very honorable and stately function. More respect should be shown to this sacred site that reflected the tragedy of so many innocent and unknowing people who had suffered so extremely from this misadventure and which had destroyed the lives of so many people.

Walking over to the monument, that monolithic listing of just good guys that did not make it back, a feeling of sadness welled up in me. I fell to my knees in prayer. Tears rolled down my checks. I asked God for forgiveness for what had happened in Vietnam. I was overcome with a feeling of love and spiritual oneness with him. The tragedy of war knew no blame as the heartlessness of the ego had blasted human beings into disastrous consequences of mutual self-destruction. I surrendered and asked for knowledge of God's will for the direction life should take, for what should be done next in his world. I knelt at the wall for an hour or so in prayer and meditation. Then I went and sat on one of the nearby benches and in prolonged prayer and meditation tears continued to stream down my checks. As I did so the pain began to ease. Acceptance began to come into my heart. It was a joy to be at one with God on this solemn occasion. A feeling of enormous weight was being removed from me. The burden was easing. I had begun sharing it with both my fellows and with God and the weight of the trauma was being lifted.

Getting up to leave and return to meet my friend a different world began to emerge. The clouds had disappeared and the sun had come out. Walking back through the Mall to rejoin my friend the yelling and rambunctiousness of the kids became merriment to my ears. They were fun to watch and a joy to hear. The music from the rock band expressed a liveliness and enchantment not heard earlier. The sun shone brightly. People were happy and having a good time talking and laughing with each other. Young couples shared their enjoyment of togetherness. It was great to be alive in God's world. It was fun to be in the park on this beautiful afternoon. There was joy in the world. Let freedom ring!

Looking back this experience opened the door to growth and recovery from a vulnerable and troubling part of the past. The change that came about was the beginning of a new relationship with PTSD. We never really ever get totally and completely away from our troubled past and the trauma it has spawned, but what we can get is the opportunity to make it possible for us to manage that past without undue trepidation and disruption in our present day lives. We can become one with the moment. With that acceptance, it is possible to live with and manage our past trauma. This process was begun at the Vietnam Veterans Memorial that day. PTSD would reappear from time to time in the years to come, but it would do so on very manageable terms which, with the help of God, the negative impact from it could be significantly reduced. And there was certainly no need to use drugs and alcohol to do so. In a change from the past, I could also turn to the Veterans' Administration for help. Such would not have been possible on early return from the war because treatment facilities for PTSD were not readily available, but that would have made no difference anyway because I would never have utilized the opportunity if they had been available. PTSD was something that I would handle on my own. But in the aftermath of the experience at the Vietnam Veterans Memorial and the growth reflected in taking the Twelve Steps, the Veterans Administration Hospital and its mental health system was now something that could be taken advantage of. They became a part of recovery. Today I make full use of all the medical facilities that the VA has to offer because that is where I belong and feel most at home. And that is with the other veterans from our many different conflicts around the world.

Closely paralleled to PTSD from Vietnam were issues of codependency. It is a word that I had never known before recovery and it is one that is frequently hard to define. Perhaps it is more closely akin to fleas on a dog hopping from one place to another. It was, basically, for me trying to make others responsible for my own happiness. "If only so-and-so would do such-and-such" I would be happy. The codependency centered around trying to have other people meet my needs no matter what those needs were or who they were in life. I would become attached to people in frequently unhealthy relationships – unhealthy in the way in which I wanted to control their actions or for them to act in such a way that they made me feel happy and complete. I was dependent upon others for contentedness with life. It was something I never realized during active addiction and was totally unaware of its existence. Yet without realizing it, it had played a major role in life.

A few years into recovery, in one such codependent incident, I was reeling from somebody else's reaction to the perception of how I thought they should behave. They had contemptuously rejected it. It occurred two or three years into sobriety and it was about the same time as dealing with the PTSD issues. God must have known that this was a good opportunity to have some significant spiritual growth come my way and that I was ready to make additional changes. In what could only have been a God moment I was in a large bookstore and there was prominently displayed on a table in the front of the store a number of books that had been significantly marked down in price. In fact, most of them were half-priced. My own penchant for penury would not normally allow me to pay full price for much of anything especially books. But one tome was prominently displayed on top of the stack. It was Melody Beattie's **Codependent No More**[2] and not only was that book there but her second book **Beyond Codependency**[3] was included in the same volume – two for the price of one and it had been marked to half the normal cost!

Apparently God knew how to get my attention. I picked the book up and started reading. I could not believe some of the things she was saying. In many instances they fitted to a T. I stood and read it for a good while. Then, without hesitation I purchased the book and headed home. Once starting reading it I couldn't put it down. Early on she gave a formal definition of a codependent. It bears repetition here: "A codependent person is one who has let another person's behavior affect him or her, and who is obsessed with controlling the person's behavior."[4] Having since been through the process of recovery on this one, I would like to add an individualized definition of codependency: "Expecting other people to bring fulfillment and happiness into your life instead of letting the God of your understanding fill the empty space within you." Taoist writer and interpreter Eva Wong explaining concepts relating to the **Tao Te Ching** hits precisely on the challenges related to the issues of codependency when she says, "People who look at others and not at themselves will see only what others have. As a result, they will seek to gratify themselves with what others have but never see what they have. They will try to emulate the thoughts and actions of others but never delight in their inborn nature. They will try to figure out what brings joy to others but will never know how to bring joy into their own lives."[5]

Beattie's definition and the discussion around it described exactly the emotions and feelings I had had over the years – to spouse, to kids, to friends, even occasionally to students that I had taught or advised. These revelations, too, went to the psychologist that I had been seeing for PTSD. We had a number of sessions to discuss what could be called my other addiction. Often, after avidly reading Beattie's works, I went to my knees in prayer. By this time prayer and asking for God's direction were becoming pretty much a multi-time per day occasion. It had emerged during a period of rapid changes coming about in life with an increasing degree of frequency. Once starting to tear down that impenetrable wall with an admission of powerlessness and the beginning of genuine surrender there seemed to be a rush toward a new life, toward a new me. It would continue almost unabated for the next couple of years.

Until discovering her writings, I really had no idea that I had gone through life with that kind of unhealthy dependency on others. Maybe that explains why I so frequently isolated to drink and drug. I would normally much rather be alone than at a bar. But by becoming aware of it, it became a negative character trait that could be worked on, so much so that I began reading all the literature about the subject that could be found including almost all of Beattie's other books looking forward to each new one as that prolific writer continued to publish additional resources on codependency. Her book **Codependents' Guide to the Twelve Steps**[6] became a vital resource for applying the steps to this newly identified and negative character trait.

My sponsor, when discussing it with him, also suggested that I go to meetings of a co-dependency twelve-step fellowship. I am very glad he did because there were people there with the same sort of unhealthy relationships that I had, but they were doing something about them. I proceeded to read all of their literature that I could get hold of as well. Things started to change. I began to realize a responsibility for my own happiness not others. Life became a lot more fun after coming to understand that it was not necessary to take responsibility for the management of other people's lives. Living became much easier. The burden of taking care of other people's happiness and success was best left for others to figure out. It sure would be a lot easier lifestyle. They could deal with their own emotions and contentedness in life. It was no longer my responsibility to handle. My only responsibility for emotional well-being was for myself and that had to be through my own initiative and in contact with the God of my understanding. The only way of helping others was to share one's experience, strength, and hope. Whether they opted to grow from that process of change that I had experienced was theirs and theirs alone to determine.

In sobriety it was possible to express emotions and feelings that relate to life's transition events without the use of chemicals. Both parents passed away after coming into the rooms of recovery. It was possible to be a part of the grievance process not isolating and drinking and drugging and feeling sorry for myself which I would have done before recovery. Instead, I could join siblings and other family members and friends and share our grief together ever thankful that God had given us the opportunity to have such good parents who had shared their values, cares, and concerns with us over the years. We had been truly blessed.

A real test of the quality of serenity and peace in life would come majorly home on January 2, 2006, with the Sago Mine Disaster in which twelve miners would die. Early in the morning that day word of the tragedy began to spread. As soon as learning of it I urgently began to try to find out about what had happened. My sponsor was an underground coal miner at that mine. He was the same sponsor who had befriended me in Wal-Mart a few years earlier and who had so gently worked with me moving through the transitions of early recover. He was also the same sponsor who had taken me through the Twelve Steps and into the wonderful life that I now had. In a panic I called his wife. She told me he had just exited the mine shortly before the explosion. A sigh of relief came over me. She further explained that he had returned to the mine in the event that he could be of help in the attempted rescue operation to try to save the other miners. Thank God he was safe. He has since retired from the mines but he is still my sponsor today.

The wall that had been built around emotions and feelings was slowly eroding away as I took the Twelve Steps making them a way of life. It was not a constant or even transition. It was very similar to the process of the Department of Highways plowing roads in the winter. A pile of ugly snow would be amassed in whatever out-of-the-way place they could shovel it into. It would be laced with ashes and salt and be an unsightly remnant of the last snowfall. Soon some of it would melt away. Then another snow would fall and more would be piled on to the existing lot. Gradually as spring approached some more of it would melt away. Eventually as the Lenten roses and daffodils began to emerge much of it would have turned to water and sludge and disappeared. It was an ongoing process of melt and re-pile until the rudiments of spring took over. The process was uneven and often ugly to watch because of all the cinders and chemicals that had been used with the plowing. But eventually the rain washed even that away and a new springtime of sun and beauty would emerge. Such was the process of recovery. The major internal conflicts that had been amassed over the years, ugly and unsightly as they were, began melting away much as the snow and ice of the West Virginia winter would have dissolved itself and disappeared. Zen Buddhist writer and teacher William Alexander writing in **Ordinary Recovery** sums it up succinctly: "When you are recovered you will know, bone deep, that there is nothing that your addiction did to you that could be undone, that has not been undone. Ordinary life awaits. The tools are the same. The problems are the same. You are transformed. Many people have had this experience. There are two truths about it. One: You can't fake it. Two: You can't deny it."[7]

Such is the way of the love of God and of recovery. It cannot be faked and it cannot be denied. We have become one with it. Recovery has become our singleness of purpose.

CHAPTER 6

A Spiritual Connection to God

"The spiritual life is not a theory, we have to live it,"[1] maintains the primary publication of the first Twelve Step Program. Making the Twelve Steps a way of life is the very last phrase of the very last step. It says "...practice these principles in all our affairs." They are the framework under which our spiritual growth can take place. They are the basis around which an interpretation and manifestation of God can come about within each of us as we reach out on our own to find the spiritual fulfillment and relationship with the higher power of our understanding that works in our lives. Curtailing the ego that manifests itself so intensely in so many addicted people becomes the objective of an emerging spirituality which can begin to manifest itself in us as we surrender and initiate the search for a way of living that will bring the contentedness, serenity, and peace of mind we have sought for so long.

Living the principles of the Twelve Steps with the spiritual growth so necessary for their nurturing means attempting to become one with God's will for whatever comes our way in life. It involves the total surrender and acceptance that are mentioned in so many of the world's spiritual expressions.

Today I know that everything is going to go my way. This may sound like an odd and ridiculous thing to say as a part of a regimen of recovery which looks toward getting out of ego and self, but upon closer examination it is not. If things are not going our way with life coming together in the manner that it should, then our will is not aligned with God's will. If we are following his will the challenges of life will be dealt with in a reasonable and effective and perhaps even a pleasant sort of way. If that does not happen then we need to get on our knees and ask God to show us what his will is for the challenges we are facing. The answers will come in the time we need to carry out what we must do. If life is getting bumpy and incoherent and appears to be falling apart then we need to look at ourselves and what we have been attempting and why it is so apparently unproductive because if what we are trying to do is not working the way we think it should then it is running contrary to God's will. The answer lies within and in the total surrender of our self-will that can so abundantly assert itself. It is only there that we will find the solution to the everyday challenges that we all encounter. A beautiful statement from the recovery literature of one of the fellowships states: "The solutions rest with me. With the help of my Higher Power, I can adorn my life with comfort, serenity and enjoyment. It does not depend on another person, and the sooner I accept this fact, the sooner I will be able to face myself realistically."[2] It is the love that we cultivate within our hearts both for ourselves and for others that sustains our accepting inclusiveness of all in the present moment of our existence.

One more related and beautiful statement from another of the fellowships says about our spiritual growth: "As our recovery progressed, we became increasingly aware of ourselves and the world around us. Our needs and wants, our assets and liabilities were revealed to us. We came to realize that we had no power to change the outside world, we could only change ourselves."[3] While most of us initially looked on the Fourth Step in probably what was its most rudimentary form, that is, trying to find out what was wrong with us as a person and what we needed to change, slowly but surely our vision of what that step was about would more fully blossom in our lives. We would come to understand that the step was much more than what it appears on the surface. It is a finding of the way of life that reflects our assets as well as our liabilities. God in fact made us all. Each of us as human beings has unique qualities which are only our own. Once this step has been taken and incorporated into a life of "practicing these principals in all our affairs" it becomes a way to continue to grow spiritually for we are innately neither good nor bad. We are ordinary human beings who have the disease of addiction. That changing of ourselves as we grow spiritually will take the form of becoming more fully a useful and productive citizen within the society in which we live as well as within our relationship with the God of our understanding. As the commentary says we grew into the fullness of ourselves. We were no longer the problem. Our problem was the disease of addiction and its associated fullness of self-inflicted suffering reflected by an ego run rampant, and for that we are building a process for subduing those willful adversities that had characterized so much of our lives. We were becoming a part of a world in consensus with others just as God intended us to be. We could not change others, but we could certainly change ourselves and our attitude toward others as we relied on our God to participate fully in our transformation to a new way of living and a new way of interacting with our fellow human beings. It becomes the fullness of the step that Richard Rohr outlined for us as a tool for inner searching. And it reflects the philosophy of most all Twelve Step programs that in the ultimate analysis we all made our own problems, and it is only we with the help of the God of our understanding who could take the necessary measures to achieve their resolution.

Much of recovery literature says that anger toward or resentment of people, things, or actions is the number one offender of addicted people and that it stands fully in the way of successful recovery from our addition. If we are angry or hold a resentment today we know that it is the ego which has created some sort of unhealthy attachment to that person, thing, or event toward which our anger or resentment is directed. So it is incumbent upon our souls to look within at the source of that attachment and upon identifying the cause of it to relinquish it by detaching with love. Our happiness in the present moment is totally dependent on the effectiveness of that detachment from these unhealthy relationships generated by the ego. Over the years we have slowly and sometimes jaggedly sought to develop this detachment so that it becomes a way of living in that such anger and resentment are gradually being eliminated from life. Detachment becomes an end in and of itself. With it we can relegate much of our ego to the garbage heap to which it belongs.

All of us will have challenges that we encounter each day. If we want we can call these problems, but they are also opportunities for growth. Both recovery literature and other spiritual literature tell us that we were the ones who caused our own problems. It is safe to say that our problems originate within us in reality and in perception. The internationally renowned master of Tibetan Buddhism Lama Zopa Rinpoche expresses it succinctly for us: "Problems and the absence of problems do not come from outside. Problems and the absence of problems, as well as all peace and all happiness, only come from your own mind. Your mind has the potential to stop the problems that come from your mind."[14] If you were like me in early recovery there was an almost incessant spawning of supposed problems created by the ego. So it is our responsibility in recovery to follow the steps to a clean and sober life, free of addiction. And that life is reached by taking the spiritual measures that permit us to achieve the inner peace and happiness and the absence of the challenges to our sober living that we ourselves have permitted our ego to create. As Zen teacher Kenneth Leong tells us, "Spiritual freedom does not mean the absence of physical constraints, but it does mean the ability to loosen oneself from the bondage of one's own ego."[5]

That means starting each day with prayer and meditation. It is the first thing I do before anything else in the morning. When I roll out of bed it is onto my knees on the floor to commune with God. Basically it is a short and simple prayer. Usually it begins with something like "God thank you for your bounty, blessing, and grace. I surrender to you praying only for knowledge of your will and the power to carry that out." The opening of the day with this prayer is based on a paraphrase of Step Eleven. It tells us to pray only for knowledge of his will and the power to carry that out. Then if there is a particular challenge or current concern that I have been facing I ask for guidance and the wisdom to do what is necessary so that the answer will come together in the context of what God would have it to be. I do not normally pray for pre-planned outcomes. Instead it is prayer asking for his help and direction on what I should be doing. Because this is the only day I have in which to blossom and enjoy the reality of life I sometimes finish it off with something like "OK, God, let's boogie." I truly do believe that God wants us to be happy and to "boogie with him" throughout the day.

Then also we can make recourse to prayer and meditation as the day unfolds with its many different implications and nuances asking his direction on matters great and small that present themselves. Intuitively, as a result, we will seem to understand subconsciously what to do because things just appear to fall into place and take care of themselves without a whole lot of effort on our behalf. Worry and concern have no part in our actions because surrender to God takes these away. They simply put egotistic dampers on anything that is unfolding. We have no control over the outcomes of what is transpiring in this day so it is imperative that we relinquish such thoughts and concerns to God knowing that when all is said and done everything will be the way God would have it to be anyway. As we accept things as they have been in the past for what they are we soon learn that there is no place for "coulda," "woulda," "shoulda," in the paradigm of a happy life.

Early on in recovery I had a real challenge with being a major control freak. It was a powerful carryover from the days of active addiction and was a reflection of the egotistical will run riot. In sobriety it would become a defect of character that it took some time to even recognize having let alone to surrender to God and attempt to do something about. Because it was so rigidly implanted and I faced such a challenge in dealing with controlism (if there is such a word – or, if not, maybe we should make it one), I eventually developed a little prayer for when such conflicts lifted their ugly heads in life. It went "God, help me do my part, then help me let go so you can do your part." This prayer coupled with a moment of meditation would usually help relieve the morass of self-induced suffering created by letting the ego run rampant in whatever I was involved in and trying to control. This was one of the major challenges in recovery from which I had to become free. Early on the extent of such controlling behavior was so intense that I often had to say that prayer and engage in meditation several times a day to let go of that little egotistic manifestation which seemed to want to control my own life (no pun intended).

Today gradually letting go and letting God be more and more an active part of life, this once continuing challenge to spirituality has played a smaller and smaller role. It is not necessary to fix it or change it or to take responsibility for somebody else's actions. Our only part is to be there if somebody reaches out for help and it is reasonably possible and prudent to respond to that request. And God will determine what form that will take. The only thing we have to offer is sharing our own experience, strength, and hope. The literature of one Twelve Step Fellowship says, "Confident belief becomes self-righteousness when we insist that others live by our values."[6] Our only role is to share that which we have experienced along the way and the strength that we have found in that process and the hope we have which is now a living and vibrant part of our lives. Early on, my sponsor also helped significantly with this problem when he told me a little quip which had assisted him enormously in recovery. That quip is "I didn't cause it, I can't fix it, and it's not my responsibility." It is a neat little quotation for those in early sobriety who have that controlling mentality. If we can memorize that short statement and let it become a working part of our day-to-day recovery, coupled with prayer and meditation, we will be going a long way toward dealing with this maladjustment toward the rest of our fellows who are perfectly capable of taking care of themselves. The result will be a happiness and relief that will almost know no bounds.

The admonition "Let Go and Let God" appears on the walls of many recovery rooms and in much of the literature of the various fellowships and spiritual traditions. It is a statement designed to convey to us that we must try to relinquish our control tendencies. But on closer examination it can mean much more. In effect, it asks us to eliminate our desires. Our happiness will be in direct proportion to the extent that we can remove our desires from our lives. This includes eliminating not only the desire for things such as material possessions, but also for events or actions in our life that we think should be this way or that way. It is the surrender of expectations that paves the way for real happiness to come about. As it is also frequently said in the recovery literature and the meeting rooms, "Today's expectations become tomorrow's resentments." One of the more pensive statements that can be heard in the rooms from persons who are new to recovery is "I am here to get my kids back" or "I'm here to make my spouse happy," or "I only came because the court said I had to." In the long run the individual must be there solely for himself or herself. We cannot do it for anyone else. That is trying to live your life through pleasing somebody else and it simply does not work.

Attempting the rigors of recovery for other people does not accomplish anything no matter how close we think we might be to those people or how important they may be in our lives. We must eliminate desire if we are to find true happiness and that includes the desire for thinking such things as getting our kids back or pleasing a significant other. As long as we cling to the notion that somehow, someway, something, or someone else will bring happiness to ourselves is letting the ego take charge of our recovery and it is letting the ego's control of desire ensconce us in the prison made of that desire. And as long as we are ego driven by desire we will still encounter the tragedies and sorrows of the past that we are trying to let go of and relinquish into the dustbin of our addiction experience. Hence, eliminating desire must become the focal point of our efforts at recovery. As we reduce our desires and our recovery proceeds and we grow spiritually we will find that God will begin to put those things in our lives that we truly do need and enjoy. They will come unexpectedly and in forms we might not have anticipated. And they will frequently be beyond anything we might have designed for ourselves that we thought we must have. God wants only for us to have and to hold those things which bring us true happiness. We cannot design any expectations that could surpass those things that he has in mind for us and that includes desiring recovery for yourself solely because you may have some type of egotistic desire to be involved with or in control of a relationship with another person or persons.

As the years have rolled by after initial recovery more and more the value and utility of prayer has emerged as a way of life. Today if encountering what would appear to be emerging as a confrontational or disarraying situation I pray a short and simple silent prayer such as "God, show me what your will is in this situation," or "God, put your words in my mouth," or "God, help me make the right decision on this" or some similar request for help. It seems to be that when this happens the potential for adversarial actions and counteractions just melts away without negative consequences. The situation gradually resolves itself with little or no significant response required on my part. Smiling and just being plain old-fashioned sociable also plays a large role in helping to make this happen. It is a resource we can fully employ as we grow spiritually and our actions begin to reflect that growth. Close distancing as well can be utilized successfully to assist with handling such a situation.

As with prayer, meditation would become increasingly a part of everyday life. A few minutes of respite and quiet letting the God of our understanding fashion a way of thinking within us each day lets us connect with those around us and with ourselves. It serves to provide a relationship with all in our lives as we become one with the eternal and let God direct our way of living. It can clear our bodies, minds, and souls and bring us into a spiritual level that exponentially increases as we become more and more accepting of God's will within us. Bonnie Duran, a practitioner of Theravada and Tibetan Buddhism, describes the results of meditation in a beautiful way. She says, "As we meditate, we can see our own propensities towards self-hate, racism, sexism, homophobia float away and we also see more clearly how those work in others."[7] Our meditative life leads us to more clearly be a part of the comprehensive totality of goodness incorporated within our lives.

Growing spiritually with the Twelve Steps interest in the texts and writings of the interpreters of the various traditions from around the world began to expand and mature accordingly. Increasingly I turned toward Buddhist, Taoist, and Gnostic literature trying to become knowledgeable of the workings and theology of the God of my understanding. New awareness of and receptivity to the world's many spiritual traditions began to evolve. For years at the institution of higher education where I worked, I had taught the World Cultures introductory course in which these various religions and spiritualties are discussed. These included Hinduism, Buddhism, Judaism, Christianity, and Islam as well as the philosophical and spiritual traditions of Taoism and Confucianism. And in Peace Corps training there had been significant discussion of Islam since we were headed to a Muslim country. But with sobriety came a renewed interest in those diverse concepts that had been formerly so routinely presented as part of the World Cultures curriculum. When we discussed these in class during the days of active addiction there certainly appeared for them to have no relevance to life as it existed. The faculty role had been to be the presenter and interpreter of detail for interested students and the repository of techniques for accessing additional sources of information of which students could avail themselves if they so choose. The spiritual concepts and interpretational philosophies imbedded in these traditions certainly did not play any significant role in my own faltering spiritual life.

Over the years of recovery, however, spirituality has evolved from incorporating the many diverse attributes of these worldly approaches to the finding of the God within by bringing together much of what they have to offer into an individual approach to a higher power. It is a blending which continues and never seems to rest except for that respite found in the meditation reflected in the ebb and flow of growth. It is in much the same context as the tender and inspiring dialog tapestry of Christianity and Taoism and Buddhism found in the beautiful rendition of the early integration of these great traditions in central Asia. In an intercultural comingling facilitated by a spatial convergence of these influences along the Silk Road in western China we find an inspirational blending of love and self-examination. It is reflected in the publication **The Lost Sutras of Jesus,** edited by Ray Riegert and Thomas Moore.[8] Because of the intercrossing of cultures from East and West in the 5th and 6th centuries we can identify monks from many different parts of the Eastern Hemisphere who came together in one place and let the wisdom of their various influences blend together in a mingling of interpretations. That blending leaves us with an enriched rendition greater than the sum of the parts which now future generations can look to as inspiration for finding ourselves in an increasingly closely interconnected world of many cultures drawing on the wealth of what came together on the Silk Road a millennium and half ago in the past. It would take a while in recovery before recognizing it.

When the children were younger we made a pretense of becoming involved in the religious life of our community. We attended the Methodist Church virtually every Sunday. Basically, this was primarily for the benefit of the children. It was also probably as much going through the motions rather than anything else. At their mother's insistence the children were also sent to Catholic elementary school mainly because she thought it would be a better education for the kids. Although not totally agreeing with that having always been a strong believer in public education, I went along just to keep peace. The kids, of course, got a full dose of the Catholic religion at that school. Neither one of them are active in the church today. I was pretty much unfazed by any of this although it was an opportunity to become familiar with some of the ritual, holidays, and comradery which existed within the church.

However, after becoming more spiritually involved in recovery this attitude and participation especially toward the idea of finding a God of our understanding that would work would see a dramatic change. In particular, in sobriety the Gnostic concepts[9] rejected by the early Christian church of looking into oneself seemed to reverberate within the philosophical approaches of the various recovery fellowships. The self-examination reflected in Logion 2 of the *Gospel of Thomas* especially resonated with this spiritually expanding nature. This gospel, which contains sayings attributed to Jesus, held that:

> Yeshua [Jesus] said:
> whoever searches
> must continue to search
> until they find.
> When they find,
> they will be disturbed;
> and being disturbed, they will marvel
> and will reign over all.[10]

Jean-Yves Leloup, a leading scholar of the Gnostic texts, interprets this logion in the following manner: "This logion describes the major stages in gnosis, which constitute a true initiatory process. The first stage is the quest; the second stage is the discovery; the third is the shock and disturbance of the discovery; the fourth is wonder and amazement; and the fifth is presence and reign over All."[11]

This appeared to be Jesus outlining what would happen in Steps Two through Nine of a Twelve Step recovery program.

It was the finding of who we are that we had never examined from the perspective of clean and sober living, yet by taking the steps we were doing that in much the same manner that this Gospel outlined for finding our relationship with the God of our understanding. The irony of this analogy is that the Big Book of Alcoholics Anonymous, which contains the original version of the Twelve Steps and is the foundation for the various other Twelve Step programs, was published in 1939 six years before the *Gospel of Thomas* was discovered in 1945 near Nag Hammadi in Upper Egypt. Scholars had known about the existence of the *Gospel of Thomas* through its Roman critics in the early growth of Christianity who labeled it as heresy and rejected it and refused to let it be incorporated into the newly-formed Bible as one of the canonical gospels. As such, it was condemned and the extant known copies of it had been destroyed at the direction of the church and the Roman authorities. As a result, no actual copy of the gospel had been found prior to the discovery at Nag Hammadi where apparently a believer in the Gnostic precepts defied his or her orders to destroy any copies and interred the gospel for safekeeping along with several other banned Gnostic texts not to be rediscovered until seventeen centuries or so had passed.

The following from Logion 3 of the *Gospel of Thomas* further enlightens what is happening when one is taking the Twelve Steps and making them a way of life:

Yeshua said:
If those who guide you say: Look,
the Kingdom is in the sky,
then the birds are closer than you.
If they say: Look
it is in the sea,
then the fish already know it.
The kingdom is inside you,

and it is outside you.
When you know yourself, then you will be known,
And you will know that you are the child of the Living Father;
But if you do not know yourself,
You will live in vain
And you will be vanity.[12]

The relationship of these passages to recovery reverberated as part of this emerging spiritual growth. Increasingly I was becoming one with acceptance of myself and with the God of my understanding. Wonder and amazement have never ceased to be a part of life as I have grown spiritually over the years of recovery.

There is no way of acknowledging the spiritual enlightenment received from the inspirational writings of Thich Nhat Hanh. The Vietnamese Zen Buddhist's numerous books have helped enormously to achieve a degree of peace and serenity never felt before. It was, in part, through the surrender that he inspires and the acceptance of his teachings that it was possible to discover fulfillment in the miracle of the present and to let go of the suffering from the past.

The reflections of the inner peace and love that radiate from his works is immense even though he himself has seen the unbelievable tragedy of active war in his own homeland and been a refugee on the world stage. I am not sure if the fact that he was Vietnamese was of any particular significance to this appreciation for his teachings. It probably was a factor, but, more importantly, it was in the surrender that he exhibited personally and that reverberates throughout his writings that my soul found solace and a path for living in the present and being one with the rest of God's people. Suffice it to say that whatever it was, his teachings helped lead to an inner peace which truly knows no bounds. The suffering I carried from post-traumatic stress for years long after the demise of the extreme violence that came from participation in war was no longer an endless part of life. It was integral to the process of recovery.

The beauty of reconciliation is within ourselves. Staying in the moment with its reflection of the wonder and awe of a Higher Power now makes possible the quiet inclusion of all in our lives. One moment that came about in this process of healing happened while reading Thomas' **At Hell's Gate**. It occurred in the text when Sister Chan Khong, a Buddhist nun, invites Thomas to visit Plum Village which is Thich Nhat Hanh's monastery in the South of France. Thomas had told her he wanted to go to Vietnam to bring about reconciliation with the past. She suggests for him to come to Plum Village first before returning to Vietnam to address his suffering. She says "If you come in summer, many Vietnamese people are there – refugees, boat people – and you can learn to know the Vietnamese in another way. Come to Plum Village; we can help you; let us help you!"[13] Reading this last sentence tears started rolling down my cheeks. There was an enormous burst of empathy and acceptance as my own suffering was being eased by these two individuals who had shared their suffering with each other. It was as if Sister Chan Khong was also inviting me to make peace with the past in full acceptance of that past which I had allowed to continue its destruction over the years. And she and the other Vietnamese of Plum Village would be willing to help.

What better essence of recovery is reflected in the writings and spirituality of Thich Nhat Hanh's than this opening paragraph from **Peace is Every Step**: "Every morning when we wake up, we have twenty-four brand-new hours to live. What a precious gift! We have the capacity to live in a way that these twenty-four hours will bring peace, joy, and happiness to ourselves and others."[14] It is a formula for beginning the day as an instrument of God's love that will flourish within us as the day progresses. We can become the love that is witnessed in all the great traditions.

As we grow spiritually we look for understanding of both ourselves and others. "Do unto others as you would have others do unto you," is the fundamental essence of Jesus' teachings. Thich Nhat Hanh provides an interpretation that renders the basis of this universal truth in **Being Peace**: "When you understand, you cannot help but love. You cannot get angry. To develop understanding, you have to practice looking at all living beings with the eyes of compassion. When you understand, you love. And when you love, you naturally act in a way that can relieve the suffering of people."[15]

An integral part of that growing love is the practice of mediation and fasting the mind. God reveals himself to us in the quietude of our environment. If our surroundings are loud and noisy and full of competing people and thoughts it is incumbent upon us that we withdraw to a place of quiet and solitude so that the spiritual connection between God and our inner selves can manifest itself within us. Calming our minds through simply relinquishing the ego which bivouacs in our psyche in the midst of the storm waiting for a moment to exert itself can be vanquished with meditation. New thoughts and ways of looking at life begin to emerge.

Complementing the *Gospel of Thomas* and the Zen teachings of Thich Nhat Hanh and incorporated into this growing spirituality has been the Middle Way of Lao-Tsu and Taoism. Finding oneself within the balance of extremes and flowing with the Tao have become the path for being in unity with God's world in a troubling today. Seeing the love reflected by Jesus is becoming a way of life that brings serenity and peace. The simple complexity of the **Tao Te Ching** helps to keep introspection and balance within the spiritual realm. Although much within the **Tao Te Ching** lends itself to a balanced life, especially pertinent in recovery has been Chapter 22.

Yield and overcome;
Bend and be straight;
Empty and be full;
Wear out and be new;
Have little and gain;
Have much and be confused.
Therefore the wise embrace the one
And set an example to all.
Not putting on display,
They shine forth.
Not justifying themselves,
They are distinguished.
Not boasting,
They receive recognition.
Not bragging,
They never falter.
They do not quarrel,
So no one quarrels with them.
Therefore the ancients say, "Yield and overcome."
Is that an empty saying?
Be truly whole,
And all things will come to you.[16]

The seeming paradoxes of Chapter 22 provide a way for living with the flow of life. It is a guiding principle that if we are a part of the natural flow of life all will come together in God's timing. It is not necessary for the individual to push and pull, scramble and intrigue, make all the waves you can, shake the tree to see what falls off, or twist and turn to become whatever it is that you think is required to control the moment. Instead it is gently moving with the flow of life in acknowledgement that if we do our small part all will come together and it will be exactly the way it is supposed to be in that moment. We are one with the world and the world is one with us. It is in balance.

The beauty of existence is apparent in the present moment and all will be well.

Staying in the moment is an undercurrent of both Buddhist and Taoist teachings. "The Tao person lives fully in every moment,"[17] says the *Tao Te Ching,* Chapter 14, based on the translation of Diane Dreher in **The Tao of Inner Peace.** She adds that "Tao people aren't haunted by ghosts of the past or phantoms of the future. They accept the gift of today and make the best use of it.[18] And Thich Nhat Hanh has a whole book on it entitled **You Are Here: Discovering the Magic of the Present Moment.**[19] His many other writings reflect much of the same concept. The spiritual literature of recovery also emphasizes that we have only the present and it is a beautiful gift from God with which we have been endowed and in which we can live freely contributing back what we have been so bounteously given to the benefit of others. Later in her writing Dreher adds, "With no time to dwell on the past or worry about the future, we're here completely, one with the moment, without separation in time or space."[20] Living in the moment has been incorporated into daily actions and gives a peacefulness and tranquility that exits without fear of what may or may not happen because that is the way this moment is right now. It makes it possible for the essence of love to become one within ourselves and with the rest of humankind as we travel the road of life. To put it in the endearing terms of the closing lines of the Chapter 19 of the *Tao Te Ching,* "Embrace simplicity. Put others first. Desire little."[21]

Living alcohol and drug free over the years has been a powerful spiritual experience in and of itself. It has brought a feeling of freedom and happiness never known before. That feeling of having become one with God's universe has permeated sobriety. The foreboding and emotions of impending doom that were so very much a part of life as an actively addicted individual are gone. There is no compulsion to use or to in any way be under the influence of any sort of chemical to get through the normal daily activities that all of us encounter as human beings living in a world striven with suffering much of it derived from egos attempting to manifest themselves in daily actions.

This release from addiction would be boldly exhibited in the result of what I would later come to find out from the Veterans' Administration medical folks was the kind of cardiac disease that was caused by exposure to Agent Orange in Vietnam. And that release became abundantly clear following one pleasant Saturday morning in June when, sitting on the front porch enjoying the serenity and peace of the West Virginia hollow up which I live, I had a massive "widow-maker" heart attack. Rather than reaching for a beer to take care of it as would have done when in active addiction, I called 911. When the Emergency Squad shortly arrived they began resuscitation and as soon as possible took me to the local Emergency Room and then on to Morgantown to Intensive Care in the cardiac unit.

After they were able to get my condition stabilized, the cardiologists and surgeons decided that open heart quadruple bypass surgery was required and they would have to move quickly. They told me of their decision and requested approval to proceed. I told them that they could begin but they could not use any narcotic drugs. They maintained that they would not proceed without drugs because the intensity of the pain would be more than anyone could bear. There was a lingering fear of relapse into the addiction of choice if I had the feeling again of drugs in my system and getting a buzz. They also told me discretely that if they did not operate I was probably not going to make it. So reluctantly I concurred for them to proceed even though being very fearful of relapse and returning to the tired old worn out and egoistic addictive ways of the past. My prayers to God reflected this concern as I asked him what to do and the course of action that should taken. Succinctly the response came, "Do it. I will take care of you." It seemed to be the intuitive understanding of the recovered addict receiving God's grace.

It is hard to explain the rest of this experience in adequate terms. The pain was the most intense I have ever felt. It ensconced my body as nothing else before had ever done. It had an intensity almost beyond description. After the surgery barely alert to my surroundings, I lay on the gurney totally helpless and could do nothing for myself. Between the pain, the trauma, and the drugs I lay in total surrender. All I could do for prayer was to thank God for all the wonderful people that he had put in my life and upon whom I had by now become totally dependent. It was not possible to move and it seemed there were tubes and needles and other medical paraphernalia going into and out of all parts of my body. Remarkably, with the intensity of the pain the large quantity of narcotics they were pumping directly into my system did not seem to bring about any sort of enjoyable, pleasurable, or tension releasing buzz of any sort that might have occurred as in the past. It is my understanding from the health care professionals that this was because the pain absolved any truly mind-altering experience from being felt as the drugs languished through the body attempting to diminish the terrible pain associated with the surgery and doing what they were supposed to do.

Slowly but surely I began to become more alert and cognizant of surroundings. Gradually the pain began to subside somewhat. After a couple of days following the surgery as the pain was ebbing slightly away the drugs did begin to cause a bit of a buzz. Much of life had been spent chasing that kind of buzz. Now there was one beginning to come over me that was being injected by the medical staff and in quantity as much as I might have wanted or thought was needed. But as that pain subsided there is only one word to describe the feeling as the buzz became more and more pronounced. That word is "repulsive." The feelings were of absolute revulsion to the chemicals coming into my body. They were as repugnant as repugnant could get. As the healing process began the repulsiveness of the buzz became far greater than the intensity of the pain. So much so that I requested the nursing staff to disconnect them. They did. And even though laying there for several more days in painful recovery there was a feeling of serenity and peace that all was well. As the drugs wore off the sunlight of the spirit came increasingly into my life and the joy of living returned. The nursing staff could not quite figure out why I wanted the narcotics discontinued. Maybe they thought I might be crazy or somehow did not have it all together. However, they did shut off the narcotics when requested because at this point the massive pain of the surgery and its aftermath that they had been concerned about was over. They did not really care after initial recovery from the surgery and down-grade from intensive care had begun if I wanted to refuse narcotics or to keep them from coming into my body. They found, also, some non-narcotic pain relievers which helped a little with the intense pain. I never told them about my true past with chemicals.

The nursing staff were great and were a real pleasure to interface with. Several of them even told me it was fun to have me as a patient. As recovery from the surgery continued during the last few days in the hospital I was able to laugh and joke with them and especially to thank them for all that they had done to help keep me alive. Later, after requesting the medical records to review with my primary care physician, in the first line of the narrative section of the report, to my surprise, they identified me as "a very pleasant gentleman." Such would never have been the case if I had continued taking drugs. Instead, God removed the problem and I could be civil and polite and caring to those who were so intently watching over me. This is one of the bounties of recovery and living in the moment.

It is for this reason that I am very dubious of the suggestion in some of the medical community that various addictive drugs that are frequently prescribed in recovery programs are a reasonable continuing treatment for the disease. To switch from one addictive substance to another is precisely that. It is simply a change of chemicals and dependency. Regardless of what the intent of the drug is, it shuts one off from the sunlight of the spirit because it emasculates one from the vibrancy of the God within us. Working with a great number and variety of addicted people over the years, especially with Twelfth Step work, it seems that no drug should be prescribed without some plan for ultimately getting the patient off that drug. The abuse of these treatment drugs is a substantive point in question. They are a rapidly expanding problem in and of themselves based on experiences reaching out to other addicts. This is especially true of our area of West Virginia where many of them have become common street drugs just as heroin, meth, and pain killers are. They float in the free market and are available if the price is right just as with all the other illegal drugs. That in and of itself negates any positive accomplishment that could possibly occur from their long-term use by the addict attempting to recover. If the active addicts in the street can continue to buy these treatment drugs to get high on how in the world could they be prescribed as a way to get clean and sober?

The answer to addiction lies in finding a relationship with the God of one's understanding. It used to be that getting a "buzz" was pretty much the ultimate experience in life. Although we had to maintain the responsibilities that were incumbent upon us in whatever position God had put us, the ultimate goal once we had met those responsibilities was to get a good buzz going and keep it going as long as we could. Taking the Twelve Steps of recovery and finding the spirituality within the context of the God of our understanding has led to a different buzz. Today the high that I chased for so long comes simply and sweetly from God. It is far more exhilarating than any chemical high that was ever attempted and it is freely given. There are no ill and negative side effects, no legal consequences, no rueful mornings after, no adverse encounters with law enforcement. Instead there is the sweet grace of God wafting across our world and providing us with a fealty to his essence that takes us one moment at a time to an ultimate bounty that we could never have envisioned before. God is love. "The Kingdom is inside you and it is outside you."

Living a life of surrender to God has replaced the life of surrender to chemicals. Surrender was an alien concept to most of us. The word was not even in our vocabularies. We were tough. And I had proven it over and over again with past experiences in Africa and Asia and other parts of the world. Our lives, we thought, were replete with exhibitions of strength and ability. Although never admitting it when in active addiction every time I picked up a chemical of some sort it meant surrender to that chemical. Because the result was always the same. I ended up using so much that I passed out someplace and had no control over the amount consumed. Today I know that the first one is the one that sets off the compulsion for more and more. Once letting go and letting God it was instead the call of Sophia – it meant surrender in the same way I did with chemicals – the same surrender process that is underway seeking after the right course that God wants us to follow. That is a life of balance, of accepting the responsibilities and the pleasures that God provides for us, of becoming one with the Tao.

Each of us are made as significant and distinct individuals with our own talents, skills, physical and emotional uniqueness, and all the other individual traits and characteristics that God has bestowed on us and wants us to have. To dismiss them for whatever reason either inwardly or as "people pleasing" for others is contrary to God's will for us. We are all precious and beautiful in the eyes of God just as we are made. Love conquers all. And Dreher would add, "The power of love brings our lives dramatic immediacy. With no time to dwell on the past or worry about the future, we're here completely, one with the moment, without separation in time or space."[22] There are no exceptions.

The concept of "Do unto others as you would have others do unto you" includes for us to participate in all his bounty but through reasonable actions and respect for others and inclusive of the balance reflective of the Christ, the Buddha and the Tao in each of us. Every person must find his or her own way through this potpourri of extremes to which we are invited everyday by the simple fact that we inhabit the ever-changing Earth. It is for this reason that it is incumbent upon us to eat reasonably, work reasonably, exercise reasonably, play reasonably and strive to become one with his world in our daily thoughts and actions one moment at a time. This entails extending our love to all who are in God's world regardless of the differences we think should exist and which can divide us into so many different subsets and genres which are all irrelevant to our existence. The literature of one Twelve Step fellowship describes it in a very proficient way: "God has given no one the right to humiliate another. In every one of His children there are qualities that should command our respect, and to withhold it is a wrong that will return to wound us."[23]

Today, Original Sin, which I was so confused and questioning about as an adolescent, is an untethered ego which can run rampant through our lives if we let it. The world's spiritual traditions viewed within their fundamental contexts of surrender and love eliminate the adverse effects of that Original Sin mitigating it to the trash heap of expended raw expectations of the ego. Instead, within us we have a serene and peaceful existence that reflects our surrender and staying in the moment knowing that everything in this moment is just as it should be. With this there is no guilt or feeling of inferiority that needs external salvation, no fear of some abhorrent afterlife if we do not pursue some rigid structural absolution, but instead a loving, caring, and companionable Force that walks with us each moment and to which we can turn releasing the malevolence of the ego and finding the sustenance for all things that we face as we move gently through our current physical incarnation.

A special word about our sexuality should be added to this bounty that comes about from our spiritual growth in recovery. One of the anomalies of the many different approaches to God and sexuality has often been denial or condemnation that somehow the individual's sexuality was in one respect or another antithetical to God and to the role it plays in our relationship with God. For some reason this sexuality has had to be repressed if he or she were to find God. An interpretation I have found useful in arriving at a functional relationship with the God of our understanding on this issue is from Thomas Moore writing in **A Religion of One's Own**: "Many spiritual people are confused about eros and sexuality. They believe in virtue and purity and end up repressing their sexuality. But repressed, it really catches fire. How many spiritual leaders have succumbed to sexual desire in inappropriate ways and lost their standing and their jobs? *Imagine eroticism in the best possible light, as the foundation of your spirituality and it will work for you rather than against you.*"[24] [Emphasis added.] The inclusion of our sexuality in our spiritual lives is a blessing that God has bestowed upon us as a part of his love for us, and it is because of that magnanimous bestowal that it is a gift for us to use reasonably and responsibly as we would any of his blessings. We should embrace our own sexuality and respect others as they embrace theirs in the way that God created us all individually to do.

Just as God has created us all differently in other aspects of our lives so too do vastly different sexual traits make us all Godly-unique people. God intended for us to enjoy sex or he would not have supplied us with the interest or ability to be sexually active. Such actions range from the most common worldwide form of sexual expression, i.e., solo, to a vast gamut of different types of activities about which a book could be written. Indeed, many books have been written over the centuries about the various manifestations of sexual activity abounding around the world. To suggest that God did not want us to be sexually active is to deny God's interest and concern for us. This applies also to the individuals with whom we enjoy and appreciate our sexual expression. Although most people are heterosexual many others have different forms of sexual relationships and some even prefer none at all. It is both holy and acceptable to be in mutually consenting relationships no matter how they express themselves. Do what comes naturally for you as it was presented to you by God. It is key that whatever relationship we have sexually with others is based on full and total respect toward each other and ourselves and not as a means of exploitation, shame, or guilt. A sexual relationship is not to be used or abused as a method of control or domination over another. It is to be cherished as an intimacy even if it is in just this moment, and in fact it is only in just this moment that we have any relationship. This too applies to sex workers who have been scorned over the generations and often frequently reviled and persecuted. Respect rather than contempt is incumbent upon the acceptance of people just as they are. "Do unto others as you would have others do unto you." The God of our understanding has created you uniquely you with all the warts and wonderful assets that he wanted us to have. So be thankful to your Higher Power for creating you in the moment that you are in acknowledging that the only constant in life is change and that whatever change that might be encountered on the road to recovery will come in God's timing as we plod along on our new lives of self-discovery and spiritual fulfillment.

In similar vein we are born with our genitals and equipped to function with a penis or a vagina one of which was given to each of us by God to greater enjoy the gift of our sexuality. To circumcise or otherwise mutilate children's sexual organs on some pretense that they will be more interested in reading religious literature, or that they somehow need to have remnants of androgyny removed from them, or that it is supposedly a beneficial thing for the child is countering the will of God who created us in the natural way that he wanted us. As Logion 53 of the *Gospel of Thomas* essentially says, in part, "Jesus said: If God had wanted you circumcised you would have been born that way."[25]

These forms of altering the genitals of our children have ramifications especially in Africa. It is difficult or perhaps better explained as hypocrisy to try to convince an African elder that it is all right to alter in a life transition ceremony the way a boy is made by God, but it is not all right to make a similar transitional alteration to a girl. To the elders the rituals of changing from a child to an adult are similar. Attempts to bring an end to the ritualized mutilation of young girls in some African societies will continue to be fruitless as long as a similar ritual is performed on and accepted as normal for boys.

Let's let each individual boy or girl grow up so they may fully enjoy the natural sexual experiences that God created for him or her. It is the decision of the individual in discourse with the God of their understanding as to whether or how to alter his or her body in any way including the genitals. For adults to presume or confiscate a child's right to genital integrity is an extreme manifestation of the ego in action. Let us allow our children to play with a full deck when they are old enough to play in the natural way that God created them to play.

As we grow spiritually we can become one with all the Twelve-Step programs and with the panoply of the world's spiritual traditions. This is true because through our own suffering and recovery we have learned how to identify with the suffering of others. Even though our particular disease has taken this form or that form of suffering once we recognize it, it does not preclude us from having the empathy and understanding for others who are facing different challenges of recovery from their suffering even though they might not be in the same box or category as our own. As we get out of self and let the ego rescind itself into the depths of oblivion to which it belongs within our lives we move gradually to that understanding which lets us become one with all others who suffer. Although its application is in regard to the LGBTQ+ community about which he writes, Tomas Prower's dictum "By not having labels and not belonging to a specific group, we belong everywhere"[26] becomes truth. It is equally appropriate for all those of us who suffer from being different whatever its form from the mainstream of humanity anywhere.

It is difficult to believe that an infinite God would lockstep human beings into the box of pre-structured orthodox religion with no room to express an appreciation for the vast number of diverse attributes with which he has created each and every one of us who are components of that creation. The expression of our uniqueness in surrender to the God of our understanding is fully amplified through our respect for others and their expression of themselves just as God has created them. That acceptance of ourselves and others is a major contributor to our happiness in this life. As we accept others and ourselves as creations of the God of our understanding as we were made to be, our happiness and joy in this life increase exponentially. How many times have people said to me "you are so happy – how do you do it?" It is simple to explain. As I have grown spiritually, I have come to accept people, places, and things as they are and that is the way they were meant to be at the moment. All we have to offer others is our experience, strength, and hope. If somebody is out of sorts with himself or herself it is only that person who can make the changes within that will bring the serenity and peace to which they aspire. Nobody else can do it for them. Hence we must respect who they are as they are. Their approach to their religion and spiritually is uniquely theirs to determine. We cannot enter into their souls or psyches and make any necessary changes for them. When we can accept that looking only at ourselves for change is the only change that we can make, the degree of our happiness increases enormously. As it says in the Big Book of Alcoholics Anonymous "We are certain God wants us to be happy, joyous, and free."[27]

CHAPTER 7

One Day at a Time

The prolific spiritual writer and Buddhist nun, Pema Chodron, charmingly describes what awakening can do for our lives. She writes, "The awakened people I have known are all very playful, curious, and unthreatened by things. They go into situations with their eyes and their hearts wide open. They have a real appetite for life instead of an appetite for aggression. They are, it seems, not afraid to be insecure."[1] Such describes what can come from surrendering, accepting the moment, and reaching out to others the hand of recovery which comes through taking the Twelve Steps and making them a way of life.

Fva Wong relates much the same concept in the manner of the Tao when she is describing the sage. She says, "Because he has transcended happiness and sadness, he is content and joyful at all times. His joy comes from the depths of his spirit, although he does not show it externally. Because he is joyful inside, he does not see himself through the eyes of others. He cultivates stillness and clarity because he knows that craving and hating come from thoughts and desires. The sage does not experience excitement, anger, happiness, and pain because he is at one with all things and is beyond truth and falsehood."[2]

Probably the most beautiful thing about living in recovery is the magnificence of God's world as it expresses itself in each day. No longer do the fears, the anxieties, the obsession with control or with making money, the perceived need to create superfluous plans, the uneasiness of the existence of our role as a human being proliferate our lives. Instead, it is a true joy to be alive and to be able to be a part of the spiritual quintessentialism of human interactions. Every day brings a new empowerment, a new enlightenment, a new way of looking at things. In practice life has become a fun adventure of being part of each moment in which we exist. This is true even with the coming of the vagaries of aging which cannot dilute this true source of happiness and serenity.

The obsession to drink or use is gone. But it is far more than that. As a whole, it is indescribable, but in its parts it is a tranquility, an inner peace, an acceptance of the spiritual relationship with the God of our understanding that orders our lives in a fashion we had never dreamed. We are at one with God's world. Tranquility has become the essence of our interaction with events, places, and changes that are a part of the way God intended us to come together. From carrying the weight of the world we can carry our own small load which makes some contribution, however insignificant we might think it is, to our fellows. God is supplying us each day with the succulent nourishment of spiritual growth which sustains our efforts from minute to minute. That becomes readily apparent as we move into that new relationship with the world and its people which arises within us. And it becomes an operating force as we live our lives in our accepted new situation as it is characterized by the love we can bring to this Earth no matter what our station in life nor how we may have become a part of it. We belong to a new world in which we have a place to make a unique contribution large or small. We are moving out of the self and the ego that has motivated us over the years.

Our life is today in this minute. Everything is just as it should be. We continue to grow whether that be through adversity or love. It becomes apparent that the spiritual growth that is a continuing factor in our lives as long as we are actively practicing the Twelve Steps in all our affairs comes from the challenges we face as we take each day one at a time (or perhaps more appropriately staying in the moment even one minute at a time if that is warranted). For within each adversity there is spiritual growth if we approach it from the point of view of surrendering that adversity to the God of our understanding. Each adversity comes with a set of unique circumstances that will provide a lesson for this spiritual growth to come about. It is a growth which it is incumbent upon us to accept as it happens. It will be within God's timing and it will be the opportunity for us to move forward spiritually because our dependence will be on his provision of the tools we need to handle it.

Some matters of reconciliation with our past emerge in unexpected ways. Just when you think you are out of the prison of Post-Traumatic Stress Disorder it explodes to haunt again. But with spiritual recovery there is a support mechanism within our souls that permeates each new experience as we work our way through the various dimensions of that relived experience. On May 29, 2016, I was discussing with a young man his taking of the Twelve Steps as a path for recovery. We were talking about powerlessness and related to him how I thought I was so tough to be recruited by quasi-governmental agents or mercenaries or whatever they were at the end of the tour in Vietnam and how I thought I could handle just about anything in life when in active addiction. The explosion happened after the young man had left. I went out to get something to eat. Returning home from the restaurant an incredible outburst welled up inside me and exploded in anger as I was driving – so much so that it was difficult to control the vehicle. For the first time since it had happened in September of 1969 the threats to me and my family that had accompanied the rejection of the offer to become a mercenary surged into my mind and emotions. Although remembering the threats to me personally, this was the first time I had remembered them threatening my parents both of whom were deceased by this time. Screaming and swearing about the threat to family I had this tremendous urge to blast away at some paper target and empty my pistol on it. The rage was intense – unbelievably intense. To think that our own government could threaten American citizens because we would not get involved in their extralegal, covert, and backhanded activities to subvert an occurrence in another land that some philosophical dreadnaught in Washington whose answer to every problem was to interject his own values and actions into a situation. What rubbish!

The rage was the most intense in years. I went upstairs to the bedroom (which was where the pistol was kept) and fell to my knees in prayer – prayer to the same God who kept me from drinking and drugging every day. In moments some serenity began returning. Holding the phone in my hand which I rarely did when praying the name of a friend in recovery – a veteran who worked with other veterans – shortly appeared in the missed calls. He would be at the meeting that evening and I could talk to him. It was almost time to leave. I got ready and headed for the meeting. He was not there. So I called him and began to tell him what had happened. Even though he had not planned on going to the meeting that evening he insisted on coming over. We talked at length in the parking lot as though God was working through him. Serenity returned. The explosion of rage dissipated into the calmness of God's protection that evening. By reaching out for help he had answered.

Not long afterwards, in June I had a jaw tooth pulled. It had finally split beyond repair and I was in quite a bit of pain from the extraction and the accompanying oral surgery. I had taken no narcotic painkillers because the pain of the buzzed sensation from them would be far greater than the physical pain of the extraction. Early on the next morning, while sleeping, a violent thunderstorm broke out. A loud clap of thunder from lightening that must have struck very close to the house slammed into the bedroom. I think I may have been laying on the side where the tooth had been pulled. Suddenly awakened, without realizing it, I bolted from the bed and yelled "Incoming rounds! I've been hit!" Apparently, I must have thought I had been hit because of being in such intense jaw pain from the tooth being removed, and the loud clap of thunder and flash of lightening certainly replicated what happens when you are on the receiving end of incoming action. Soon I realized I was in my own bedroom during a thunderstorm. Calmness returned. I thanked God for being with me in this unanticipated time of returning to the past and took a couple of acetaminophen and went back to sleep in serenity and peace.

Although there is probably no complete recovery from Post-Traumatic Stress Disorder the Twelve Steps have made it possible to come to terms with what had happened in Vietnam and its aftermath. It is possible to live with it and sometimes the forces at work in the trauma take some strange forms. It is not unusual, for example, to have dreams about this experience even though almost half a century has transpired. However, the dreams are frequently revolved around the same theme. That is, they involve some sort of surrender, and they may go something like this: our unit has been surrounded and we are trying to find some way of surrender because we are out of ammunition and there is no way of escape. Usually the problem is we cannot communicate with them for whatever reason. There is no major fear or insecurity that characterizes these dreams. Usually I will awaken when we have exhausted all our resources for ending the encounter. I am not sure what all this means. Probably somebody more knowledgeable about the psychology of past traumas could explain it better, but today I know it is a harmless dream. They used to be annoying, but really they are not anymore. It is just a passing transition that occurs during sleep sometimes. Ironically, no one ever gets killed or wounded in these dreams and there is normally little extreme violence. It is more a matter of process than of slaughter.

God gives us a route to erase our suffering through a closeness to him which is expressed in our love and appreciation of others. As we continue on the path of kindness and acceptance of all God's people his will becomes manifest in us. No matter what the outcome we think we should have that word that every soldier and every addict has an absolute foreboding about emerges. That very word surrender – surrender to a power greater than ourselves – is an action that makes it possible for us to have the serenity and peace to glide effortlessly toward a oneness with him. For with that surrender we begin the process of growing spiritually that will carry us to a realm which we have never before known. As one Twelve-Step Fellowships puts it, "Recovery begins with surrender."[3] And with recovery we can rejoin the society from which our addiction has diverted us. We can become active and involved making a positive contribution in a sane and sober manner.

Ever since being a teenager I had been interested in politics and the political process at work in a democracy. While growing up discussing feelings and emotions at our home was not really acceptable, political discourse occasionally was. My own inclinations as a teen were far more libertarian at that age perhaps reflecting a youthful disinclination to submit to authority or an independence that was based on feelings of alienation or not belonging. After coming into the rooms of recovery I had long since jettisoned that well-worn copy of Goldwater's **Conscience of a Conservative** because concern for working people and equal justice for all of us had overcome and exceeded the libertine. And, although familiar with the writings of Ayn Rand, she was always way too extreme and far out to take any serious interest in her form of individualist philosophy.

Interest in the political process would continue for many decades as it still does today. Pacifist feelings and concerns for working people and those marginalized for whatever reason would become markedly more pronounced in graduate school and with the political and social involvement which characterized life as a doctoral student. The result of this interest was that throughout life there would frequently be some role, usually minor, in working with various political campaigns over the years both during active addition and after the beginnings of recovery. In active addiction the best I could do was work on the sidelines helping various candidates with similar views. That was also where the booze, which was often such an integral part of so many political campaigns, could be found. Belief in and support of candidates was directly proportional to the degree to which they reflected my own personal values. With reentry into society in the aftermath of the Vietnam War and graduate school there developed a focal point for the fuller incorporation of these values into daily life. These included concern for all people especially as it related to their political, social, and economic inclusion into the full fabric of American society. It was accompanied by a loathing for war and violence as a policy for solving disagreements that emerged between people and nations which thought they had no alternative to such reprobate actions in the absence of other mechanisms for peaceful resolution of their conflicts.

Once coming into the rooms of recovery momentarily interest in politics and political campaigns became somewhat diluted because of other priorities focusing on reclaiming life and restoring sanity. But after a few years I became reinvolved and once again commenced work for candidates who supported similar values of inclusion and equality under the law. The nature of that involvement would change however. A few years into recovery the institution at which I worked decided to trim its staff of senior people and replace them with more entry level faculty for a lot less money. So they offered everyone even remotely close to retirement a buyout if they would just remove themselves from the college's payroll as soon as possible. After thinking long and hard about it I came to believe it was time to move on. I had been at the institution by this point for 27 years. So I took the offer and decided to retire to Charlottesville, Virginia, where my daughter and grandchildren lived. It did not take long to realize though, that, delightful a city as Charlottesville was, my roots were still very much in Appalachia. So within a year the decision had been made to return to hometown Elkins where I had been born and had spent most of childhood. Although Mom had passed away Dad was still living at the time and it was a little incumbent upon me to be with him during the remaining years. It was probably a good idea since shortly after relocating to West Virginia my daughter would leave Charlottesville for Seattle and within a couple of years of that move to the United Kingdom with the three grandchildren to go to graduate school at the University of Manchester. They have remained there ever since.

A couple years after retirement I got a call from a neighbor who telephoned early one morning so early in fact that he woke me up. He said he thought I should run for city council and he knew other people whose support he could enlist if I would run. I said no, hung up the phone, and went back to sleep. But my thoughts returned to the idea throughout the day and later in the afternoon I stopped by his office to talk to him about it. During active addiction it was something that would never have occurred to me and if it had I would have been inwardly terrified of publicly standing as a candidate for elective office. It was one thing to work in campaigns and quite another to actually be the candidate. But when he offered to help organize a campaign – and he himself had previously served on city council – I became increasingly interested in it. After talking with a few friends and family members in the ward I decided to file. Various individuals in our family had lived in the ward for years. It was the same ward that my grandfather had represented on city council for a couple of terms during the 1920s and 1930s.

The incumbent councilman who was currently serving had initially indicated that he was moving out of the ward and hence would be ineligible to run for reelection. He had been a good councilman and that is why long term residents were actively looking for somebody as well qualified as he to replace him. However, he ultimately changed his mind about moving out of the ward and at the last minute he reconsidered his decision and filed late in the filing period for reelection. I had been around politics long enough to know to get commitments early on if you could and I had done that. The result was that we were able to put together an effective campaign and upset an incumbent even though he was a good councilperson and I could have easily voted for him myself.

As was normal practice the mayor assigned each council member to various committees. After some lobbying she appointed me to Finance, Personnel, and Water. The Water Committee was a key activity at the time because the mayor and previous councils had initiated an enormous water generating and distribution project which would be the largest public works project in the history of the county. The mayor had asked me to be chair of the committee whose responsibility it was to oversee the project, because, as she said during the process, she thought I had the requisite expertise based on experience with state academic administrative responsibilities to steer the project through the necessary regulatory and funding bureaucracies to a successful conclusion. For some reason the city had never instituted a city manager form of government, and so much of the administrative initiative was carried out by the mayor, various committees with oversight responsibilities, or individual directors in charge of specific offices or functions.

It was on the Finance Committee, however, that red flags would pop up at the very first meeting. In West Virginia, municipalities utilize similar accounting and financial administrative systems as state government agencies including state institutions of higher education. At that first meeting as we began discussing the expenditures of the city and the budget that the city was operating under, it became immediately clear that the activities that were being carried out were outside the scope of normal accounting procedures required of state agencies. There was also no transparency. Once the budget had been prepared and approved by Council and the State Auditor's Office no one could view it until the fiscal year was over. Thus it was impossible to know at any given time how much money had been expended and what the expenditures were for or what the remaining balance for the year was. Also funds appeared to be indiscriminately moved around among lines items. Not sure how to handle the situation I eventually discussed it with some of the other members of the committee. None of them had had experience operating under normal state fiscal accounting procedures although the chair of the committee indicated that he too felt something was wrong. Others were comfortable with the situation since the state auditors had passed the city in their annual review albeit with a number of auditory exceptions.

Two years into the council term the incumbent mayor decided that she was not going to run for reelection. Instead she asked me to run. What a surprise and shock. I had spent all kinds of time during an active addictive career trying to get ahead scratching and clawing along the way with few satisfying results, and now an incumbent elected official was asking me to run as her replacement, and she had pledged the support of her rather vast network of colleagues and associations to help in the campaign if agreeing to run. Such are the results of actively working a Twelve-Step program and living under the auspices and direction of the God of your understanding.

Several friends and family members also volunteered to be part of the campaign but probably the greatest single source of help came when a retired chief-of-staff for a former Republican governor who had also served as a high ranking member of President Reagan's administration volunteered to be the campaign manager. This was a real first. Never in my drinking and drugging career would I ever have thought of running for public office let alone receiving help from a bipartisan group of people such as the one that was about to be assembled. But so it was to be.

Fortunately, both council and mayor's offices in the municipality size class Elkins is were non-partisan. Here I was a Democratic activist who had long been involved in various campaigns being voluntarily assisted in a major way by a Republican partisan who had had some significant political successes in his life. And I had been encouraged to run by a retiring elected non-partisan mayor who had a long history as a Republican activist. Yet that is exactly what was in the process of coming about. This was something coming together in a living way that could never have been envisioned prior to recovery.

With the help of a wide variety of people we won. It was a coalition of conservative and mainstream Republicans, conservative and Obama Democrats, veterans, business people, regular working people, fundamentalist Christians, liberal Christians, family, and many others. We even had people who lived outside the city limits and hence could not vote in the election who volunteered to help contact voters who did live within the city and who could vote. I am not sure exactly how all these folks came together, but it happened. It reflected the philosophy of life and living witnessed by Chapter 22 of the **Tao Te Ching**.

The principles of the Twelve Steps coupled with the introspective guidance of the Gnostic, Buddhist, and Taoist traditions made it possible to accomplish a great many objectives as mayor. The most important was the continuance of engineering work and securing of favorable funding for the water plant and distribution system which would eventually exceed $37 million. Another major achievement was the reorganization of the city administration from a compendium of small isolated and relatively scattered offices into a central office fully visible and adjacent to the Police Department so that employees could be cross-trained and also not be intimidated by angry patrons because they were off some place in offices by themselves. All of these employees had been women and because some tended to be located in relatively isolated offices and not visible to other offices or the police they were sometimes threatened and bullied by patrons who were angry about a water or sewer bill or about some other kind of municipal administrative function that did not meet with their satisfaction. Because all these employees were physically relocated together we could cross-train and provide a secondary backup if the person primarily responsible for a function was not at work that day for some reason. We were also able to address the odd financial management system that the city utilized and that had become apparent at that first Finance Committee meeting. This was made possible, in part, when we were able to hire a CPA administrator who knew exactly how the state accounting system worked. She was able to coordinate directly with the mayor and other administrative officers in conjunction with the State Auditor's Office to bring the system into full compliance with standard state accounting practices and in the process saved the city substantial amounts of tax dollars in administrative costs. We were also able to bring complete transparency to the financial record keeping system. Following the conclusion of the final year of the second term as mayor we were able to receive a perfect rating from the State Auditor's office without a single exception. It was the first time anyone living could remember that ever having happened in the city's annual auditory review process.

It was the responsibility of the mayor to appoint citizens to serve on a wide variety of boards and committees that in one way or another made recommendations on various city functions. Wherever possible I tried to be as diverse and inclusive as possibly with the appointments. One of these boards was the Zoning Appeals Board. I was familiar with it since Dad had served on it for many years before his final retirement. He had about the time he was initially appointed made the comment that the board was composed of older men with balance and maturity to evaluate the appeals. This became too great an opportunity for change when one of the board's current members retired. We began to actively recruit a woman to serve on it. It was not long until a young professional woman who ran an accounting service volunteered in response to our outreach. She had excellent credentials. And so she became the first woman to serve on the Zoning Appeals Board. It was shortly after her appointment that two more members of the board who happened to be good friends with each other also decided to retire. So two more women were recruited. In this case both were professionals but a little bit older than the first appointee. Now the board had a female majority. And soon thereafter yet another retirement came about, but, alas, we could not fill it before leaving office so we still had a board with three women, one man, and a vacancy. The board functioned very effectively and served the purpose for which it was constituted. So, Dad, we can get good results if we mix it up a little bit and let everybody have a chance to be involved.

At the expiration of the first mayor's term I was encouraged and decided to run for a second term. We were beginning to see some substantive accomplishments and by and large people seemed pleased with what was happening. I was excited about it because it was an opportunity to bring to fruition some of the major administrative undertakings and infrastructure rebuilding that was in process. The election was a sweep with our coalition carrying all five wards in the city. It also put in office a council that supported more whole-heartedly the changes we were undertaking. This term proved to be a little more contentious than the first one perhaps because of the extensive changes that were coming about. Much was being accomplished because people were working together and bringing to fruition some long overdue improvements to the way the city operated and to its infrastructure.

But as all successful politicos know the greater the changes the harder is the keeping together of a coalition, and our coalition had been so diverse that it is a wonder that it stayed together as long as it did and got the results that it was able to. It was not to last much longer however. It was impossible to keep such a diverse group functioning and soon it began to splinter as eventually all political coalitions do. Recognizing that it was crumbling I almost decided not to run, but was encouraged by some to seek a third term. In reality I could not generate the enthusiasm that had propelled the first two mayoral elections and quite frankly my heart was not in it.

Throughout the campaign I kept thinking why am I doing this? So it was that in a three way race the splintered coalition that had been so effective in the previous two elections fell completely apart and a new mayor was elected. It is strange that in recovery when you feel that you are really not doing what God wants you to do you can sense it even though it might be a very laudable and respectable venture that you are undertaking. It simply is not the right thing for you at that juncture of your life. Such was the case in the attempt for a third term as mayor. The enthusiasm required for winning simply was not there. In a three-way race when the ballots were counted I came in second. Although no one got a majority there was no run-off because there were no provisions for it in the city charter. The winner regardless of the percentage of the cast ballots received was the victor.

In looking back I now know God had other plans. Soon after leaving office I had the massive heart attack mentioned earlier. There would be a series of cardio-related challenges in the next year or so. Had I been reelected for that third term it would have been impossible to have completed it for health reasons. But what God was doing was preparing me for a bout with narcotic drugs for medical purposes in which he provided the experience of having so many drugs in my system, being fearful of relapse, but being absolutely repulsed by them when beginning to feel the buzz that they caused coming over me. He had bestowed the opportunity for being intimately involved in the political process, something that would never have been done in active addiction, then he made me a witness to his power at work in redirecting this addict as an example of his power in a sober existence. I would never have had such an experience to share had the course of life been otherwise. Today it is possible to share with others in recovery this experience, strength, and hope in dealing with our addictions which comes from the God of our understanding. And I have shared it on many occasions when asked to speak. I think God was preparing me to do just that, creating an example for those severely addicted to have hope of recovery and to know that his power could relieve the addict of the bondage of chemicals. One had only to surrender and ask for God's help and it would happen.

During the tenure as city council member and mayor, even though I had become an elected official with the responsibilities incumbent upon the offices, I still continued working occasionally in other political campaigns. Senator Barack Obama had spoken at the annual Jefferson-Jackson Day Dinner in Charleston a few years before being elected mayor, and I was thrilled with what he had to say. He could be a rejuvenator of the Democratic Party as a champion for working people. So when he announced his first run for President I identified with his campaign. I was probably the only elected official in Randolph County to do so, but that was OK. It was exciting to be able to help out, however minimally, in his primary campaign and even more so after he received the Democratic nomination.

During his first primary season I was in a small group of people at a political rally discussing his candidacy. A slightly-built woman perhaps in her forties, in an almost desperately plaintiff voice, made this comment, and I quote, "If Obama gets elected we won't have any meat to eat this winter." Odd as it may seem to others from outside the mountains her concern stemmed from the fear circulated by the gun lobbies and other opponents of Obama that he was going to take their hunting rifles and shotguns away. To her this takeaway was defined by the concept that any sort of gun regulation would result in the confiscation of all hunting guns and rifles. The ridiculous nonsense that a large number of gun huggers and opponents of change put forward regarding attempts at some kind of regulation has had a needlessly negative impact on making adjustments in this direction. As a result of this propaganda from the gun lobby, Obama's campaign represented for many Appalachians an underlying economic challenge to obtaining prevailing food sources from their land in a diet that was often sparse in store-purchased meat especially in winter. People in many of the rural areas of Appalachia, particularly in West Virginia, frequently do not have the financial resources to buy much meat for their families in winter. As a result, many folks take advantage of the abundant supply of deer, squirrels, rabbits, and occasionally bear that inhabit the narrow valleys and abandoned corn fields that characterize so much of the region. When the Department of Natural Resources permits it, some families will slaughter and preserve as many as half a dozen deer for use during the winter months. These are normally accompanied by a variety of smaller game. I doubt that there is a single soul in urban America who would have been able to grasp the economic consequences of this woman's comment about Obama and not having enough meat to eat in the winter. Opponents of any sort of gun regulation have exploited this fear factor significantly. And this characteristic of the mountain socio-economic fabric might also go a long way to clarifying why so many people have been described unwittingly, and perhaps derogatorily, by others outside the mountains as taking solace in "clinging to their guns."

In similar vein, as with so many other misconceptions, the disease of addiction has been stereotyped by those who may or may not have been affected by it. Sometimes it seems the stereotype parallels that of the stereotype about Appalachian peoples in general. This preconceived idea that there is a unitary type of people who are characterized by such-and-so and exhibit the same traits without substantive differences within the class. This is simply not the case in either instance. And in fact, some of us fit into both categories (and maybe a few others!). But we cannot be put into either box encompassing a pre-described set of stultifying social, economic or political parameters over which as descriptors we have no method of countering.

A real addict has no control over his addiction, hence, the wording of the first step, "We admitted we were powerless...." For some non-addicts to presume, as some writers have done, about both addiction and Appalachia that we had some sort of control is simply not true. Instead, they look at the widespread poverty and addiction and even sometimes go so far as to suggest that somehow it is because of the so-called Scots-Irish background which gave us some sort of different gene characteristics even though it is doubtful that the majority of Appalachians are even descended from this immigrant group. They allege that this has sometimes, somehow been a contributing factor in the opioid epidemic when, in fact, their stereotype is essentially wrong, especially in West Virginia, where there has been significant ethnic diversity. I would suggest that external exploitation on a vast scale especially by outside corporate groups springing from both American and foreign entrepreneurs has been a major contributing factor. That exploitation has had its own particular international component in that many of the mining and other industrial activities that came to the Appalachians in the late 19th and early 20th centuries have included especially substantial numbers of British capitalists and other European investors. They differed little in their attitudes toward Appalachians which were similar to their attitudes toward the Africans and Asians whom they also imperialistically exploited at this same time in history. It could be suggested as well that the relative isolation of many of our communities has been another contributing factor. The mountains that cover much of the coal, oil, and natural gas in the region provided for an isolation from others who, although they are often times physically in close lineal proximity, have historically been relatively very detached from each other because of the difficulty of transportation and communication across those very mountains. The degree of isolation is significant. I live up a "holler" in West Virginia. It is peaceful and quite because my home is the only one up it. And it is isolated from even the closest neighbor. That is not to say that I don't get out of the hollow frequently because I do. But this is of my own choosing. I am not locked into the hollow because of economic dependency on it and consequently isolated from others in our local society.

Some of this isolation, however, is beginning to be abated with modern freeways and electronic communication. That factor has made it easier to bring in outside drugs and other intoxicants but frankly they complement the extensive and historically illegal domestic production of marijuana which has paralleled the equally extensive and historically illegal production of moonshine both of which have been traditional industries in an economy which has sometimes had significant impediments to supporting all the population it contains. Regardless of the mitigating factors, each addict and each Appalachian is a different person created individually by God and each has a path that should be seen as uniquely his or her own. This is true both for recovery and for socio-economic resiliency.

It is unfortunate that political discussion in the United States has come to include terms such as "deplorables" and "fake news". Individuals who have concerns about their well-being and that of their families are indeed very legitimate to them as their environment and experiences have led them to interpret their concerns. All individuals have been created by God, and have his love to take refuge in. To use such terms is akin to using any other of the extensive and repulsive vocabulary many of our American people utilize because somebody else is a little different. We need not elaborate on it here – we are all entirely too familiar with this kind of talk. In fact, every one of us has fears, concerns, feelings, and emotions that we have to deal with every day. In going back over these letters from Somalia and Vietnam as well as other inspirational readings, I believe this feeling of community has been true within me for a long time. One letter from the Peace Corps in 1964 sums it up: "I guess I've found out that the one thing that's common to all the people of the earth is that each and every one of them has personal feelings and emotions. That each one is a human being."[4] This holds just as true today as when it was originally written over half a century ago.

Any category or label that puts another human being in a box with certain supposed identifying traits is a dehumanizing process that makes it easier to scratch that person off the list of those who are acceptable in our lives. Recall the Vietnamese who were locked into the bamboo cages by GIs at LZ Bronco. To do that to other human beings is only possible if we can somehow make them less than human. Look also at the massive incarceration of people in our own prison system. Somehow they have to be made "less than" for us to be able to continue that practice as a society. When we make someone "less than," we have nothing to preclude us from dispatching that person to somewhere other than within the fellowship of humanity. The word "hillbilly" is in that category. Somehow if we can denigrate some white people – conveniently ignoring the fact that there are numerous black and Latino Appalachians – we can somehow dispose of these people as an embarrassing side show of our country's whiteness. It is especially grating to hear supposed scholars (or at least people who have achieved paper to hang on the wall announcing their graduation frequently from leading universities) to use such terminology. Putting anyone in a box and determining a separate set of rules for them deprives them of the uniqueness that God has created for each of them. This is true whether it is physical characteristics such as skin color, country of origin, sexual preferences, handicap, gender, or any other point of difference that the individual might have been bequeathed by God. It is also true with writers who tell the stories of their own dysfunctional families, interesting as they may be, and pretend that they represent all people from a specific socio-geographic area.

Part of the legacy of recovery is carrying the message to others. Many of the fellowships suggest that if we feel we are having challenges to our own recovery from within then we need to reach out to another who is addicted to that substance or character trait to which we dedicated so much of our time, financial resources, and emotional allegiance. They add that it is important to our own recovery that we need to recount our struggles and successful efforts to remove that addiction from our own psyches and personalities. We do this by sharing our experience, strength, and hope especially relating to the spiritual awakening that has led us to finding a power greater than ourselves. To go even further it is sometimes said we have to "give it away to keep it."

The most common way of sharing is recounting our stories in the meetings or one-on-one with each another. It is a mutual discourse of sharing and listening. Our spirituality resonates with each of us as we interrelate our stories of where we have been, where we are right now, and the hopes we have for the future. Our conversations are in the moment and it is in that moment that we transcend the differences and become one with the God of our understanding. We hear those facets of recovery which lead us to our spiritual growth. Rosa Zubizaretta, writing about practice within the Buddhist community, says, "Whether one-on-one or in group settings, simple yet skilled listening allows us to honor our suffering, our conflicts, and our differences – the truth of our relative experience – as well as our absolute nature, the interdependent radiance within us all."[5] It is from the beauty of this shared experience that we grow.

By extending the hand of fellowship to others we are living the life that Jesus and so many others in the world's religious traditions have called for us to do. If we are to find true happiness this is the route we must go. Sharing one's experience, strength, and hope with another addicted person is what we have to offer. We cannot make the other person recover – only God can do that – and we have long since quit playing God. But what we do have to offer is the understanding of what the addicted person is going through at least in its physical aspects and even to a certain extent in its emotional and spiritual turmoil which we as individuals have experienced in our own lives. When newcomers enter the rooms they are virtually all stultifyingly frightened because most of us could not imagine life without our chemical of choice. This is true as well for our other behavioral and social dependencies around which the various Twelve-Step programs have evolved including all those which are not chemically-based in nature.

At meetings a simple hello and handshake go a long way in mitigating the adverse effects of this initial contact. Then when one starts up a conversation, even if it is such a simple thing as inviting the person to have a cup of coffee or tea, a new bond is beginning to break through that initial reticence. In addition, asking the person if he or she has been to a meeting before can kindle that flicker of hope. Even if the person says nothing some friendly smiles or simple words of welcome can go a long way. I have frequently told newcomers I was scared to death too when first coming into the rooms (which is the absolute truth). That often seems to break the ice a little. As folks listen many of them will begin to understand as others share their stories of what it was like, what happened, and what it is like now. Many newcomers often do not understand as lots of us laugh and joke around before or after the meeting with other members in what seems a lack of concern for our propensity to use our chemical of choice or the probability that we might within the next few minutes. Many of them think how could that not be a problem for us? And how is it possible that we can be so congenial and jovial about the serious challenges that we face? Yet it is with deadly earnestness that we take our recovery and the return to sanity that it entails. But it works.

Often helpful in this initial process of recovery is the acronym HALT frequently found in the various fellowships. It means don't let yourself get too Hungry, Angry, Lonely, or Tired. In other words we can introduce the balance of the Tao without beginning any discussion of spirituality which the new person is probably very far away from comprehending early on anyway. Most of us have been in somewhat of a la-la-land emotional state when we first began the process of recovery. HALT recognizes the need to feel the even flow of life which as addicted people we have not had present in our lives. It recreates a touch of the balance of the Tao without the immediate intellectually surrendering dynamics of the Twelve Steps which will come eventually as the individual moves through the process of creating a new way of life based on surrender, recovery and spirituality.

It is when the topic comes up about getting a sponsor that sometimes there is a little hesitation on the part of the newcomer. Most of us have become so distrustful of others by the time we get into the rooms that we are sometimes reluctant to take this next very important action. However, if we find someone we are comfortable with, it certainly behooves us to reach out for help especially since this action goes a long way to ease our transition into a smoother recovery, and it substantially enhances the probability that long-term sobriety can characterize our life. If we are at the point of true surrender we will take advantage of what others in the rooms have to offer who have already been through the process and are willing to help in any way they can.

On the other hand, if we are the one being asked to become a sponsor we are taking on both a responsibility and an opportunity. The responsibility is that we work with the sponsee so that he or she gradually learns to understand the steps and that they are creating a new way of living not just eliminating their problem with addiction or behavior. His or her recovery relies on finding an adequate spiritual replacement for the empty hole in us that we tried to fill with drugs or alcohol or various dysfunctional character traits. Access to that spiritual replacement comes with successfully taking the steps and making them a way of life.

The opportunity in sponsorship, of course, is that it is there that we can grow with the sponsee spiritually as we go through the steps together. It has been my experience that every time I study and review the steps with another person I learn more and experience more. Perhaps it is because of spending so much time in an academic career around young people, but it seems that most of my sponsees over the years have been in their twenties and thirties. This is also a time when young people face the various challenges of life that virtually all people of that age face so sometimes the situation can frequently get complicated. But if it is something that we have had other experiences to share with them it is certainly most important that we do so. Lots of grief can sometimes be prevented with our sharing with another. Most of us are not lawyers, bankers, bed and breakfast providers, physicians, marriage counselors, or other professionals who normally provide services to third parties as well as to alcoholics. What we can do, however, is share our experience in utilizing the Twelve Steps to address these issues and to deal with the challenges of everyday living.

We cannot in any way, however, take recovery measures for them. When the first step says "We admitted we were powerless…" that statement may be extrapolated to include powerlessness over anyone else's problems that they face. All we can do is offer our experience, strength, and hope. Believe me I have had to learn this the hard way. Early on while sponsoring other guys I thought, "C'mon, you can do this." Yes, they can do this if they are honest, open-minded, and willing. But they have to put some effort into it and be capable, at least minimally, of surrendering their addiction to the God of their understanding. If they are to find any peace and serenity in life at all they are going to have to surrender a lot of other stuff over which they think they have some sort of power. In effect, they are essentially powerless over most of what they believe they should have some control over and which they regard that is essential in their lives that they continue to exercise such control.

Those three key words – honesty, open-mindedness, and willingness – are the essential ingredients for someone coming into the rooms of recovery for the first time. For without them it is impossible to make any progress at all. They are the key factors of change that are essential to finding the happiness to which we aspire. With them, on the other hand, the individual can create a life that is boundless in its serenity and peace.

Honesty, in particular, heads the list for without the self-searching inside oneself that is required for growth any change is impossible. How many times has it been said throughout history "The truth shall set you free" and how many of the ancient and medieval scholars from the various traditions and cultures around the world have said "Know thyself." To know ourselves we must be thoroughly honest about looking at our own attributes – good and bad – that compose us as human beings. If we are less than honest this is an impossible assignment and one that we cannot carry out in its absence.

Honesty is searching for the truth for without the truth about ourselves and the identification of who we truly are our lives cannot change. The Buddhist Lama Anam Thuban sums it up when he says, "Through embracing and living the truth, we realize inner freedom, which is the only nirvana to be found. Liberation is the cessation of all mistaken beliefs."[6]

Open-mindedness makes it possible for us to allow into ourselves more and more of God's world. In essence, if everything is created by God then for us to receive we have to open our minds and hearts to it. Any artificial or prejudicial concepts (and alcohol and other drugs are part of this) block us off from the sunlight of the spirit. God's grace will come to us if we are open to receiving it, and we do this by surrendering the precepts we have created within the wall we have built around ourselves. That wall is the structure which imprisons us just as much as it shuts out the truth. We must become willing to tear down this wall and not build another. Again Lama Anam Thuban puts it beautifully when he says, "When we open our hearts and our minds completely, we are in a place where we can experience something new, a new truth, a new reality, a miracle that we haven't experienced in the past. We can see things differently and they present new, expanded opportunities, new horizons."[7]

And finally is the willingness to change. If we are honest and open God will enter our life bringing happiness, serenity, and peace. All this will come in parallel to the degree to which we completely surrender and are honest and open enough to let him enter our spiritual being. A oneness with him will bring us closer and closer and his bounty will shed on us in ways that we never thought possible and perhaps in ways that we could never have imagined before. When our bodies and emotions were poisoned with chemicals and the associated insanity that came with them, we had no way to envision any sort of growth and change that might have been possible.

With recovery we will appreciate or even realize in fact that we have received his bounty over the years even though because of our addiction we may have been unwilling and unaware that his grace had entered us because the chemicals of our disease smothered our souls. But we never realize this until we established that spiritual connection with him through the honesty, open-mindedness and willingness that we now let be a part of our lives. With our addiction we had shut ourselves off from receiving what he has always had in place for us. It is available to us whenever we want it through the surrender which is an absolute first action in our recovery.

With these – honesty, open-mindedness, and willingness – the stage is set for making changes. Sometimes it is difficult for newcomers to grasp these concepts. When one does, a gradual rebirth begins to come about. It is an evolving process which continues as our recovery progresses. Watching others grow physically, emotionally, and spiritually over the years is one of the most personally fulfilling and beautiful events that can happen in the recovered person's life. But the opposite is true if the individual cannot or will not grab the lifelines of hope that are offered to him. Often this failure or refusal leads to jails, Institutions, or death. When this has happened to people we have worked with it sure can be tough to take. Most of us cannot help asking ourselves what did we do wrong or what should we have done differently but did not. There is only one answer to that question and that answer is "nothing." We have to truly believe "we admitted we were powerless...." Because in fact we are. The only thing we have to offer is our experience, strength, and hope. If that hits home and helps somebody it was God at work through us in that person's life. We can hope and pray for them but they have to grow in their own experience as they reach out to the God of their understanding if in fact they do. We cannot reach out to God for them. We risk becoming enablers if we think somehow we can help them find in their own thoughts and actions what they, in fact, must find within themselves. No one has the right to interfere or meddle in another's spiritual change and its associated growth within the individual. This practice is called enabling. We are only harming our own spirituality and spiritual awakening if we do, and we are, in reality, preventing the other person from hitting the bottom that he or she must first hit if they are going to bring about the changes internally within themselves that are so necessary to confront their own addictions and meet the challenges of overcoming them.

But many of us in recovery will be the first to admit that it is hard to get that concept from the head to the heart, and many have had to learn this the hard way. It is only through experience and prayer that this concept begins to become firmly implanted in our own psyches. Certainly, it is our attachment that is a manifestation of our ego at full speed, but it seems that by sharing our experience, strength, and hope also creates bonds of attachment that it is difficult from which to detach. Spiritual readings, especially of the Buddhist and Taoist traditions, have helped enormously to detach with love. As with others, I am still very much a "work in progress."

Over the years we as addicted people have experienced a number of tragic endings that have taken place among others attempting recovery. These have included suicides, homicide, incarceration and many other tragedies related to the inability to surrender and let go of the ego. But perhaps some of the hardest of these to take have been those without a known ending. The disappearances of people without notice leave one in a state of unknowing...what happened to so-and-so? Where have they disappeared to? It's almost like they fell off the edge of the earth never to be seen or heard from again. That remains in God's domain and that is where that we shall leave it. But on the other hand if an addicted person wants to find a way of life in which he or she can function as the genuine loving, caring, and forgiving participant in the human society of God's creation released from the confines of the ego they can find a life they never realized before. And who knows what beautiful and exciting experiences await them in that recovery. Their free spirit will become alive at last.

The Cool Wind blows gently with the rhythm of life.

Epilogue

If anyone can see themselves anywhere in the pages of this book I encourage you to look at yourself and know that you are not alone with any dependent characteristic you may recognize on your journey through life. If you have a hang-up or addiction that controls you even if you genuinely believe you are managing it take a closer look. This is particularly true if it has become an obsession over which you have little or no control. There is a way of dealing with anything on the emotional and spiritual plane that stands in the way of our freedom as an individual. Don't let your life revolve around it. Life is way more fun when we don't have any addiction to drugs or alcohol or to other people, places, or things that we feel we must have in our lives. We don't.

There are all kinds of Twelve-Step programs that address your issue and the people who participate in these fellowships will have the same hang-up you do. Getting involved in the process of recovery you will find there are all kinds of great people in the fellowships – and a few jerks – who identify with the suffering you are going through. They can be a sounding board and a way of identifying with the origins of what causes you to suffer that you probably never knew existed. You are, indeed, not the only one. There are comrades who face the same challenges you face whether they be physical or emotional. They seek the spiritual growth necessary so that they may separate themselves from whatever dependency they have that causes their suffering. There is help and understanding. And they are willing to share their experience, strength, and hope.

In closing I would like to make one final plea to all those out there who think they may have an addiction problem. This plea especially goes out to those who are having some success in their careers or what they consider their marginal spiritual identity with the way things are going in their lives but for some reason that addiction is, probably very quietly, keeping them from fulfilling their role in life. If things seem to get upside down no matter how hard you try and you in any way turn to booze or pot or some harder drug to get the momentary relief you crave you might have a problem. This is especially true if you want to have only a small quantity such as a couple of drinks or a joint but end up having many more, then you are probably a candidate for becoming another victim of some addiction which your ego has led you to believe is the elixir for the challenges in your life. It is not. It is only burying your problems behind a wall that is shutting you off from the sun light of the spirit. Take the opportunity now to deal with it. Go to a Twelve-Step meeting of some kind. There are many out there to choose from especially in more urban areas. It will only cost you an hour or so of your time and the opportunities for growth beyond your addiction are unfathomable. There will be some surrender involved and sometimes the ego dies very, very slowly. But the rewards are infinite. Not dealing with your addiction has, ultimately, the final outcome of jails, institutions, or death. For those who are honest, open-minded, and willing the change in life will bring a serenity and peace within them that knows no bounds. That new life will find a high that is way greater than anything you've ever gotten from chemicals or other addictions, and its sweetness will eviscerate your whole being just in this moment.

Endnotes

CHAPTER 1 – Trying to Grow Up

[1] Twelve Step programs grew out of the Oxford Movement of the early 19th century which sought answers to the challenges facing humankind through surrender to God, letting go, and helping others. The original Twelve Step program upon which the others are based is Alcoholics Anonymous which was developed by Bill Wilson and Dr. Bob Smith in Akron and New York City in the 1930s.

[2] For a list of some of the various Twelve Step programs and other recovery fellowships, see Verne Becker, general ed., **Recovery Devotional Bible** (Grand Rapids MI: Zondervan, New International Version), 1436. This work also contains a section entitled "The Spiritual Roots of the Twelve Steps".

[3] The Manhattan Project was the process in which the atomic bomb was developed. It was under the leadership of War Department Army Service Forces Corps of Engineers and was officially called Manhattan District.

[4] Formally West Virginia Industrial School for Boys, Pruntytown, West Virginia.

CHAPTER 2 – Introduction to a Wider World

[1] Personal letter, November 6, 1964. Author's possession.

[2] Personal letter December 15, 1964 – Author's possession

[3] Qat is a mild narcotic that is chewed. It is a green leafy plant and it is the leaves that are chewed but not swallowed. It is consumed in many parts of the Horn of Africa to get a buzz.

[4] *Shifta* are bandits in the Horn of Africa who prey on railroads and other forms of ground transportation. They were usually mounted

on horseback and carried rifles of some sort. They could be of any number of ethnicities.

5   Personal letter, December 30-, 1965 - Author's possession.

6   Personal letter, November 16, 1964 - Author's possession.

7   Personal letter, November 24, 10964 - Author's possession.

8   Personal letter, January 17, 1965 - Author's possession.

9   Personal letter, February 19, 1965 - Author's possession.

10   Personal letter, February 25, 1965 - Authors possession.

11   Personal letter, October 13, 1965 – Author's possession.

12   *Ibid.*

CHAPTER 3 - Vietnam

1   Slang term for shanties used either for offices or billets that GIs lived in. They had plywood floors and wooden ribbing which held up canvas sides and tops.

2   Infantry personnel on assignment to operations in the field.

3   This slang refers to the actual performance of duties in the field.

4   This was written during the collapsing stages of European imperialism in Africa when traditional societies which had been pulverized by European occupiers were becoming independent entities. Political, social, and economic vacuums were rapidly emerging in these former colonies which often precipitated armed and frequently brutal conflict to resolve issues of state control. The media especially made reference to what they termed "savage" actions, actions that were not much different from what was happening in Vietnam.

5   Personal letter October 25, – Author's possession.

6   Personal letter November 5, – Author's possession.

7   For confidentiality purposes the name of the city has been omitted.

8   A grenade launcher.

9   Personal letter April 22, – Author's possession.

10   Personal letter April 30, – Author's possession.

11   In this case the term refers to career NCOs.

12   Personal letter June 9, – Author's possession.

13   Basically a procedure equivalent to a civilian grand jury investigation.

14   Personal letter February 13, – Author's possession.

15   Personal letter February 24, – Author's possession.

16 Personal letter February 24, – Author's possession.
17 Personal letter March 23, – Author's possession.
18 GI slang for the Viet Cong.
19 For those unfamiliar with battle situation preparation, soldiers were required to lace a dog tag into the shoe string of one of their boots. They also wore a dog tag around their neck. Because it was so easy to lose a dog tag on a necklace around your neck during a combat situation, the one in the boot was a backup for identification purposes. Dog tags carried your name, serial number, blood type, and religion.
20 A soldier with less than a hundred days left in the normal one year tour of duty.
21 Personal letter May 15, – Author's possession.
22 Personal letter May 21, – Author's possession.
23 Short drops are latrines in which a large wash-tub type bucket is placed under a seat which collects the fecal matter as it drops down. They had to be emptied from time to time and the military used Vietnamese employees rather than GIs for this purpose.
24 A piss tube was a urinal constructed by putting a drain pipe obliquely into the ground with the open end covered with screening. Even though it was out in the open it tended to be a space where men could gather to talk privately especially since everything else on the LZ was very open and lent itself to no privacy at all.

CHAPTER 4 – PTSD, Addiction, and a Professional Life

1 Reprinted in the San Juan Star, February 18, 2015, 25.
2 Personal letter September 15, 1965 – Author's possession.
3 Claude Anshin Thomas, *At Hell's Gate: A Soldier's Journey from War to Peace* (Boston: Shambhala, 2006), 153.
4 Ibid., 53
5 *Daily Athenaeum*, October 14, 1971 and October 15, 1971.
6 See Henry Louis Gates, Jr., *Colored People: A Memoir* (New York: Alford A. Knopf, 1994) for an interesting reflection on his childhood in Appalachia.
7 See Ken Fones-Wolf and Ronald L. Lewis, Transnational West Virginia: Ethnic Communities and Economic Change, 1840-1940 (Morgantown WV: West Virginia University Press, 2002). For a

biographical statistical listing of the diverse nationalities reflected in this massive intrusion of different nationalities into one relatively small West Virginia county during its Industrial Revolution, see Agnes A. Ferruso, *Naturalization Records of Tucker County, West Virginia 1856-1954* (Parsons WV: McClain Printing Company, 1995).

[8]   Talbott, I. D., "African Agriculture" in W. R. Ochieng' and R. M. Maxon, eds., *An Economic History of Kenya* (Nairobi: East African Educational Publishers Ltd., 1992.)

CHAPTER 5 - Recovery

[1]   Richard Rohr, *Breathing Under Water: Spirituality and the Twelve Steps* (Cincinnati: St. Anthony Messenger Press, 2011), 35.

[2]   Beatty, Melody, *Codependent No More & Beyond Codependency,* (New York: MJF Books, 1990).

[3]   *Ibid.*

[4]   *Ibid.*, 36.

[5]   Eva Wong, editor and translator, *Being Taoist: Wisdom for Living a Balanced Life,* (Boston: Shambhala, 2015), 135.

[6]   Beatty, Melody, *Codependents' Guide to the Twelve Steps,* (New York: FIRESIDE/PARKSIDE, 1990).

[7]   William Alexander, *Ordinary Recovery: Mindfulness, Alcoholism, and the Path of Lifelong Sobriety* (Boston: Shambhala, 2010), 61.

CHAPTER 6 – A Spiritual Connection to God

[1]   *Alcoholics Anonymous: The Story of How Many Thousands of Men and Women Have Recovered from Alcoholism* (New York: Alcoholics Anonymous World Services, Inc., 4th ed., 2001), 53. (Note: Usually referred to as the Big Book of Alcoholics Anonymous.)

[2]   *One Day at a Time in Al-Anon* (Virginia Beach VA: Al-Anon Family Groups, 2000), 228.

[3]   *Narcotics Anonymous* (Chatsworth CA: Narcotics Anonymous World Services, Inc., 6th ed., 2008), 101.

[4]   Lama Zopa Rinpoche, *How to be Happy* (Boston: Wisdom Publications, eds. Josh Bartok and Ailsa Cameron, 2nd ed., 2008), 3.

[5]   Kenneth S. Leong, *The Zen Teachings of Jesus* (New York: Crossroad, revised and expanded edition, 2001), 59.

[6]   *It Works: How and Why* (Chatsworth CA: Narcotics Anonymous World Services, Inc., 1993), 63.

[7]   Bonnie Duran, "Race, Racism, and the Dharma" in Hilda Gutierrez Baldoquin, ed., Dharma, /Color, and Culture: New Voices in Western Buddhism (Berkeley CA: Parallax Press, 2004), 167-8.

[8]   Ray Tiegert and Thomas Moore, eds., *The Lost Sutras of Jesus: Unlocking the Ancient Wisdom of the Xian Monks* (Berkeley CA: Seastone, John Babcock, trans., 2003).

[9]   Taking a look at the literature which did not make it into the canonical Bible was encouraged by the same student who stayed in my home at the tail end of my active addiction and who had taught me the joys and techniques of boating. He had studied this spirituality for some time and even gave me my first Gnostic literature to review.

[10] Jean-Yves Leloup, *The Gospel of Thomas: The Gnostic Wisdom of Jesus* (Rochester VT: Inner Traditions, 2005), English translation and notes by Joseph Rowe, 63.

[11] Ibid.

[12] Ibid., 67

[13] Thomas, 43.

[14] Thich Nhat Hanh, *Peace is Every Step: The Path of Mindfulness in Everyday Life* (London: Rider, 1995), 5.

[15] Thich Nhat Hanh, *Being Peace* (Berkeley CA: Parallax Press, 1996), 14-15. Arnold Kotler, ed.

[16] Lao Tsu, *Tao Te Ching* (New York: Vintage Books, 2011), translated by Gia-Fu Feng and Jane English with Toinette Lippe, 24.

[17] Diane Dreher, *The Tao of Inner Peace* (New York: Plume, 2000), 21.

[18] Ibid.

[19] Thich Nhat Hanh, *You Are Here: Discovering the Magic of the Present Moment* (Boston: Shambhala Publications, Inc.), 2001

[20] Dreher, 221.

[21] Lao Tzu, *Tao Te Ching* (London: Arcturus Publishing, Ltd., translated by John H. McDonald, 2018), 52.

[22] Ibid., 219.

[23] *One Day at a Time in Al-Anon* (Virginia Beach VA: Al-Anon Family Groups, 2000), 264.

[24] Thomas Moore, *A Religion of One's Own: A Guide to Creating a Personal Spirituality in a Secular World* (New York: Avery), 116.

25 See, for example, Leloup, 148, and Davies, Stevan, translator and annotator, *The Gospel of Thomas Annotated and Explained* (Woodstock VT: Skylight Paths Publishing, 2006), 70-71.

26 Tomas Prower, *Queer Magic: LGBT+ Spirituality and Culture From Around the World* (Woodbury MN: Llewellyn Publications, 2018), 202.

27 *Alcoholics Anonymous*, 133.

CHAPTER 7 – One Day at a Time

1 Pema Chodron, *Practicing Peace in Times of War* (Boston & London: Shambhala, 2007), 94.

2 Wong, 113.

3 *Narcotics Anonymous Basic Text*, 89

4 Personal letter, November 6, 1964. – Author's possession.

5 Rosa Zubizaretta, "How Can I Be a Buddhist if I Don't Like to Sit?: Learning to Listen with Love to Self and Others," in Baldoquin, ed., 204.

6 Anam Thubten, *No Self, No Problem: Awakening to Our True Nature* (Boston & London: Shambhala, Sharon Roe, ed., 2013), 29.

7 *Ibid.* 31.

Bibliography

Alcoholics Anonymous: The Story of How Many Thousands of Men and Women Have Recovered from Alcoholism. New York: Alcoholics Anonymous World Services, 2001, 4th ed. This is the Big Book of Alcoholics Anonymous.

Alexander, William. *Ordinary Recovery: Mindfulness, Alcoholism, and the Path of Life Recovery.* Boston: Shambhala, 2010).

Aronson, Martin, ed. *Jesus and Lao Tzu: The Parallel Sayings.* Berkeley CA: Seastone, 2003.

Baldoquin, Hilda Gutierrez. *Dharma, Color, and Culture: New Voices in Western Buddhism.* Berkeley CA: Parallax Press, 2004.

Betty, Melody. *Codependent No More & Beyond Codependency.* New York: MJF Books, 1990.

————. *Codependent's Guide to the Twelve Steps.* New York: FIRESIDE/PARKSIDE, 1990.

Becker, Verne, general ed. *Recovery Devotional Bible.* Grand Rapids MI: Zondervan, New International Version, 1993.

Bourgeault, Cynthia. *The Wisdom Jesus: Transforming Heart and Mind – a New Perspective on Christ and His Message* (Boston: Shambhala, 2008).

Chodron, Pema. *Practicing Peace in Times of War.* Boston & London: Shambhala, 2007.

        . *Taking the Leap: Freeing Ourselves from Old Habits and Fears.* Boston: Shambhala, 2009.

Chopra, Deepak. *The Third Jesus: The Christ We Cannot Ignore.* New York: Three Rivers Press, 2008.

Dalai Lama. *Beyond Religion: Ethics for a Whole World.* London: Ebury Publishing, 2013.

Davies, Stevan, translator and annotator. *The Gospel of Thomas Annotated and Explained.* Woodstock VT: Skylight Paths Publishing, 2006.

Deng Ming-Dao. *365 Tao: Daily Meditations.* New York: HarperOne, 1992.

Dreher, Diane. *The Tao of Inner Peace* (New York: Plume, 2000).

Ferruso, Agnes A. *Naturalization Records of Tucker County, West Virginia 1856-1954.* Parsons WV: McClain Printing Company, 1995.

Flanagan, Eileen. *The Wisdom to Know the Difference* (New York: MJF Books, 2009).

Fones-Wolf, Ken, and Ronal L. Lewis, eds. *Transnational West Virginia: Ethnic Communities and Economic Change, 1840-1940.* Morgantown WV: West Virginia University Press, 2002.

Gates, Henry Louis, Jr. *Colored People: A Memoir.* New York: Alfred A. Knopf, 1994.

Gregory, Jason. *Effortless Living: Wu-Wei and the Spontaneous State of Natural Harmony.* Rochester VT: Inner Traditions, 2018.

_____. *Fasting the Mind: Spiritual Exercises for Psychic Detox.* Rochester VT: Inner Traditions, 2017.

_____. *The Science and Practice of Humility: The Path to Ultimate Freedom.* Rochester VT: Inner Traditions, 2014.

It Works: How and Why. Chatsworth CA: Narcotics Anonymous World Services, 1993.

Jacobs, Alan. *When Jesus Lived in India.* London: Watson Publishing, 2009.

Lao Tzu, *Tao Te Ching.* London: Arcturus Publishing, Ltd., translated by John H. McDonald, 2018.

_____. *Tao Te Ching.* New York: Vintage Books, 2011, translated by Gia-Fu Feng and Jane English, 2011.

Leloup, Jean-Yves. *Compassion and Meditation: The Spiritual Dynamic Between Buddhism and Christianity.* Rochester VT: Inner Traditions, Joseph Rowe, trans., 2009.

_____. *The Gospel of Thomas: The Gnostic Wisdom of Jesus.* Rochester VT: Inner Traditions, 2005.

Leong, Kenneth S. *The Zen Teachings of Jesus.* New York: Crossroad, revised and expanded edition, 2001.

Miller, Joanne P. *Zen and the Gospel of Thomas.* Somerville MA: Wisdom Publications, 2018.

Moore, Thomas. *A Religion of One's Own: A Guide to Creating a Personal Spirituality in a Secular World.* New York: Avery, 2015.

Narcotics Anonymous, 6th ed. Chatsworth CA: Narcotics Anonymous World Services, 2008. This is the Basic Text of Narcotics Anonymous.

Nhat Hanh, Thich. *Being Peace.* Berkeley CA: Parallax Press, 1996.

. *Peace is Every Step: The Path of Mindfulness in Everyday Life.* London: Rider, 1995.

. *You Are Here: Discovering the Magic of the Present Moment.* Boston: Shambhala Publications, 2001.

Ochieng", W. R., and R. M. Maxon, eds. *An Economic History of Kenya.* Nairobi: East African Educational Publishers, Ltd. 1992.

One Day at a Time in Al-Anon. Virginia Beach VA: Al-Anon Family Groups, 2000.

Prower, Tomas. *Queer Magic: LGBT+ Spirituality and Culture From Around the World.* Woodbury MN: Llewellyn Publications, 2018.

Richo, David. *The Power of Grace: Recognizing Unexpected Gifts on Our Path.* Boston: Shambhala, 2014.

Rinpoche, Lama Zopa. *How to be Happy.* Boston: Wisdom Publications, Josh Bartok and Ailsa Cameron eds., 2nd ed., 2008.

Rohr, Richard. *Breathing Under Water: Spirituality and the Twelve Steps.* Cincinnati: St. Anthony Messenger Press, 2011.

Thubten, Anam. *No Self, No Problem: Awakening to Our True Nature*. Boston & London: Shambhala, Sharon Roe, ed., 2013.

Tiegert, Ray, and Thomas Moore, eds. *The Lost Sutras of Jesus: Unlocking the Ancient Wisdom of the Xian Monks*. Berkeley CA: Seastone, John Babcock, trans., 2003.

Trunga, Chogyam. *Smile at Fear: Awakening the True Heart of Bravery*. Boston: Shambhala, 2010.

Wong, Eva, editor and translator. *Being Taoist: Wisdom for Living a Balanced Life*. Boston: Shambhala, 2010.

Printed in the United States
By Bookmasters